DUNCAN LARCOMBE is an award-winning British journalist and commentator who spent more than ten years working as royal editor for the *Sun* newspaper in London. He also worked as the paper's defence editor, reporting from the front line with British and American troops in Afghanistan. As well as writing, he is a regular royal commentator with US network ABC. He has been married for sixteen years and is the father of two daughters.

PRINCE
THE INSIDE STORY
HARRY

DUNCAN LARCOMBE

HarperCollins*Publishers*

HarperCollins*Publishers*
1 London Bridge Street
London SE1 9GF

www.harpercollins.co.uk

First published by HarperCollins*Publishers* 2017
This edition published 2018

3 5 7 9 10 8 6 4 2

© Duncan Larcombe 2017, 2018

Duncan Larcombe asserts the moral right
to be identified as the author of this work

A catalogue record of this book is
available from the British Library

ISBN 978-0-00-819648-6

Printed and bound in the United States of America by
LSC Communications

For more information visit: www.harpercollins.co.uk/green

To two legendary royal reporters, Harry Arnold for the Sun and James Whitaker for the Mirror, who were inspirational as both mentors and friends

CONTENTS

CHAPTER 1

DRESSING DOWN

'HELLO, CLARENCE HOUSE Press Office, how can I help?'

It was the sort of call every reporter dreams of making. A world exclusive which would be followed by TV, press and radio outlets in every corner of the planet.

'Hello, it's Duncan Larcombe calling from the *Sun*. We have a picture of Prince Harry wearing a Nazi outfit to a fancy dress party. I'm giving you the heads-up because we're planning to run the picture in tomorrow's paper.'

There was an unusually long pause, then the predictable response: 'We will call you back.'

The picture wasn't a fake. To everyone in the *Sun* newsroom's astonishment, the young, popular prince had made one of the biggest gaffes in modern Royal history. To make matters worse for the 20-year-old, his antics at a private party in West Littleton, Wiltshire, in January 2005, coincided with the 60th anniversary of the liberation of the Nazis' notorious Auschwitz death camp. As world leaders, former prisoners and plane-loads of news reporters prepared to descend on Poland to remember the 1.1 million who died at the camp, the young British Royal had given them all something to comment on.

Within twelve hours of that call to Harry's media advisers, he would find himself in the eye of a global storm of criticism.

Everyone knew German blood runs through the veins of the British Royal family. But was this careless choice of outfit finally proof the House of Windsor harboured secret sympathies with the fascist regime all along? At the very least, was Prince Harry's stupidity a sign of a young Royal who had fallen off the rails and was out of control in the years since his mother's tragic death? How could a young prince, with an army of media advisers, make such a glaring error of judgement?

Big questions always follow a big exclusive. But Harry will never forget the afternoon of 12 January 2005 when his father's press adviser called him to break the bad news of the *Sun*'s scoop.

Over the years Harry has joked about all kinds of stories that have been written about him. His sense of humour is one of his greatest assets. But never once has he made light of, or even discussed off the record, that fateful party and the swastika wrapped around his left arm.

The story sent shockwaves through the palace. Prince Charles was furious with his youngest son. Even the Queen began to question where her grandson's life was heading. But now, more than a decade since the infamous event, such fears have proved unfounded. Although the Nazi uniform gaffe was by no means the last time the men in grey suits at the palace have had to frantically try to deflect criticism away from Harry, today Prince Harry is the most popular Royal after the Monarch. Despite a string of incidents that would normally be enough to destroy the career of an aspiring public figure, Harry has a mysterious gift. The more scrapes he gets into, the more the public seem to love him. He is the Royal most men would like to have a beer with, and most women would like to mother, or more.

* * *

AT THE *Sun* offices in Wapping, east London, the morning of 12 January 2005 started like any other. The newsroom was hectic as usual. The newsdesk team were busy answering calls from readers and reporters while trying to prepare for the morning conference with the editor.

Every day at 11.30 a.m. the news editor and other senior staff had to face the dreaded 'news conference' with the boss. It was, and still is, the daily meeting they all feared. It was their job to present a list of stories ready for the next day's paper. Get it wrong, and the editor would hit the roof. If the news list was weak, the news editor would be shouted at, or worse – the news list might be ripped up in front of all the executives. If the news editor was shouted at, the news reporters would get the blame. They would in turn be shouted at, or worse.

That day, like any other, the news list had its usual blend of showbiz stories, crime, health and politics exclusives served up by the forty-strong team of news reporters. There was also a splattering of typically *Sun* 'off the wall' stories aimed at entertaining the readers and making them laugh. The morning conference therefore went OK, with no shouting from the editor, but no real interest in the suggestions for the next day's paper. A score draw for the news editor and another daily nightmare put to bed.

While the conference had been in full swing one of the juniors on the newsdesk had been manning the phones. He took a call from the paper's Thames Valley district reporter Jamie Pyatt. A former news editor himself, Pyatt was one of the most respected members of the *Sun*'s team of reporters, and the desk naturally took tips from him very seriously.

Pyatt recalls: 'I took a call from one of my long-term contacts. He was a young lad and I knew he was well connected with the princes. He asked if the *Sun* would be interested in a picture of Prince William wearing a gorilla outfit to a fancy dress party.

Obviously a picture of the future king in any sort of unusual outfit would be very newsworthy.'

Pyatt arranged to meet the source an hour later and phoned the newsdesk to tell them about the tip. There was nothing unusual about a reporter heading off to meet a source. The newsdesk were all too aware that more often than not the tip would fall down. But they arranged for Pyatt to link up with a photographer to meet his source and kept their fingers crossed the picture would be good enough quality to make the paper. They also knew that as a seasoned and experienced reporter, Pyatt would instantly sense if the picture was part of an elaborate hoax.

When you are dealing with pictures of a Royal, alarm bells always ring. Publishing a picture of a Royal that then turns out to be a hoax could cost even the editor her job. The Royal family is so high profile that if you get it wrong the paper becomes the story. The *Sun* was famously once hoodwinked by a set of pictures of Princess Diana training at a gym. It was only after the snaps were published that it emerged it wasn't the Princess of Wales working out. It was a lookalike and the paper had been the victim of an elaborate hoax.

Within an hour Pyatt pulled into a Burger King at a motorway services to meet his source. 'He was a young lad, just after a few quid to help with his university bills. He had about eleven prints showing a bloke at a party dressed as a gorilla. He insisted it was Prince William but not one of the pictures showed William's face.

'I was a bit disappointed, and so was the lad when I explained we couldn't use the pictures just on his say-so. There is a big difference between a picture of a bloke in a gorilla suit, and a picture that proved the person in the suit was the future king of England.'

As Pyatt prepared to head off back to his office in Windsor, his source tried another tack. He asked: 'Is a picture of Prince Harry at the same party any good?'

Pyatt replied: 'Well, that depends on what it shows, what was he dressed as?'

The source then uttered the words that within hours would be repeated by millions of people all over the world.

'Harry is dressed in a Nazi outfit.'

The source then handed Pyatt the final picture in his set. It showed the third in line to the British throne standing with a drink in one hand, a cigarette in the other, surrounded by other partygoers. To Pyatt's astonishment the young prince was sporting a full German Afrika Korps uniform from the Second World War. On Harry's left arm, in plain sight, was an armband with the hated Nazi swastika.

There are moments in a reporter's career when you have to keep calm and not panic the source by letting your true feelings show. The last thing you want is for them to change their mind and decide the impact of the story might be too big, too controversial. Like a car salesman being offered a rare gem, you have to stay calm and keep your poker face on.

'I couldn't believe what I was looking at,' Pyatt recalled. 'The tipster clearly had no idea what would happen if we published this picture. I knew I needed to stay calm because the last thing I wanted to do was risk him getting cold feet. I was pretty sure he was inside William's social circle and was obviously taking a gamble by coming to the *Sun*. If I appeared too keen he might be spooked and refuse to hand over the picture.

'In my head I could hardly believe what I was looking at. The picture was so clear and the swastika on Harry's arm just leaped out at me. The hardest thing was to take the picture in my hand without ripping off his arm. I knew at that second I wasn't leaving Burger King without that picture.'

Pyatt played it cool and said he needed to ring the office to find out whether they were interested. The priority now was for the photographer to copy the picture and send it as soon as possible to the office.

'I called the office and said what we had. They were expecting a picture of William in a gorilla suit. That would have made a good page lead. But what we were sitting on was a world exclusive. It was very exciting, but the office were terrified this was a sting, that the picture was a hoax. When you get in this situation all kinds of paranoia kicks in. I couldn't see how the picture could have been altered, but you can never be 100 per cent sure.'

Pyatt was told to get hold of the negatives. These were the days before mobile phones had cameras that were good enough to take digital pictures of the quality needed to put in a newspaper. The photos had been taken on a happy snap camera that used film rather than the modern digital images, and the source had already had them developed, but even pictures printed from negatives could be doctored. It was entirely possible Harry's head had been cleverly superimposed onto someone else's body. If the *Sun* ran a fake picture like that, the editor would almost certainly lose her job.

The young tipster, who remained convinced that the paper would be more interested in the snaps of William, pulled out the negatives and handed them to Pyatt. The photographer then cast his expert eye over them and it all seemed to add up. Still there was hesitation.

'The office took the view that this picture was too good to be true,' Pyatt recalled. 'They kept asking me was I actually holding it in my hand, and did I think it was real.'

Although the morning news conference was over, a story like this needed the editor's immediate attention. To get this close to a world exclusive and then for things to go wrong fell well beyond the pay grade of the news and picture desks. The editor was informed, and she shared the scepticism of her juniors.

The order came down the line. We had to be 100 per cent sure the picture was not a hoax. The only way this picture could be run was if Harry's media advisers confirmed its authenticity. Only then could the danger of it being a hoax be eliminated. There was always a risk that by tipping the palace off before publication, they would try and kill the story, maybe even get the lawyers involved to block publication. But the risk of getting it wrong on a story like this far outweighed these concerns. As a result, I was asked to 'put in the call' to Clarence House.

In 2005 Harry and William's press affairs were still dealt with by the Prince of Wales's media team, a band of highly paid civil servants brought in to oversee and manage the affairs of Clarence House. They were famously fierce.

Only a year earlier the *Sun* had run a picture of Prince William skiing with his new girlfriend, the middle-class daughter of a former air stewardess. No one had previously used a picture of Kate Middleton, and by running that picture the *Sun* were breaking an agreement that had stood in place since the fall-out from the death of Princess Diana in 1997. It had been agreed that while the young princes were in full-time education they were 'off limits' to the press. In return Clarence House would issue the occasional picture and some words about the boys. The agreement was taken so seriously that national papers, including the *Sun*, refused to let their reporters and photographers even set foot in St Andrews University in Scotland, where William was studying for his degree.

No one in the media was entirely comfortable with this arrangement. The British Royal family enjoy a position of being 'above politics', and this all seemed generally to have the backing of the deeply patriotic British public. But because they are not elected, there is no real way of bringing them to account. So to ban the media from placing any scrutiny on William and Harry was indeed a big call.

The media team at Clarence House knew they were on borrowed time. William was coming to the end of his time at St Andrews. And Harry, whose A level results at Eton had been mediocre, had embarked on an extended 'gap year' rather than remain in full-time education. Before long Harry was likely to be seen as 'fair game' by the press, and it was the Clarence House team's job to try and ensure this prospect was delayed for as long as possible. So receiving the Nazi call from Britain's biggest-selling newspaper had implications that went far beyond what might appear on the *Sun*'s front page the following day.

As civil servants, the Clarence House press office staff were there to defend the Royals. But they were not there to defend the indefensible. Nor would they risk lying to a journalist. After hearing about my call, the Prince of Wales's Communications Director, Paddy Harverson, knew what was coming. A former head of media at Manchester United Football Club, Harverson was razor-sharp at protecting his clients by deflecting trouble. But there are times when even a seasoned spin doctor has to hold up his hands and admit defeat. As soon as he had been made aware of the Nazi call, Harverson got in touch with Harry. He needed to know if it was true. If it was, he was going to have to draw on every ounce of his experience to try and limit the damage.

At four o'clock that afternoon my phone rang again. It was Harverson. He confirmed that Harry and his brother had attended a fancy dress party in the sleepy village of West Littleton, Wiltshire, just a few days earlier. And in fairness to Clarence House, a decision had clearly been made to hold up their hands to the gaffe. The only request was for us not to go in 'too hard' on the prince, to play the story straight and prominently include a statement issued on his behalf.

Harverson read over the statement from Harry. It ended: 'I am very sorry if I have caused any offence. It was a poor choice of costume and I apologize.'

I called the office to tell them the story was copper-bottomed. The picture was not a hoax and Harry had issued an immediate apology.

That was it. We had everything we needed. Pyatt had secured the picture, and now we had confirmation it was the real deal. The office immediately went into overdrive; the editor was informed and the genius team of subeditors were put into action to start drawing up the pages for the next day's paper.

There is an expression in Fleet Street that 'it's never easy'. But for once it was. Shortly afterwards, the editor took a call from Harverson. He wanted to know how we were running the picture and reiterated that he hoped the *Sun* would not to go in too hard on the prince.

That is exactly how the story was put across. *Sun* readers are generally pro-Royal, and the paper reflects that view. The last thing the *Sun* wanted to do was plunge the knife into a young Royal who most people back then remembered as a tragic teenager bowing his head at his mother's funeral. Harry was very popular, even if his reputation as a party-loving prince was growing momentum.

But others were not so sympathetic. By the time the first edition of the paper appeared, the story was already out there. The *Daily Mirror*'s legendary Royal correspondent James Whitaker had been invited to give his views on the gaffe on the ITV's *News At Ten*. In his famously grand accent, Whitaker told viewers this was a disaster for Prince Harry. He said that the image of him donning a Nazi costume would dog the young Royal for the rest of his life.

Sitting at home watching the story break, I can remember wondering whether Prince Harry would ever know how close he came to the story never seeing the light of day. If Pyatt's tipster had produced a photograph proving that it was William in the gorilla outfit, then that might well have been the end of the matter. Maybe Pyatt would have left the Burger King that day with a strong page lead picture of the future king in his pocket, blissfully unaware of what William's younger brother had decided to wear to the same party.

In reality Harry had to face the music. The next day the story was being repeated all over the world. It led the news bulletins at home. TV crews from the UK, Australia, America, Germany, France and even Japan were camped outside Clarence House in London reporting on the fall-out. Harry stayed well away from the cameras. He was instructed to keep a low profile while the media team at Clarence House dealt with hundreds of follow-up calls from all over the planet.

Among the most damning criticism came from Israel. Silvan Shalom, the then Israeli foreign minister, said: 'Anybody who tries to pass it off as bad taste must be made aware that this can encourage others to think that perhaps that period was not as bad as we teach the young generation in the free world.'

The then Conservative leader Michael Howard, himself of Romanian-Jewish descent, ripped into Harry, demanding he should make a public apology. 'It would be appropriate to hear from him in person,' Howard said. 'It might be appropriate for him to tell us himself just how contrite he is.'

People even began to suggest that Harry's antics should prevent him from becoming an Army officer. Since his days with the cadet force at school Harry had long dreamed of joining the Army. A senior Royal like him had very limited career options after finishing full-time education. There is no way the third in line to the throne can join a private sector firm. He would risk being accused of gifting his employers an unfair advantage over their competitors because of his Royal roots. Nor would it be likely someone in Harry's position could work in the public sector because of the attention he would attract. If he worked at a hospital or a school, how could his protection officers keep him safe? So a career in the military was one of the few options open to the young Royal.

By the time the Nazi story broke Harry had already been accepted into the famous Royal Military Academy at Sandhurst. He was only three months away from starting forty-four weeks of intensive training aimed at making him into an Army officer. This was Harry's dream and he had worked extremely hard getting through the Regular Commissions Board selection course. But now he was facing murmurs that risked ending his future career before it had even started. Former Armed Forces Minister and Labour MP Doug Henderson said his error of judgement demonstrated Harry was unfit to join the British Army. 'I don't think that this young man is suitable,' said Henderson.

Harry was under attack from all sides. A senior Royal source recalled the pressure the prince was under. 'The Nazi outfit was a foolish mistake, and that is all. But in the wake of it coming to light Harry was being put up as public enemy number one. His advisers remained calm and were convinced the story would fade away. They advised against him making any public statements, or doing anything that would fuel the story. He had issued an apology and they felt that was all he could do. There were suggestions that Harry should travel to Auschwitz but that was quickly rejected because it come across as a cynical stunt. Harry was desperate to do something to put it right, but his hands were tied.'

Surrounded by his father's advisers, and still facing a barrage of criticism, Harry turned to the one person he knew would be on his side.

For the previous nine months he had been in a relationship with a pretty university student called Chelsy Davy. Born in Zimbabwe and the daughter of a wealthy businessman, Chelsy was a breath of fresh air for the young Royal. The pair had met the previous April while Harry was on a visit to Cape Town in South Africa. They had become very close and the prince even joined Chelsy and her family on a Christmas holiday on the remote island of Bazaruto off the coast of Mozambique.

Harry and Chelsy's whirlwind romance was unlike anything he had experienced before. Chelsy, who was twenty, was studying law at the University of Cape Town. Not only was she intelligent, she was also athletic and extremely attractive, with long blonde hair and piercing blue eyes, and shared with him a love of Africa and the outdoors.

But most important of all, it was not Harry's position that attracted the free-spirited Chelsy. She was not in the least bit interested in all the trappings of the Royal family, fame or the limelight. It is no surprise that it was Chelsy that Harry turned to for support when the story broke.

The source added: 'Harry was infatuated with Chelsy. He had never met anyone like her before. When the Nazi row erupted he turned to her for comfort. She agreed to fly over to the UK to visit Harry as soon as possible and that made a world of difference to him. He was desperate to see her and take his mind off the storm that surrounded him.'

This was the first, but by no means the last time Harry sought comfort from his first true love. Chelsy's steady outlook was exactly the kind of cool-headedness Harry craved. Over the coming months and years she provided him with the vital support he needed. In those dark days Harry had been blown away by the negative reaction to his choice of fancy dress outfit.

Reflecting on the story now, it was nothing more than a silly mistake, an act of carelessness which simply hadn't been thought through. The reaction around the world was grossly over the top. He could never have foreseen that what he thought would just get a laugh at a party of 250 youngsters would become a talking point across the globe.

Since the death of his mother, Harry had grown up in relative anonymity, away from the media glare. Perhaps the most significant and lasting effect of his choice of party outfit was to bring forward the point where Clarence House could no longer justify keeping him away from the media spotlight. And that above all is what Harry would have regretted about the whole sorry episode. Scoring an own goal of that scale is the very last thing that would have been on his mind when he and William went to a small fancy dress shop to get ready for their pal's party.

In reality it was one of many storms Harry was going to ride out over the coming years. Looking back, the Nazi gaffe did him no long-term harm whatsoever. James Whitaker's prediction that the prince would be blighted by the story for the rest of his life was wide of the mark. But it was enough to remind Harry of the things that were important in life and the dangerous path he trod as the media microscope once again began to focus on everything he did.

CHAPTER 2

THE GAP YEAR

EVERYONE REMEMBERS WHERE they were the day Princess Diana died. It was a tragic event that dominated the news all over the world. In the UK it was the only story being reported, and most of the papers even put black borders around their front pages as a mark of respect.

In the small hours of 31 August 1997, Diana and her boyfriend Dodi Al-Fayed were being driven by chauffeur Henri Paul away from the Ritz Paris hotel when disaster struck. Their Mercedes smashed into a pillar in the Pont de l'Alma underpass as they tried a high-speed escape from the chasing paparazzi. Within hours the People's Princess was pronounced dead. The most photographed woman in the world had been killed as her lover's security team played cat and mouse with photographers desperate for a rare shot of the couple together.

Whatever the rights and wrongs of what happened, this tragic event would change the way British newspapers in particular would cover the Royal family. After Diana's death, things were never going to be the same again. The backlash against the media was instant, but the fall-out would continue for many years to come.

As it happens, the terrible news came through just three days after I had begun my first job in journalism. I could not have predicted, as a young cub reporter on a local paper, what a long-term impact those events in Paris were to have on my career.

I had always been a fan of the Royal family as individuals, even though as an institution I felt it was perhaps outdated and anti-democratic. As a politics graduate I had written countless essays on whether Britain would be better as a republic. In fact, I always felt the Royals represented little more than a living museum, a throwback to the Empire that people just enjoyed gawping at.

The goldfish bowl they occupied must have been, I thought, a hellish place to live. No palace, privilege or position could be worth the life sentence of being trapped in the spotlight purely because of an accident of birth. I would rather have been born into the Addams Family than the House of Windsor, and that remains my view.

My desire to become a journalist had nothing to do with Royal coverage or the high-profile tabloid soap opera that had been played out since Diana's marriage to the Prince of Wales began to unravel. I was interested in meeting people, writing and having a job that would get me out of the office.

Now, as a trainee reporter for the *Tonbridge Courier* in Kent, I was tasked with trying to get some kind of local angle on the story. The chief reporter decided to send me down to the railway station to try and speak to people about the biggest story for decades.

The outpouring of public grief centred on the gates of Kensington Palace in London. Thousands of people were flocking to Diana's home in the capital to lay flowers and messages in response to the awful news. I was asked to go down to Tonbridge station to see if I could find anyone who had made that pilgrimage and interview them for the following week's edition. With the exception of writing about morris dancers visiting a Tonbridge pub, this was my first assignment as a reporter. My shoes had been proudly polished and I was wearing a brand new suit with a tie bought for me by my mother as a reward for getting through my interview with the paper.

I was so excited about getting a job as a reporter. I had only just graduated from university and this was my dream career. The local paper would train me and although the pay was dreadful, at least I didn't have to fork out on a post-graduate journalism course with no guarantee of a job at the end.

So the first trip out of the tiny office above a shop in Tonbridge High Street was a real milestone for me. It was the first time I would meet the public face-to-face, and with a bit of luck get some good quotes and my first byline in that week's edition.

Finding people that fitted the bill wasn't difficult. Dozens were setting off or returning from London on the train in their bid to pay their respects. I pulled out my brand-new notepad and approached two middle-aged women who had clearly just returned from Kensington Palace.

'Hello,' I said. 'I'm really sorry to bother you but I'm a reporter from the *Tonbridge Courier*. I am trying to speak to anyone local who has been up to Kensington Palace to lay flowers.'

The reply I was given is ingrained in my memory.

'Why don't you fuck off and leave us alone,' snarled one of the women.

'Your lot killed Diana, you're nothing but scum,' barked her friend.

As first interviews go, it's fair to say mine wasn't the best start. I was so shocked by their response and didn't dare try and explain how it was my first week on the job. After trying for another hour I finally gave up. Everyone was angry and all I was doing was gifting them a chance to vent their spleen. Heading back to the office, braced for the inevitable telling-off for failing in the task, I was still in shock. I thought: 'Do people really hate the press this much? Surely members of the public can see the difference between a local reporter trying his best and the big national papers that pursued her with such an obsession?'

From the moment of Diana's death, journalism in the UK changed. The very same people who flocked to the newsagents to buy papers showing pictures of Diana, the people who fuelled the demand for these pictures, were now turning on the newsmen and women who satisfied their demand. We were the enemy. In their eyes we were indeed 'scum'.

As a result of this public backlash, in 1999 a new set of rules was introduced to stop the press from hounding the Royals. Harry, who was then only fourteen, and his 16-year-old brother William were to have particular protection. It was agreed that while they remained in full-time education, they were to be 'off limits' to the press. The only pictures that were to be published of the boys were those taken by accredited photographers and released with the authorization of the palace.

It was a concession almost all editors agreed to. The flag-waving, pro-Royal public loved to read about their favourite family, but Diana's death drew a new line in the sand. From that moment on the teenage princes were to be treated with kid gloves by the media and any journalist who stepped outside this agreement faced being named and shamed.

In most respects the post-Diana arrangements worked well. The princes were left alone to continue their education at Eton College, in Berkshire, one of the world's best and most expensive private schools. For the next six years, every now and then the palace would arrange for William and Harry to be photographed and these pictures would be released to the media for their consumption.

Diana was such a big seller for the British tabloids in particular. At the height of her popularity, a mere picture of her in a new dress would make front-page news. And a front page with Diana would sell like hot cakes. Editors quickly realized she was a gift from the tabloid gods. But following her death, there was a general reluctance to allow history to repeat itself with her sons. Generally, papers steered well clear of publishing pictures and stories of the boys. And in this unprecedented media vacuum William and Harry were allowed to enjoy their teenage years in relative normality.

That should really have been the end of the matter. The only problem was that the princes, and Harry in particular, had taken their mother's death very hard. He was not academic and his mother's death in many ways gave Harry the freedom to react like any teenager who was never likely to excel in his studies. He became rebellious. In fact, he revelled in being the class clown. Rather than befriend fellow pupils who sat at the front of the class, handed their homework in on time and studied hard for exams, Harry chose a different path. He chose to sit at the back of the class, rarely finished his homework on time and the less said about his exams the better.

One fellow Etonian recalled: 'Harry was a rebel. His protection officers were always in the background and everyone knew who he was. But apart from that, you would never know he was a Royal, and a senior one at that. He gravitated towards the other boys who were often in trouble, who didn't seem to care about getting on with schoolwork.

'Harry seemed to take the view that Eton was about having fun. He always played the fool and even then had a way of acting up, going a bit further than anyone else. He was very popular and even the teachers doted on him. He had that way of messing about and pushing it to the limit without upsetting the masters enough to get into real trouble. His group of friends were very similar but Harry was definitely the ringleader.'

Harry's antics at Eton went largely unreported, not least because of the agreement with the press. But in January 2002 the world's press got their first opportunity to reveal how Harry had adjusted to life away from the cameras since his mother's death. The *News of the World* revealed that the prince, then just sixteen years old, had experimented with cannabis.

The paper told how in the summer of 2001, Harry had made the most of being left home alone by his father and elder brother at the Prince of Wales's Highgrove estate in Gloucestershire. Harry and his under-age chums had apparently been drinking at the Rattlebone Inn, three miles up the road from Highgrove. He was then alleged to have carried on partying into the early hours after inviting his pals back to the secluded manor. It was during this infamous night out Harry is alleged to have smoked a cannabis joint in front of his friends.

Prince Charles was reportedly made aware of what went on by a member of Highgrove staff who caught a whiff of the class C drug on the prince. However, the scandal remained a closely guarded secret for nearly six months before the *News of the World* ran its famous 'Harry's Drug Shame' front page.

When that story broke there was no official denial. A spokesman said at the time of the revelations: 'This is a serious matter which was resolved within the family and is now in the past and closed.' It was also revealed that Prince Charles had sat down with Harry to discuss the matter before deciding to take his youngest son on a secret visit to a drug rehabilitation centre in south London.

The reaction to the story was illuminating. Here was the third in line to the British throne admitting that he had at the very least experimented with an illegal drug. And for the first time a newspaper had stepped outside the post-Diana agreement and published a sensational story about the behaviour of one of the princes.

While the 'men in grey suits' were furious the story had made it into the public arena, there was no way they could argue the public did not have a right to know what had happened. The statement confirming the story made the news all over the world, and to this day the general public have a vague recollection that Prince Harry has dabbled in drugs.

But very few people condemned the prince for his behaviour. There was still a lot of sympathy for him, and rather than debate whether Harry should be condemned for his behaviour, the public mood was one of anger that he had been exposed. The then Liberal Democrat leader Charles Kennedy even went on television to repeat his view that cannabis as a drug should be declassified and made legal.

This remarkable reaction showed the public generally supported Harry and if given the choice would side with the young Royal ahead of any newspaper. It became clear that the public feeling, even after nearly five years since Diana's death, remained firmly behind her children rather than the media.

In 2004 the agreement over media coverage of the princes was still in place, as the newspapers were reluctant to break it. Seven years after the events in Paris, and public feelings towards the press were still raw.

Prince Harry had left Eton College after his A levels in 2003, in which he had secured a B in art and a D in geography. Despite attending one of the world's most prestigious schools, he had scraped through and only just achieved the minimum results required to allow him to apply to join the Army's officer training course. No one dared criticize his results. Not even when it later emerged that his former art teacher had helped Harry with parts of his coursework did anyone poke fun at him.

By his own admission Harry is not academically minded. He suffers from mild dyslexia and was far more suited to the challenges of Eton's CCF (Combined Cadet Force) corps, where he achieved the highest rank in his last term at school. The general consensus was that having to cope with the tragic death of his mother, coupled with the pressure of being a young Royal, more than excused his below-average exam results.

With a place at Sandhurst secured, however, Harry made a mistake that would haunt him for many years to come. Rather than head straight into the British Army, the young prince chose to take a 'gap year'.

Had Harry gone straight to Sandhurst in 2003 after getting his exam results there is little doubt the media restrictions would have remained in place. The military academy is after all a college of learning. There, young cadets are made into officers. They take exams, learn basic infantry skills and much, much more. It would have been very difficult for any news organization to argue that Sandhurst could not be deemed 'full-time education', and the prince would have been left alone.

However, Harry followed in the footsteps of so many ordinary teenage school leavers and decided to embark on what would turn out to be eighteen months of travelling, partying and high jinks. Unfortunately for Harry, he was not an 'ordinary teenage school leaver', and this decision left him open to the kind of scrutiny that his palace advisers had fought so hard to avoid.

One palace source explained: 'At the time Harry left Eton it was hoped he would focus on going to Sandhurst. Clearly his one great passion, and something he was very good at, was the school cadet corps. At that time Harry was very vulnerable. He was still very damaged by the death of his mother and people noticed he carried a lot of anger. Going into the military would have, with hindsight, helped this young prince face and deal with his demons.

'But instead he was absolutely adamant that he would take a break. He wanted the freedom to travel, to let his hair down and see the world. No one around him at that time was able to persuade him not to take a gap year and his aides were told to make a press statement confirming his time out.'

Harry spent time on an Australian ranch and was spotted cheering on the England rugby team as they lifted the World Cup in November 2003. He then travelled to South Africa and made the very worthy decision to set up a charity in memory of his mother. But the rest of the time the prince spent living in his apartment at St James's Palace in central London surrounded by the handful of people he considered friends.

In October 2004, soon after his return from South Africa, Harry set off for a night out at the Pangaea club in London's West End. Surrounded by his chums, Harry drank and enjoyed the evening as if he didn't have a care in the world. The exclusive club seemed to be a safe haven for the prince. Just a stone's throw from his palace apartment, here he could enjoy a night out safe in the knowledge that the club's security and his own detail of Met Police protection officers would keep any unwanted attention at bay.

Sadly, however, the same could not be said for the short walk he would inevitably need to take between leaving the club and jumping into one of the waiting protection officers' vehicles. At 3 a.m. Harry emerged from the club to be confronted by the one thing he hated more than anything, a pack of paparazzi.

There is a common misconception about press photographers. Paparazzi is a word generally and erroneously used to describe just about any group of photographers with a camera. In fact, paparazzi is quite a narrow term which only applies to freelance snappers who trade in pictures of celebrities, royals and anyone else they hope to make money from.

A press photographer is generally an accredited photojournalist who has had training and is commissioned by newspapers to take pictures. If a press photographer behaves badly, hurls abuse or harasses their target, they risk the wrath of their employers. As a result they are forced to ensure their pictures are taken legitimately, as they cannot risk their reputations by taking shortcuts or stepping outside the rules of engagement agreed by the Society of Editors.

But in these days of digital photography and a heightened public obsession with the cult of celebrity, there is little or nothing to stop just about anyone from picking up a camera and chancing their luck. In London's West End these 'bounty hunters' patrol the nightclub doors looking for famous targets. With the success of Twitter, their sources are unlimited. One tweet from a member of the public boasting about a celebrity face in the crowd, and the paparazzi can pounce.

On that night the photographers were aware that Harry was partying in Piccadilly and it would only be a matter of time before he would have to emerge.

It needs to be stressed here it was not at all underhand or illegal for them to patiently wait outside a club for someone famous to emerge. If celebrities choose to make a splash in a public place then they are 'fair game' in the eyes of the law. But a young Royal emerging from a club in the small hours will inevitably not see it in those terms, and when the little group of photographers' flashes started to go off in the October darkness, Harry was furious.

Accounts differ about what actually happened that night. It was claimed that Harry deliberately stepped back out of his Royal protection officer's vehicle to make a lunge at one of the photographers. In the scuffle that followed, the snapper in question was left with a cut lip. Clarence House later insisted that it was Harry who had been hit in the face with a camera, and that he instinctively reacted by pushing the camera away.

Whatever the truth of the ugly incident, it made little difference to the consequences. The following morning images emerged in London's *Evening Standard* showing the prince lashing out before being physically lifted away by one of his most trusted protection officers and bundled into the waiting vehicle. In an interview accompanying the pictures, photographer Chris Uncle said: 'Prince Harry looked like he was inside the car and we were still all taking pictures.

'Then suddenly he burst out of the car and lunged towards me as I was still taking pictures. He lashed out and then deliberately pushed my camera into my face.'

Another photographer backed up the claim. 'He was halfway getting into the back of the car when he suddenly reacted and lunged at him and grabbed his camera and pushed him against the wall.'

Harry's media team at Clarence House were forced onto the back foot and released a statement defending the prince. But the incident made headlines all over the world and whether he liked it or not, questions were being asked about whether Prince Harry was in meltdown.

Since he left Eton, the public had seen very little of Harry. The only images of him showed a young man enjoying what could only be described as the mother of all gap years. Although there had been focus on his Sentebale charity set up to help the forgotten AIDS orphans of the tiny kingdom of Lesotho in Southern Africa, relatively little had emerged to show Harry in a good light. The timing of the nightclub incident was therefore all the more unfortunate for him. There was very little his advisers could point to in his defence. These unprecedented pictures of a young Royal in a fracas simply fuelled the feeling that the prince should have already knuckled down to his military career rather than waste time partying and travelling the world.

Several months later I discussed what actually took place with one of the people who was there with Harry as it happened. 'It was in many ways a storm in a teacup,' he said. 'Harry felt he was threatened by how close the photographers came. They were right up in his face, their flashes firing off like disco strobes. He was very upset and angry when he got back into the car. As he was driven off, the red mist had clearly got the better of him. His face was bright red with rage and he was swearing and cursing. After that he was just upset and kept asking what could be done about the incident.'

At that time Harry's anger towards the paparazzi was all-consuming. It is hard to imagine just how much the 20-year-old prince was upset by what happened. The combination of an angry young man, a few late-night drinks and a confrontation with the one thing he hated the most was all too much for Harry.

By the time the story had been reported all over the world, editors and Royal watchers were beginning to reach the conclusion that a closer eye could be laid on the young prince. While the post-Diana agreement was still in place to an extent, opinions varied as to whether a gap year constituted an end to full-time education, or whether it was, in a loose way, still part of his growing up.

The work Harry had done in Lesotho was winning him many plaudits. He was showing a mature side, a side determined to continue his mother's legacy. He even invited a small group of newsmen along with him on one of his trips to launch the charity and throw the spotlight on the terrible plight of the orphans he had met.

Lesotho, the small kingdom land locked by South Africa, had one of the world's highest AIDS and HIV rates. It was, and still is, so bad that the life expectancy for an adult is a mere thirty years. Harry visited the country and saw at first hand the horrors being suffered by the young people of Lesotho. Because of the AIDS epidemic, an entire generation of adults is missing. The majority of people are either below eighteen or grandparents. What struck Harry was the way these children seemed to have been forgotten by the outside world, and he made a profound and genuine pledge to make a difference.

During his trip with the media, an ITV documentary was made, which did indeed throw a light on what was going on. For Harry, and his advisers, this was a coup. Like his mother, the prince was using his Royal fame to focus a spotlight on people the world had forgotten. To this day Harry has kept his pledge to the children of Lesotho. Sentebale – which means 'Forget Me Not' – continues its essential work in Lesotho.

But in October 2004, Harry's decision to invite the media to follow the work of his new charity in some ways fuelled the calls for the prince to be put under more scrutiny. Cynical minds started to argue that if it was OK for the media to report on the very worthy things Harry was up to, why should they not report on his other antics? It was an age-old debate that was starting to emerge within the British media. Everyone liked Harry, but how much longer could the press sit back and allow his advisers to call all the shots?

Even then, there was a public fascination with Harry. He did not seem like the other Royals. He was not like the other Royals. His natural way with people, and in particular children, came across in bucket-loads as he bounced a little orphan on his knee for the cameras. It was clear he had that natural gift when meeting people for instantly making them feel like the only people in the world that mattered.

Following the media coverage in Lesotho, pledges of support and money started to roll in. Sentebale was up and running with Harry at the helm. Harry was an emerging star. But everyone was eager to see the other side of his personality – the party-loving, laid-back lad with a glint in his eye and a lust for life. A prince who was fun to be around was a prince people wanted to know more about.

The row over him smoking cannabis, followed by the high-profile clash with photographers, opened the door to this hunger for information. The agreement to leave him alone was being put under pressure and as Harry headed towards the end of 2004, he must have sensed things were all about to change.

It wasn't long before the press got a sniff of one very significant change that Harry had been keeping secret since April that year. Away from the cameras, away from the front-page stories, he had fallen head over heels in love.

CHAPTER 3

THE ROYAL JOB

'WHAT DO YOU think about doing the Royal job?' asked my news editor Chris Pharo in his typically abrupt, no-nonsense way. I was walking the dog when he rang and I was caught completely off guard. I'd never considered covering the Royal beat at the *Sun*, and the call came right out of the blue.

In the days of Diana, the Royal job was the stuff of legends. I had heard stories about what it was like following one of the most talked-about women on the planet to all corners of the globe. The Royal patch was indeed a plum job then. Because stories and pictures of Diana were such a huge seller, the budget for covering them was equally large.

It was rumoured that when Charles and Diana went on honeymoon following their wedding in 1981, a team from the *Sun* had chartered a private jet to scour the Mediterranean to find the yacht they were holidaying on. The bill for the plane alone was £50,000, and although that was split between several newspapers, it still amounted to a vast sum of money.

My colleague and legendary Royal reporter Charlie Rae would often share stories about flying the world in First Class, staying at some of the best hotels in some of the finest locations. As a general rule, Royals only go to nice places. So, for the reporter lucky enough to be dispatched to cover them, this meant jetting off to ski slopes, safari lodges, and exclusive resorts I could only dream of.

Since qualifying as a journalist I had moved on from the morris dancer exclusives at the *Tonbridge Courier*, eventually getting a full-time job at the *Sun* in 2001. The paper was a daunting place to work. Everything happened at 100 miles an hour and the daily pressure was immense. Walking into the *Sun* newsroom for the first time was a day no reporter would ever forget.

In 2001 the *Sun* was still put together on the seventh floor of the print works on the vast News International site dubbed Fortress Wapping. At the height of his dispute with the print unions in the mid Eighties, Rupert Murdoch famously outflanked the strikers by moving his entire UK newspaper operation to a nine-acre site in the run-down area of Wapping, on the edge of the City of London.

The site was ideal because it really was like a fortress. High stone walls and huge fences protected an oasis safe from the rioting protesters and picket lines that threatened to bring the news operation to its knees. The site was dominated by the huge print works which in 1986 had been state of the art, requiring far fewer printers to operate. In 2001 the *News of the World*, *The Times*, the *Sunday Times* and the *Sun* editions still rolled off the presses there before being loaded onto hundreds of lorries to be dispatched throughout the UK.

The *Sun* newsroom was a dark, imposing place housed on the top floor above the print rooms. When, each evening, the print run began, the floors shook and everyone arriving for a late shift had to run the gauntlet of lorries and forklift trucks as they rolled in and out of the building. But it was in this dirty, almost threadbare room where Britain's biggest newspaper was put together by the army of sub-editors, journalists and support staff every day of the year except Christmas Eve.

Stepping out of the stainless steel lift and walking towards the metal-framed glass doors of the paper's newsroom, you were instantly reminded of the place you were entering. All along the corridor leading to the newsroom were huge copies of legendary *Sun* front pages, encased in frames, proudly shown off like hunting trophies in a colonial palace. Above the fingerprint-smudged glass doors hung a red and white sign saying: 'Walk Tall – You're entering Sun country'.

In reality, being lucky enough to do casual shifts at the *Sun* meant keeping your head down, doing what you were told and trying to make the most out of any assignment you were handed. After more than a year of casual shifts I was offered a staff contract at the paper. I left my job with a press agency and grabbed the opportunity with both hands.

By November 2004, when my boss sounded me out about doing the Royal beat, I had worked on all kinds of general news stories. As a general reporter I had worked on what felt like everything. Covering the TV show *Big Brother* in the days when people still watched it in their millions. Working with the team who covered the Soham murders of 10-year-olds Holly Wells and Jessica Chapman. Then following the trial of their killer, Ian Huntley. When a group of Leicester City soccer players had been falsely accused of raping three girls in a Spanish hotel I had spent a month chasing the story.

I had been sworn at by Posh Spice on the ski slopes of Verbier, shaved my head into stripes in an appallingly unsuccessful bid to look like David Beckham with braids. Under instruction from the newsdesk I'd even pushed a Dalek onto the set of *Doctor Who* in protest at the producers refusing to bring back the infamous Kaled mutants everyone remembered from their childhood.

It is fair to say there was never a dull day at the *Sun*, and this was an environment I adored. But until that phone call I had never given any thought to the job of covering the Royals for the

Sun. Royal coverage at that time consisted of writing up the stories and pictures on William and Harry with which the media were spoon-fed by the palace. Or filling in a picture caption as Prince Charles pulled a funny face while visiting an organic yoghurt factory somewhere in the West Country. While the Royal job was prestigious and meant travelling to some great places all over the world, it was not something that had ever appealed.

The reason the news editor was sounding me out was quite simple. It was November 2004. Prince Harry had been charging all over the world on what was fast becoming the longest 'gap year' in history – he would not arrive at Sandhurst until May 2005. Away from the cameras it had been revealed that the 20-year-old prince had been secretly dating a young Zimbabwean student. Just days before that call, the *Mail on Sunday* had revealed that Harry had taken Chelsy Davy for a two-week holiday in Argentina at a remote polo lodge near the capital Buenos Aires.

This was the first time 19-year-old Chelsy's name had emerged, and the paper made great play of how the pair were clearly a couple. It claimed they had spent almost the entire trip side by side. Quoting a source at the El Remanso polo lodge, the paper revealed: 'Harry and Chelsy were like any young couple in love, kissing and holding hands, and he seemed quite besotted.

'They looked madly in love and at one point Harry admitted she was his first true love. They did all the normal things young people do. We held a small barbecue and they sat beside each other and were laughing and joking. She seemed very relaxed in his company.'

According to the report, Harry even flew Chelsy out on a hunting expedition to a private game lodge in the province of Entre Rios during the visit. They quoted another source who said: 'When they went on the hunting trip, where they were mostly shooting pigeons, someone got out a small camera. Harry seemed quite agitated about having their picture taken together.

'It is obvious he is besotted with her ... When someone asked how long they had been going out together she blushed and said, "Eight months".

'Harry seemed very protective of her and often had an arm around her shoulders. She was definitely a calming influence on him. We had some drinks at the barbecue but he had only one beer and half a glass of wine.

'Chelsy was sweet and was very proud of Harry when they were hunting, as he is a very good shot. They flew in together on a private plane and left together. There was no doubt they were a couple.'

In their exclusive story, the *Mail on Sunday* also quoted Chelsy herself. At the time she was living with her brother Shaun in a house owned by their parents in the swanky Cape Town suburb of Newlands. When the paper knocked on Chelsy's door, the unsuspecting teenager let slip that she had known Harry since she was at school.

This was the excuse Fleet Street had been waiting for. Less than a month after his row with the photographers, it had been revealed that Harry had jetted off in secret, with his Met Police body-guards in tow, to enjoy a romantic break with Chelsy. The palace had remained tight-lipped and the whole romance had been going on in secret for several months.

Sadly for Harry – and any senior Royals – his love life is considered 'fair game'. Throughout modern history, newspapers and commentators have viewed the private relationships of Royalty as something the public are entitled to know about. With all the privilege and patronage comes the convention that the tax-paying public have a right – within reason – to know about those people who may have become romantically linked to the most important family in Britain. And because Harry had enjoyed living the high life since leaving school, it was going to be very difficult for his palace advisers to argue that he was still in full-time education, and that the post-Diana agreement should stay in place.

'I want you to go to Cape Town and follow up the story about Harry's new girlfriend,' continued my news editor.

I had never been sent on a job outside Europe before, and the instruction to go to South Africa sounded like one of the best assignments I had ever been given.

There was a lot riding on the trip. The *Sun*'s editor was understandably furious that the *Mail on Sunday* had beaten us to the story about Chelsy. But virtually nothing more was known about this beautiful blonde who had seemingly stolen Harry's heart. It was obvious most of Fleet Street would be sending staff out to find out more. This would be a high-pressure race to come up with the goods, but I was determined to give it a go.

The flight to Cape Town was hideous. Twelve hours on a packed British Airways 747 flight. It was November, the start of South Africa's long hot summer, and that meant seats had been booked up long in advance. The photographer and I had to cram into the last two available, sandwiched in the centre aisle of economy class for the inevitably sleepless overnight flight.

By the time we landed in Cape Town I was already beginning to regret agreeing to the assignment. I knew that as soon as I turned my phone back on the pressure would start. Sure enough, my phone started to bleep as soon as it connected to the local signal.

'Call the office, urgent', barked the message.

I was still waiting in a long queue at passport control when I phoned the newsdesk to tell them I had arrived.

'Well, have you got anything yet?' came the response. The only thing I had was what felt like a rotten hangover from being crammed in an overnight flight for twelve hours and a suspicion I might have a deep vein thrombosis in my legs, which were numb from being stuck in the same position since 10 p.m. the night before.

If this was what Royal reporting involved, then it was a far cry from the glamorous, plum job my colleagues had always described. We were desperate for a shower and some sleep, but instead we headed straight from the airport to Chelsy's address in Newlands.

Chelsy and her brother lived in an expensive area of Cape Town in a detatched house halfway down a quiet suburban road. Like any nice property in Cape Town, her white-washed home was surrounded by high walls, electric gates and razor wire. Directly opposite was a school playing field where wealthy South African families sent their children. The tree-lined street felt like a haven, worlds away from the run-down shacks of the townships we had driven past on the way from the airport.

Cape Town is a city of huge contrasts. The poor are extremely poor, forced to beg at traffic lights or pack into rusty white mini-buses in the hope of finding a day's labour. And the wealthy are extremely wealthy, living the dream life in well presented detached homes where housekeepers and gardeners cost less than £10 a day.

Chelsy's home was owned by her father Charles, a wealthy businessman from Zimbabwe who had bought the place as one of his many investments and to provide his two children with somewhere comfortable to live while they studied at the prestigious University of Cape Town.

It was no surprise to find we had company outside the house. There were at least ten other cars with photographers and reporters waiting for Chelsy to emerge. By now the race to find out more about Harry's new girlfriend had well and truly started. If the UK papers hadn't sent their own staff, they were employing Cape Town-based freelance reporters and photographers, all of whom had made a pilgrimage to Chelsy's plush home.

A story about a UK celebrity always felt like a big deal. I was well used to heading out to a ski slope, or a European beach resort following a tip that someone from *Big Brother* or a Premiership football team had been spotted. But when it comes to the UK Royal family, you are entering a different league. A story about Jade Goody would have found its way into the pages of the *Sun*, *Daily Star* or *Mail on Sunday*. But a story about Prince Harry, the third in line to the British throne, would make headlines in the UK, across Europe, America and Australia, in fact in most places in the Western world. And the chance to reveal more about Harry's first ever serious girlfriend was big news. For freelance photographers just one decent picture of Chelsy could be worth tens of thousands of pounds, as newspapers and magazines around the world waded into the *Mail on Sunday*'s exclusive.

Understandably, Chelsy had 'gone to ground'. She may have been caught out when approached for the first time by a journalist a few days earlier, but by now she was under strict instructions to say nothing to reporters and to try to keep a low profile.

Knocking on her door would have been a total waste of time. That opportunity had gone. So we set about trying to see who our competition was. What other papers had sent from London, and who were the reporters out there.

Journalists will always try and establish who they are up against, especially if they have been sent 6,000 miles for a story. With newsdesks screaming for results, there is a strange bond that quickly grows between the reporters on the ground. In reality working for a national newspaper meant getting to know reporters and photographers from rival papers, and spending more time with them than your own colleagues.

In Cape Town that week there were staff from the *Mirror*, the *Mail*, the *Mail on Sunday*, the *News of the World* and the *Daily Express*, all tasked with finding Chelsy. Without any obvious signs of the 19-year-old, the job now was to track down relatives and friends of Chelsy who might be willing to speak or hand over pictures. The clock was ticking and the newsdesk back in London was desperate for something.

Eventually we got a breakthrough. We had been told Chelsy had flown to Durban, a two-hour flight east of Cape Town. Her father had another property up the coast from Durban in an exclusive resort called Umhlanga Rocks, popular with wealthy young South Africans and with a reputation as a seaside party town. Better still, we were told that Chelsy was expecting a visitor for the weekend: Prince Harry.

Any attempt by the palace to play down the stories of Harry's new girlfriend would go out of the window if they were spotted together in Umhlanga Rocks. Harry was clearly taking every possible moment to see Chelsy – his gap year had turned into a romantic break and he was smitten.

It was clear too that Chelsy was a very popular student. She loved to party and enjoyed a close-knit circle of good friends. Long before Harry had come onto the scene, the 19-year-old was the sort of student who would hang out with the crowd. Cape Town has an amazing night life, with clubs, bars and restaurants to rival any city in the world. And for well-off students it is a playground for beautiful young people, a place to show off their athletic bodies and tanned skin. We were offered a picture of her wearing a little black dress, holding a glass of champagne in one hand while she danced on a table. It was taken during a typical night out in one of Cape Town's exclusive clubs, where Chelsy was clearly well known.

The manager of one of the clubs – the Rhodes House – described how Chelsy and Harry had enjoyed a night there during one of his secret visits to Cape Town in April that year. 'Chelsy and her friends were regulars at the Rhodes House,' Jack revealed. 'In April 2004 Prince Harry came to the club. He was on his gap year and had stopped in Cape Town while on a visit to Southern Africa. He arrived with his security team and a couple of other pals. A little later he was seen leaning out of the window and shouting down to a group of girls outside.

'It was only later we realized it was Chelsy. She came upstairs and joined Harry's group in the VIP area. At that time no one put two and two together, but it is clear looking back that they already knew each other.

'They were careful not to draw too much attention to themselves but Cape Town is the sort of place where it's not unusual to spot famous people. Lots of films and adverts are shot here and in the summer months we have super-models and famous sports stars here a lot of the time. It's a laid-back place and people don't really take any notice of famous faces in the crowd. I can well see why Prince Harry felt he could come here and let his hair down in a way he would never be able to in London. People just aren't that bothered.'

We were booked on the first flight to Durban the following day, which was a Sunday. I decided to get an early night because we had to get up at 5 a.m. and I knew it was going to be very busy. Having got to sleep pretty quickly I was soon awoken by a phone call from London. It was the night news editor.

'Harry and Chelsy have been pictured together in Durban,' he said. 'They are on the front of tomorrow's *Mail on Sunday*. The pictures are not very good quality but it looks like they are on a balcony together and you can clearly see it's them.'

In fairness to the *Mail on Sunday*, they had made the most of their head start on the Chelsy exclusive and had already sent some local freelance photographers to Durban. But the pressure was now on. We had to try and match those pictures in time for the *Sun*'s next edition of the paper on Monday or I could forget about doing the Royal job.

We arrived in Umhlanga Rocks by 11 a.m., determined to get something for ourselves. The resort was very busy with young beautiful blonde girls who all looked like Chelsy. Everywhere we looked it was as though our eyes were playing tricks. Chelsy is very much the typical white South African beauty. With her long blonde hair, athletic body and sun-kissed skin, at Umhlanga Rocks she blended in like a chameleon. This was going to be far more difficult than we thought.

Chelsy and Harry were staying in a plush apartment block overlooking the Indian Ocean. The modern building boasted its own security and each of the 20 or so apartments had large layered sun decks to the rear that wouldn't have looked out of place on the back of a large cruise ship. It was surrounded by large walls topped with electric fences and it was almost impossible to see inside.

Impossible, that is, except from a large tower block of holiday apartments right next door. It was obvious that the freelance photographer had staked out the couple from the roof of the building, waiting for the best moment to get their picture. The photographer and I took one look at this vantage point and immediately agreed we could not stay. The rules were quite clear that taking a picture from private land onto private land fell well outside the then Press Complaints Commission guidelines. Also the roof of the private block was accessed by a door which had almost certainly been forcibly prized open. It seemed to have been damaged in the process, and there was no way in those circumstances a picture from that position could be used.

So instead we waited in the centre of town in the hope that Harry and Chelsy might slip out of their apartment for some lunch. After driving around the resort we finally spotted a small group of youngsters enjoying a lunch outside a café called Zack's. They were sitting in a courtyard on picnic benches and under the shade of some large umbrellas.

Sitting with his back to us in a grey T-shirt was a ginger-haired guy with a pair of sunglasses tucked behind his ears. I had never seen Prince Harry in the flesh before that moment, but there was no mistaking him. To his side Chelsy's long blonde hair waved in the breeze. She was wearing a figure-hugging turquoise shirt over a black bikini top. The couple were sitting side by side and looked completely relaxed with each other.

Chelsy's brother Shaun and his girlfriend were sitting opposite, while a small group of Harry's police protection officers sat discreetly at a table nearby. Their policy, as ever, was to draw as little attention as possible to their principal. They were even dressed like other holidaymakers in shorts and open-necked shirts, and quietly sipped coffee as the group enjoyed their lunch.

Even though dozens of people walked past, it was clear no one had a clue who was sitting right there. It was obvious even then that this was paradise for Harry. He had grown up in castles and palaces, been greeted by crowds of people since the day he was born, always stared at, always under the spotlight. But here in Umhlanga Rocks he was anonymous. No one even gave him a second look. And better still, he was with Chelsy.

Their eight-month romance had brought them to the place where she enjoyed holidays as a youngster. The laid-back, sun-kissed resort must have seemed like a world away from the busy bars of London. Harry seemed equally relaxed with Shaun, Chelsy's 21-year-old brother and best friend. The siblings shared their parents' house in Cape Town and were extremely close. If Harry was to have any chance with Chelsy, Shaun's seal of approval was vital.

One of the great paradoxes of Royal life is that the family who probably meet and greet more people than any other rarely make friends. For Harry his friends consisted of a handful of school chums, cousins close to him in age and the triple-barrelled children of his father's wealthy landed friends. Sure there were the usual polo pals and hangers-on, but Harry has never really warmed to this crowd.

Making new friends is a near impossibility for someone in Harry's position. He can't wander down to the pub or nip to the football to meet a group of his friends' pals. Nor, at that stage, did

Harry benefit from making friends at work. He'd never done a day's real work in his life.

So it was little surprise that the duo of Chelsy and Shaun seemed like a breath of fresh air to the 20-year-old. At last he had met someone who didn't seem to care about his royal status. Chelsy was an intelligent, outgoing African. Although she had been educated privately in England, she had never lost her Zimbabwean twang. She didn't seem interested in palaces or privilege, she was only interested in Harry the way he was.

Shaun also seemed down-to-earth and at ease in Harry's company. He often mocked the prince with put-downs and jokes at his expense. At times Chelsy and Shaun even ganged up on Harry, pulling his leg and making his odd comments the butt of their jokes.

This was incredible for Harry. A new circle of friends who could be trusted and most important of all, make him feel normal. In their relaxed company he could be himself, play the fool, make jokes at his own expense and entertain them with his silly remarks and wicked sense of humour.

Even during lunch Harry let this side of his character shine through. At one point the waiter brought over two cocktails Harry had ordered without telling his lunch companions. The large glasses contained what appeared to be a mixture of orange juice and grenadine.

'Come on, Chelsy – let's have sex on the beach,' Harry was overheard saying. The famous cocktail – with its risqué name – was enough to make the table fall about laughing. Harry was in heaven and could barely hide his excitement. The couple kissed and held hands as they tucked into the drink.

After lunch the group headed into a surf shop before splitting up to return to the nearby penthouse apartment. This was when one of the most iconic pictures of Chelsy was taken. Slowly walking back, she looked incredible in her tight top and pink sarong.

Her outfit showed off her tanned and athletic body. This girl may have already made headlines but now the world could be left in no doubt as to how she caught the attention of one of the planet's most eligible bachelors.

Harry may have ticked the box of being accepted by Chelsy's protective brother but he faced another, more daunting challenge the following day. He had been invited to join the Davy family for their pre-Christmas holiday in Mozambique. The group were due to fly there from Durban and join Chelsy's parents, Beverly and Charles, on the remote island of Bazaruto. This was to be Harry's first encounter with Mr and Mrs Davy.

Harry would have met them earlier but for one inconvenient fact: Charles Davy was a wealthy businessman who lived near Bulawayo, Zimbabwe. The country was run by Robert Mugabe's repressive government, which had overseen the removal of many white farms in recent years. Horrific stories had emerged from Zimbabwe as families, many of whom had farmed the land for generations, were forced out of their homes by violent gangs.

A few months earlier Harry had asked his father if it would be possible for him to go to Zimbabwe and visit the Davy ranch. But he had been told in no uncertain terms that this was out of the question. Even if Harry's safety could have been protected, the political fall-out of a senior British Royal making a private visit to Zimbabwe would have been immense.

The advice was spot on. The following year when Prince Charles accidentally shook the hands of Mugabe at Pope John Paul's funeral he found himself at the centre of a political storm.

But joining the Davys on their annual holiday in Mozambique seemed like the perfect solution for Harry and Chelsy. The island resort really is an undiscovered paradise. Its white sand beaches, palm trees and log cabins make it one of the most exclusive and secluded getaways on the planet. Here, Harry could take time to get to know the Davys while feasting on fresh fish and langoust-ines landed the same day by hotel staff.

The tiny resort had its own airstrip to fly wealthy guests in and out. The area was so remote it barely had any roads, just miles and miles of sandy beaches and untouched lagoons. Ironically, among the handful of those lucky enough to have discovered Bazaruto was the Zimbabwean president himself, who was a regular visitor. But fortunately for Harry, there was no chance of Mugabe's visit clashing with his.

By now several newspapers had arrived in Umhlanga Rocks and were being sent to Mozambique as the Chelsy story gained momentum. We flew with other journalists from Durban to the nearest airport on the mainland. Bazaruto is fifteen miles off the coast of Mozambique, so the nearest airfield was a place called Vilanculos, a small fishing town with not much more than a shed for an airport.

We had accommodation booked on the island, but after look-ing at the resort website we decided there was no way we could stay there. The resort only had about a dozen beachside lodges and one communal bar area, dining room and outdoor swimming pool. The last thing Harry would want to see was a bunch of Fleet Street hacks tucking into cocktails in the only bar. So instead we headed for a small hotel on the mainland, which was several miles away from the prince but as close as we could realistically get.

The following day the journalists from the UK decided to rent a boat to go and look at Bazaruto and get a feel for the place for the inevitable story that would follow. Tasked with the job of travelling to the island on behalf of the group, I set off in a small fishing boat manned by two local guys who were happy to sacri-fice a day's catch to become a water taxi.

Looking back, there is no way I would have attempted the journey had I known just how far, and how perilous it was going to be. The resort was at the far end of the island and this meant three and a half hours in a tiny boat through shark-infested waters. If anything went wrong, the nearest hospital was a six-hour drive away, and the waters off the coast of Mozambique had no coastguard or emergency services.

After bumping up and down in the boat for what felt like days, we finally arrived in a secluded bay where the Royal party were staying. There was no doubt this was one of the most beautiful and remote places I had ever seen. The crystal clear blue sea, the white sand and sight of palm trees looked to me like paradise on earth.

Soaking wet and relieved to be finally in the shelter away from the choppy swell of the Indian Ocean, I could just make out a man walking down to the water's edge. As we got within feet of the shore I could see who the man waiting for me was. It was Harry's number one protection officer; a loyal and professional police officer who had been by Harry's side since he was a small boy. We had met briefly back in Umhlanga Rocks after pictures had been taken of Harry and Chelsy eating lunch at Zack's.

The officer – who I have agreed not to name – stood on the beach with his arms folded. I could only make out one or two huts in the bay, and his footsteps were the only ones on the entire beach.

After taking one look at my soaked clothes he started to smile. He could see how relieved I was to have made it to dry land and must have known what a dangerous journey I had made.

I immediately apologized for arriving on the island. It was so obvious that this remote location was clearly no place for us to try and get pictures of Harry.

The protection officer seemed grateful when I assured him this was going to be my one and only time on Bazaruto, and that I had come on behalf of the other journalists to get a look at the place for our stories, then I was off.

To my surprise he then asked me for a favour. He said: 'Do you know a reporter from the *News of the World* called Sarah Arnold?'

Of course I did. She was a well-known and popular journalist on our sister paper. Only a few months earlier I'd met her on a job in Switzerland covering a story about Victoria Beckham.

'Why do you ask?' I replied.

'Because she is here on the island with a photographer and they are pretending to be on honeymoon. We know who she is because we've seen her passport. Harry is extremely angry about it and if she doesn't leave he will have no choice but to fly home.'

The officer asked me if I could have a gentle word in her ear to suggest she leave the island and head back to the mainland with me.

Even though the *News of the World* and the *Sun* were written in the same building, in adjacent newsrooms, we were still fierce rivals. Also, I thought, if she and the photographer stayed on the island, Harry and Chelsy would simply head home.

Most importantly, the kind-hearted policeman offered to have a word with the hotel manager to see if I could hitch a ride on his next flight back to Vilanculos, meaning I didn't have to set foot on that clapped-out old boat again.

I agreed to go and speak to Sarah and pass on the message. She was sitting on the terrace near the hotel pool. The photographer was by her side, although neither of them had notepads or cameras. There were only a small handful of other holidaymakers in the area, but I suggested to Sarah that we head off for a quiet chat along the beach.

To my astonishment the pair of them stayed in character. They said they were on honeymoon and demanded I leave them alone. They even threatened to call security if I did not do as they demanded.

I said: 'Have you two been drinking the seawater? I've been asked to point out that they know you are from the *News of the World* and if you don't leave then Harry will fly home.'

Despite my best efforts, there was nothing I could do to persuade them. I walked back to find the protection officer, who had been watching from a distance. To my surprise he was standing there with someone else. It seemed Prince Harry had decided to come over to see if I had succeeded.

'Well,' I said. 'You are right about who they are but I have a bit of a problem.'

Harry and his protection officer looked at me, confused.

I explained: 'They won't get out of character. They are adamant they are just a normal honeymoon couple. In fact, they said if I didn't stop pestering them they would call security.'

Harry and the officer burst out laughing before the officer replied: 'Thanks for trying.' We all shook hands and I wished Harry a good holiday, repeating my promise that I was heading back to the mainland, where I would stay.

It was only a few days later, when my office had finally given up on the waiting game and called us off the job, that I eventually saw the 'honeymooners'. They were waiting for a flight back to South Africa. It was an awkward moment, to say the least, but I later found out they had been thrown off the island shortly after I had gone.

It was a very surreal way of meeting a prince, but it taught me a valuable lesson. Harry doesn't like the press, but if you are prepared to compromise and show willing, he can see the funny side of what we do.

CHAPTER 4

KLOSTERS

'I'LL BE THERE, with a glass of brandy, smoking a big fat cigar with my dad,' said a bleary-eyed Harry.

It was the early hours of 31 March 2005 and I was in a Swiss nightclub in the company of Prince William and his high-spirited younger brother, Harry. In just a few hours' time we were all due on a hillside in the posh resort of Klosters for the official ski photocall with Prince Charles. It was the first time I had spoken to Harry since the *Sun* broke the story of him wearing the Nazi outfit to a fancy dress party.

I must confess I was very worried about what he would say to me. My name was on the story and since then I had been asked to talk about the partying prince on television. The story broke in January 2005 and since then the young prince had been under fire from all over the world. Inevitably Harry was criticized for his judgement, and the impact his seemingly wayward behaviour was having on 'the Firm', and people were questioning whether he was spiralling out of control.

One thing that has always surprised me about William and Harry is the interest they take in what is written about them. They are well aware that because of their accident of birth they will be the focus of media attention from before they were born, through-out their lives and after they are dead.

Many celebrities, politicians and famous people can only cope with negative press by pretending it is not there. As a general rule, they choose to avoid reading the bulk of the negative comments in a bid to keep their sanity or at the very least to prevent their large egos from taking a battering. Like actors refusing to read negative reviews of their work, they tend to cherry pick the best bits of media coverage as a way of coping with life under the spotlight.

In these circumstances it would be reasonable to assume the young princes simply refuse to pick up a newspaper for fear of seeing mistruths or criticism of them splashed across the pages. At the very least they could be forgiven for leaving their army of media advisers to 'deal' with the bad stuff and allow them to get on with their lives.

Nothing could be further from the truth. At times both the boys have demonstrated to me that they appear to read every word that is written about them. Certainly as far as the British tabloid papers are concerned, William and Harry seem to have an intense interest in what is said about them.

In the wake of the Nazi storm I had already been warned about this by the Prince of Wales's media team at Clarence House. 'You realize they (William and Harry) take a very keen interest in what people write about them,' warned one of Prince Charles's senior press advisers less than a week after the Harry the Nazi front page.

They went on to explain how both the boys kept in regular contact with the press office, asking for cuttings to be read to them and often demanding action if they felt stories were inaccurate or unfair. Even then Clarence House was well known for using the Press Complaints Commission and an aggressive legal firm to instantly seek some kind of redress if that was what the Royals demanded.

Some might think this egotistical, even vain, but that is far from fair. As far as the young princes are concerned, they have a duty to protect their reputations from inaccurate statements made about them. In their eyes this is nothing more than the 'rules of engagement' with the media. If criticism is fair, if the stories are accurate, then they are both big enough to take it on the chin. And they often do. But there has to be a line in the sand, a point beyond which they feel they can't just sit back and not say anything.

Behind the scenes there is a constant conversation going on between the Royal PR advisers and those members of the media who write stories about them. Both Harry and William are sensitive. They really do care about how they come across and will react with fury if this line has been crossed.

When the Nazi uniform story broke, Harry faced a very difficult few weeks. He knew he had made a mistake and he knew it would take a very long time to repair the damage. But, even as a relatively immature 20-year-old, he was also well aware that the story was accurate and he had no choice but to take the storm of criticism, even the parts which were unfair, on the chin. He lay low for six weeks, and the controversy had died down by the time he was due to join his brother on Prince Charles's annual ski trip to Klosters.

This was a regular date in the calendar for the family, a time to enjoy a favourite pastime with their father, a chance to hook up with friends and to hit the slopes at high speed. But over the years a convention had grown in a bid to ensure their ski holiday antics would remain largely unreported. The select group of Royal reporters and photographers would be invited to Klosters for an official photocall with the princes.

This idea began way back in the days when the princes were very young and Charles and Diana were desperate to try and give them as normal a ski holiday as possible. In return for being allowed to take pictures and throw a limited number of questions at the Royals, the media agreed to leave them alone once the photocall had taken place.

By and large over the years this unofficial arrangement had worked. It was not ideal for the Royals, who would much rather have enjoyed a holiday far away from any media attention. Nor was it ideal for the journalists, many of whom were uncomfortable with agreeing to take part in what was really nothing more than a staged event.

But in March 2005 there was particular interest in the annual photo opportunity. Yes, it was to be one of the first few times Harry would pose for the cameras following his recent embarrassment. But there were two bigger reasons the pressmen and women would flock to the exclusive Swiss resort that year.

Prince Charles was just weeks away from marrying Camilla Parker Bowles. The 'third person' in the future king's marriage to Diana was finally going to cement her place within the Royal family. She didn't join them on the trip, and this was going to be the last time William and Harry would spend a holiday away together without the woman famously dubbed a 'Rottweiler' by their late mother.

And the other reason why newspapers and television stations were more than happy to fork out a small fortune for their staff to stay in one of the world's most expensive ski resorts was to do with Prince William. In their wisdom, William and Charles had agreed to let Kate Middleton join them on the slopes that year. The couple were in their final few months at St Andrews University and their long-term romance had become the worst kept secret in Fleet Street. While the press was voluntarily banned from bothering William and Kate at university, the fact she was out in Klosters keeping her lover company was always going to serve up a mouth-watering opportunity for them.

The combination of a long-awaited Royal wedding and the prospect of catching a rare glimpse of William and Kate together was enough to ensure the small town was going to be packed with photographers. Fortunately for Harry, his recent problems were far from the minds of the journalists who arrived in Klosters in a fleet of hire cars after the two-hour drive from Zurich.

As is the case with all official photocalls, the event was to be carefully controlled by Clarence House. Invited media were told to gather for a briefing in a hotel conference room they had rented for the occasion.

Here, the familiar faces of the 'Royal press pack' would gather to discuss the plan for the following day. The exact location had been chosen but was being kept secret for security reasons. Only this handful of seasoned Royal watchers, their photographers, cameramen and producers would be told the details of what was planned for the morning.

It was agreed that William, Harry and their father would walk to an agreed point and sit together on a wooden wall by a Swiss farm building. The backdrop had been carefully chosen to show the mountains behind and the snow-kissed resort of Klosters in all its glory. To maximize the chances of the event going smoothly the media would be kept well back behind a rope. By creating a 'press pen' away from the Royals it was hoped that pushing and shoving would be replaced by careful and orderly behaviour from the forty or so journalists who were allowed to take part.

The princes would only answer a limited number of questions and it was decided in advance who was going to be lucky enough to quiz all three the following day. It is convention when reporting on the Royals that you do not shout out questions from the pack. The British media are well accustomed to this arrangement, and the palace team orchestrating the event knew it would have been a bad career move for any of us to try and push the boundaries of what had been agreed.

After the briefing the reporters headed off for a meal to discuss the photocall and speculate as to what we might get. By Alpine standards Klosters is a very small resort. There are just a handful of restaurants and bars and a single nightclub which is barely the size of someone's front room. The plan was to have a nice meal, then head off to our small hotels for an early night.

While most of the pack did just that, I decided to pop into a hotel where I knew many of Harry and William's friends liked to hang out. The downstairs bar was packed full of well-spoken English people. The fact that Prince Charles had made Klosters his annual choice of resorts had clearly not been wasted on the plane-loads of wealthy British families who, by complete coincidence, also decided to make the annual pilgrimage to the town.

The bar was wild, with the over-stretched staff serving up expensive champagne by the ice bucket-load. This was how the other half lived. The offspring of some of the country's wealthiest families tucked into bottles of Bollinger and goldfish bowls of £90-a-time cocktails all shamelessly put down on Daddy's tab. It seemed obvious that it was not just the press who flocked to Klosters because the Royals were in town. This was the place to be seen and this was the week to be seen there.

The only issue for the young and trendy revellers that had chosen this hotel bar for a night out was that there was little or no chance of William and Harry turning up. The princes have spent much of their lives surrounded by these types: hangers-on with more money than sense. Several of them worked out that our little group must be journalists and they made a beeline for our table to tell us how they went to school at Eton and were on very good terms with the young Royals.

This is the reality of life for William and Harry. Anyone they have ever met, through school, polo matches, charity events or nightclubs, claims to be friends of the princes. This is why it is so hard for the boys to make real friends. In reality they stick to a small group of trusted pals and do not trust anyone outside that select inner circle.

After a couple of hours it was definitely time for bed. I headed off in the direction of my hotel and walked up the empty streets thinking about what an early start I had. But the route took me past the only nightclub in Klosters and curiosity clearly got the better of me. I decided to visit the Casa Antica Club for a nightcap, justifying the decision on the basis that I wanted to see what Klosters' night life was like. I had overhead several people in the last bar mention they were heading up to Casa and, as it was the town's only nightclub, I wanted to see what all the fuss was about.

The club is very small and from the outside looks like all the other Swiss chalet-style properties. I walked through the entrance and into a small foyer which led into the main bar area. Here, I instantly recognized some of the characters sitting on chairs dressed in the tell-tale smart outfits of chinos, polo tops and fleece jackets. It was the Royal protection officers, several of whom I'd met while covering Prince Harry's trip to South Africa and Mozambique three months earlier. This was clearly a sign that the boys were in the club, which came as a surprise given that tomorrow morning was the photocall and it was already well past midnight.

'Oops, sorry, guys,' I said as they all looked at me walking in. 'Don't worry, I won't come in if the boys are here – it's well past my bedtime anyway.'

They laughed and agreed that it was indeed a late night for them as well.

The life of a Royal protection officer is indeed a plum job within the Met Police. They get to travel the world guarding their 'principals' and although there is little overtime and no extra pay, they all receive an annual allowance of £15,000 for clothing. As police officers they never have to make an arrest, and because the majority of their working life is spent well outside the jurisdiction of London they simply team up with local officers, who provide the bulk of the back-up required.

The best part of being a Royal protection officer, besides the kudos of guarding the Royals, is the prospect of enjoying a lucrative security job when they take early retirement on a full pension.

What wealthy Arab or billionaire businessman wouldn't want to snap up someone whose CV boasted years of looking after the most famous family on the planet?

In my experience I have found them to be professional, polite and very good at what they do. They never like to speak to the press and, on the rare occasions when they do, remain tight-lipped and discreet as their job requires.

But there is an obvious downside to being on hand twenty-four hours a day, 365 days a year. When Harry is out with his pals they have to sit and wait nearby, never knowing when they will get to bed. As the minutes roll into hours, they must occasionally wish they'd never given up the regular shifts and generous overtime associated with being an ordinary police officer. I have never heard them complain, but the sight of them all soberly sitting in the foyer of yet another nightclub in the small hours of the morning was quite amusing.

'You don't have to leave on our account,' said one of the more senior officers in the group. 'I will go and see if the boys mind you being here if you like,' he added.

This was a generous offer, given that the role of the protection team is to ensure the safety of the boys and has nothing to do with dealing with the press on their behalf.

After a few minutes the officer returned and said it was OK for me to go in. This was an offer I couldn't refuse, because the chance of seeing William and his brother party with their pals was very rare indeed. I went into the main part of the club and went to the bar to order a drink. Although I was still in my twenties at the time I was far older than the majority of those sipping Vodka Red Bulls and drinking beer out of bottles.

The club itself was quite dark and very loud. The main bar area was in the middle of the room, with a dance floor behind and a crowded drinking area at the front. It was a tiny place and that night there was barely room to move.

Sitting on stools at the far end of the long bar were two people who were easily recognized. William and Harry were staring straight at me as I gestured to double-check they didn't mind me being there. I could see they were both laughing at my expense as they started to mimic the clumsy hand gestures I was making in a bid to make sure I was not encroaching on their turf.

I respectfully stayed at my end of the bar and ordered a drink. If they were happy for me to be there I didn't want to blow it by rushing over and getting in the way. Besides, if Harry wanted to let rip at me for the Nazi story, then tonight I was a sitting duck.

After a few minutes I realized I needed to use the toilet, which meant walking straight past where Harry was now sitting on his own after William had disappeared into an adjoining room. My respect for their personal space was one thing, but it didn't extend as far as deciding to wet myself in the corner of a crowded club. So I slowly made my way through the crowds in the direction of the toilets, which were up a flight of stairs directly behind the barstool where Harry was sitting.

As I got right up close to the young Royal he smiled and said hello. By now I had no time to get into conversation with anyone because my priority was to answer the call of nature. But I had just enough time to say hello back and looked at Harry to joke: 'It's very late, are you sure you're going to be there for the photo-call tomorrow?'

Harry grinned and replied: 'I'll be there, with a glass of brandy, smoking a big fat cigar with my dad.'

I laughed and nodded back at what was clearly a risky comment from a prince everybody in the media had been branding boozy. I carried on past and went upstairs into the gents toilets.

Within seconds, as I stood at the urinal, I was aware of a flash going off. Looking round I saw Harry holding a small disposable camera and falling about laughing. He had followed me upstairs and decided it would be funny to get a bit of revenge on a member of the press by taking my picture for a change.

'Leave me alone, you paparazzi scumbag,' I barked at Harry, which only caused him to laugh even more. The other half a dozen or so people in the gents heard the exchange and they too started to laugh.

This candid moment was, I was later to learn, typical of the third in line to the throne. He has a very down-to-earth, spontaneous sense of humour and an opportunity for a gag like this was too good to miss. Harry was in his element fooling around and making everyone around him feel at ease. From that moment on I realized that the prince we had all written about was a far more natural and fun-loving young man than he was given the credit for.

If Harry has the chance to say or do something funny, he will. This spontaneity and ability to play the fool, even at his own expense, is a key reason why he has risen to become one of the most popular members of the Royal family in history.

I returned downstairs still laughing at what had happened. So much for me expecting to be shouted at for writing the Nazi story. It was clear he had no intention of bringing that up; he was just wanting to enjoy a night out before the boredom of posing for the cameras once again as a member of the Royal family.

Instead of returning to where I had been standing I decided to take my drink out to the foyer, where the protection officers still sat waiting for the signal the boys were ready to call it a night.

I sat down next to one of the officers and we started chatting about rugby and anything other than our jobs. After a few minutes a young reveller appeared out of a side room wearing nothing but a pair of silk boxer shorts. The lad clearly knew the protection officers and in a bid to find somewhere to sit and talk to them he jumped onto my lap. One of the officers then couldn't resist the temptation of having a bit of fun at this high-spirited reveller's expense.

He said: 'Hello, Guy, have you met the *Sun*'s new Royal correspondent, Duncan Larcombe?'

It was Guy Pelly, William and Harry's best-known pal. He had taken the rap when Harry was accused of smoking a joint in Highgrove. Since then his wild antics had often made the headlines. The son of a self-made millionaire car dealer, Pelly had struck up a close friendship with William and Harry while they were at school together at Eton.

Without a second word, Pelly jumped off my lap and ran back into the adjoining room. The incident had clearly spooked him, much to the delight of the protection officers. They definitely enjoyed the look on Pelly's face when he realized whose lap he was sitting on, wearing nothing more than his boxers.

To this day I don't know whether it was the incident with Guy Pelly which prompted William to break with Royal protocol. Bizarre as some of the things I had witnessed in less than an hour of being in that club were, nothing could have prepared me for what was to happen next.

A few minutes later I was still chatting to the protection officers when William himself came into the foyer. This was the first time I'd met the future king and I was surprised that he seemed keen to speak to me.

'What is the story in tomorrow's papers then?' he asked.

I explained that most of the papers were running pictures of him on the slopes with his girlfriend Kate Middleton. They had been taken earlier that day and with the couple looking so in love the story was bound to be splashed all over the papers.

William seemed strangely surprised by this and asked what all the fuss was about. Surely he knew the level of interest in his first serious relationship, I thought.

Kate, whom he had met at university and had been secretly dating for more than eighteen months, ticked all the right boxes. She was stunning, and came from a wealthy family but not the usual aristocratic background. Their relationship was a real love story about a young, handsome prince who had met and fallen in love with a 'commoner'. Kate had already been briefed on how to act in front of the cameras. Every time a photographer went near her she smiled and kept her mouth shut.

I asked him if he had heard the rumours that Kate was the one. His father was due to marry his true love in just a few days' time, so it was inevitable that people would be drawing comparisons between Kate and Camilla Parker Bowles. This was dodgy ground for William and I felt bad putting him on the spot. But he gave me an answer that oddly enough became more of a prophecy when we look back now.

He replied: 'I'm only twenty-two for God's sake. I don't want to get married until I'm twenty-eight or maybe thirty.'

I couldn't have imagined back then that six years later I would be sitting in Westminster Abbey watching Kate walk down the aisle while two billion people sat in front of their TV sets to see her and William tie the knot. It still makes me wonder whether William already knew that Kate really was the one and that as soon as he felt they were old enough they would get married.

Even more than his brother Harry, William's life is destined to follow a fairly rigid script. As the heir to the throne he carries the weight of expectation and is only too aware that his life is, in many respects, not his own.

But the main, and most touching part of our conversation that night, was about his kid brother. Since embarking on his gap year, Harry had been the subject of a great deal of criticism. When the Nazi story broke, people were saying he was out of control, a dangerous loose cannon whose antics risked damaging the monarchy. Now William leapt to Harry's defence, insisting the way his brother was being portrayed in the media was nothing like the real person he knew and loved. 'He's just a kid who's madly in love,' he said.

The way William defended Harry that night was very special. It was clear the two brothers were so close. They really cared about each other and William was visibly upset that Harry had endured such criticism.

Once again his words would turn out to be prophetic. Over the coming few years Harry's true colours would shine through. Yes, he would always be known as a party-loving prince but the fun-loving, caring and genuine side to the young Royal would take him from that point to becoming one of the most popular Royals. The more the public saw of Harry, the more they would come to adore him. His natural way with people and ability to come across well in front of the cameras were gifts that back then had yet to be unwrapped.

William's words also confirmed that Chelsy and Harry were head over heels in love with each other. She was not a holiday fling or someone Harry was enjoying time with before he knuckled down to military life. Chelsy clearly held a very special place in Harry's heart, and William had been listening to his brother rave about her for months. We talked for more than half an hour and William came across as a confident, friendly and trustworthy young man.

Since the tragic death of his mother, William had withdrawn into the background. He had been kept away from the cameras and allowed to finish his studies in relative peace. In that time he had met and fallen in love with Kate and his relationship with Harry had grown closer than ever. The shy, slightly awkward-looking young prince had grown up. He was confident in himself and clearly concerned for his brother.

The following day, when the press pack finally got the photo-call they had been waiting for, William and Harry famously showed just how good an asset they were to become for the Royal family. They arrived at the agreed point with the media scrum carefully positioned behind a rope a good twenty metres away. A very grumpy-looking Prince Charles arrived, flanked by his sons. His expression of unease was a possible clue as to what was about to happen.

As the three princes sat on a wooden wall while the camera shutters clicked away, the BBC's Royal correspondent Nicholas Witchell shouted out the first question. He asked Prince Charles about his upcoming nuptials, a reasonable enough question given that the wedding to Camilla was to take place the following week.

Without realizing microphones would pick up his every word, Prince Charles turned to his sons and muttered quietly: 'These bloody people. I hate doing this.' Then, in a now infamous reference to the veteran BBC reporter, he said: 'I can't bear that man. I mean he's so awful, he really is.'

Astonishingly, it was William and Harry who tried to calm their father down. William did his best to help his father through the briefing. At one stage, after a pressman urged the trio to 'look like you know each other', the two princes leaned into their father, who put his arms around them.

Charles then muttered under his breath: 'What do we do?'

William replied: 'Keep smiling, keep smiling.'

It was a cringeworthy display from Prince Charles, especially considering how many times in his life he had been expected to get through such photocalls.

As I stood in the press pen looking on, I began to wonder what kind of a night on the tiles Prince Charles must have had, to perform so badly. Harry, who I'd last seen slumped over the bar in the early hours of that morning, looked fresh-faced and relaxed. William, who had not exactly enjoyed an early night either, managed to hold the photoshoot together while his father seemed intent on messing it up.

When the TV crews finally got to edit their recordings of the encounter they couldn't believe what their small microphones placed in the snow by the princes' feet had picked up. Within minutes Prince Charles's on-screen rant was being beamed back to London. A gaffe which made him look grumpy and unprofessional. The danger with attacking the media so publicly is that they are only there as representatives of the general public.

Who wouldn't expect Prince Charles to answer a reasonable question about his upcoming wedding? And how on earth did it fall to his two young sons to placate their father and prevent even more embarrassment?

It is no surprise that this photocall was the last of its kind. The following year Clarence House announced that the Prince of Wales would no longer take his annual ski trip to Klosters. While William and Kate have returned since, for his father that photocall was perhaps the straw that broke the camel's back.

For the Royal press pack the trip to Switzerland that year was one of the most revealing moments in years. We now knew that William was to emerge from university a mature and confident young Royal. His contrasting behaviour in front of the cameras was a sign of how there really would be a danger he might one day eclipse his father in public. And thanks to William's brotherly intervention, we now knew that perhaps there was more to Harry than had met the eye.

The young prince playing pranks and making jokes on a night out in Klosters was not the person I had read about for the past few months. He wasn't out of control, he was Harry. Yes, he may have lost his temper with the photographer a few months earlier, and yes, he may have made a stupid mistake by dressing as a Nazi at a party, but there was clearly much more to Harry than this. He was in love, and his readiness to fly all over the world just to spend a few hours with Chelsy showed his passionate, almost free-spirited side. At twenty years old why shouldn't he spend as much time with Chelsy as possible? He was just weeks away from starting at Sandhurst in May, and once that ordeal got underway he was unlikely to spend any time with the girl who he clearly found captivating.

I later discovered that Harry had secretly flown Chelsy from Cape Town to England for Valentine's Day the previous month. While this romantic gesture went down well, Chelsy's visit had more significance. It was on this occasion that she met Prince Charles and was introduced to Kate Middleton. Harry had already ticked the Davy family boxes in Mozambique; now Chelsy had gained the Royal seal of approval.

The romance was blossoming at a hectic pace.

CHAPTER 5

BOTSWANA

PRINCE HARRY MIGHT have been forgiven for thinking his 2005 ski trip to Klosters was, from his own point of view, a success. Any thoughts of his Nazi gaffe dominating the news had been totally overshadowed by the fact that his brother William had taken Kate Middleton on the annual trip with Prince Charles.

The rare glimpse of Kate in public with her university sweetheart was enough to send the photographers into a frenzy. Even some of the seasoned 'old boys' of the Royal press pack found themselves grabbing their cameras and waiting for a frame of Kate as she turned up at the main ski lift each morning. This was the first time since the death of Princess Diana that any of these veteran snappers had dared try and take a Royal photograph against the wishes of the palace press office. For seven years they had obediently refrained from pursuing the young princes, only turning up to official photocalls carefully managed by the press office.

But Wills and Kate were huge news. It was the second year in a row this mysterious brunette had joined the princes on the slopes, which was inevitably seen as a sign of just how serious their relationship had become behind the closed doors of St Andrews University.

For his part, Prince Charles had also inadvertently taken the heat away from Harry with his televised rant at the BBC's Royal correspondent. His wedding to Camilla was due to take place the Friday after they returned from the slopes and again this attracted media attention all over the world.

But when Harry woke up on the last morning of his holiday that year, any thoughts that he had been able to slip under the media radar were immediately dashed. The *News of the World* had written a story claiming the 20-year-old prince had cheated on Chelsy on the same night he had laughed and joked with me in the nightclub.

For three days the paper had worked on its world exclusive, which was splashed across the tabloid's front page under the damning headline: 'Harry Cheats on Chelsy'. The scoop was based on claims made by a friend of a 17-year-old Swedish stunner called Alexia Bergstrom. According to the paper she had confessed to a friend how the randy young Royal had invited her back to his hotel in the small hours.

Chelsy meanwhile was 6,000 miles away at her home in Cape Town and was oblivious to what her boyfriend of nearly a year was claimed to have been up to.

This was a tragic blow for Harry. The girl he had fallen for was now alone in South Africa trying to come to terms with salacious claims she was the victim of a cheating boyfriend. Horrified, the prince immediately went to see his father's director of communications, Paddy Harverson, who was part of the entourage on the trip. He begged Harverson to help him because he feared the impact this sort of story would have on Chelsy.

The prince is surprisingly good at taking stories about him on the chin but, like his brother William, he has no such tolerance of stories that may affect other people in his life. Harry was extremely protective of Chelsy and furious that her name was splashed over the front pages in a negative story, purely because of her association with him.

The carefully written story was correct in every way except

one. Harry had met the Swedish beauty in the club that night and she had been invited back to the hotel. But Harry's role in the events of that evening remained purely as a 'wing man' for one of his closest pals. It wasn't Harry who had lured Alexia back to the hotel that night, it was one of Harry's friends.

A source close to the prince revealed at the time: 'This was a case of Harry playing wing man to his mate. The fact Harry was there was enough to set tongues wagging, but on this occasion it really had little if anything to do with Harry. The reality is Harry only has eyes for Chelsy. She is all he talks about and it is quite clear there is no way he would risk ruining his first serious relationship for a one-night stand.'

Despite the misunderstanding being quite swiftly sorted out, the episode certainly acted as a wake-up call to Chelsy. What was she letting herself in for by dating Harry? Her friends knew she was not interested in being famous or becoming a Royal WAG. The cost of being in a relationship with the third in line to the throne comes with its own unique baggage and challenges. The *News of the World* story was a sign of what was to come for Chelsy, and the first real doubts about whether she had a future with Harry began to worry her.

Harry flew home at the end of his ski trip wishing he could be with Chelsy and have time to sit down and explain what really happened. But it was impossible for him to fly out and see her. The following week he was going to be paraded in front of the world as his father finally married the woman who had been in the background for more than twenty-five years.

Chelsy was not a guest at the wedding. It had been decided that Prince Charles and Camilla would tie the knot in the relatively low-key surroundings of Windsor Guildhall.

Because they were both divorcees and Camilla was from a Catholic background, the wedding plans had been thrown into chaos. The Queen felt she could not attend the ceremony itself because of her official position as Defender of the Faith, the theoretical head of the Church of England. But Prince Charles was determined to press ahead with the nuptials and in an astonishing break with Royal protocol booked the closest civil registry office to Windsor Castle.

Although Her Majesty attended a service of dedication in the castle's chapel afterwards, the compromise meant the guest list for the ceremony itself was extremely limited.

A close friend of Harry revealed that even if the wedding had taken place with all the pomp and ceremony usually associated with the marriage of a future king, there is no way he would have invited Chelsy. 'The constant theme throughout Harry and Chelsy's relationship was the battle between his position and her free-spiritedness. It was clear from the start that Chelsy was not interested in becoming a princess, with all the grandeur and baggage that would entail. But what option did Harry have? He was besotted with Chelsy and the fact that she wasn't interested in all the trappings of royalty was one of the things he found so irresistible.

'This situation was a constant elephant in the room for Harry and Chelsy. Right from the start he avoided inviting her to any events that might put her off or blow his chances of continuing the relationship. Because of this, there is no way he would have invited Chelsy within 100 miles of his father's Royal wedding. Harry did everything he could to play down the Royal thing, it was a constant difficulty which in the end probably explains why they had such a rocky time.'

On the day of his father's wedding, Harry dutifully supported Prince Charles, knowing that once the day was out of the way he was free to fly out to Africa to try to build bridges with Chelsy.

He was due to start his training at the military academy in May that year, which gave him just enough time to fly out to Africa and see his sweetheart. There was no doubt in Harry's mind that he had to see her before starting at Sandhurst.

The officer training school, considered one of the finest in the world, was going to be a huge challenge for the young Royal. Harry was not academic, and the forty-four-week course would mean him having to knuckle down to sit exams on basic maths, English and military history as well as being tested on the theory of basic infantry skills. For someone who had struggled at school, this was going to be a huge hurdle. Failure in the classroom at Sandhurst would risk him being put back, or even thrown off the course.

It is a high-pressure environment for any aspiring officer cadet, with a high drop-out rate. New recruits are thrown in at the deep end with an intensive regime that tests the resolve of even the toughest. The course is designed to test every aspect of a cadet's abilities. Harry was not so worried about the gruelling training regime outside the classroom. He revelled in the challenge of being woken each day at 5 a.m. and going on military exercises, including long yomps through rugged terrain.

But if he didn't fly out to see Chelsy before his course began, Harry was all too aware that he wouldn't be able to explain about Alexia, the ski trip and the damaging headlines. For the first five weeks at Sandhurst cadets are forbidden to leave the base to see loved ones.

Harry's problem was convincing Chelsy to see him in the short window before he started at Sandhurst. Once again the couple had the added difficulty of where to go. Chelsy's home in Zimbabwe was still off limits because of the Mugabe regime. And to spend weekdays sitting around her student home in Cape Town was never going to be ideal.

Strangely, the solution for the young couple was staring Harry in the face. As a child he and William had been taken to Africa on holiday by their late mother, Princess Diana. She was keen for them to experience a true African adventure, far away from the public gaze and the lavish surroundings of Royal palaces. Diana's instinct to give her boys an experience they would never forget now gave Harry the answer he was looking for.

The landlocked Republic of Botswana was the perfect compromise. It bordered South Africa to the south and Zimbabwe to the north. But unlike the busy suburbs of Cape Town, Botswana was and remains one of the most sparsely populated nations in the world. And unlike Zimbabwe, it had enjoyed decades of peaceful democratic elections and relative political stability since becoming a republic in 1966. Harry could happily visit Botswana without any of the political controversy that would come with a trip to Zimbabwe. Here, he and Chelsy could experience the real Africa without a care in the world.

It was Diana's legendary work with the victims of HIV and AIDS that first brought Botswana to her attention. A former British protectorate, the diamond-rich country was one of the places hardest hit by the AIDS epidemic, with around a quarter of the population feared to have been infected. Despite its relative wealth by African standards, Botswana was in desperate need of Diana's high-profile intervention.

She had fallen in love with the country following an official visit there and decided to return for a holiday with her young boys. Harry and William spent days sitting around campfires, rafting on hippo- and crocodile-infested rivers, and travelling out into the wilds looking for elephants, rhinos and lions. For any child this must have seemed like the adventure of a lifetime. There is no doubt that, for Harry, his mother's decision to take him to Botswana as a child was to have a profound impact on him in later life.

Fortunately for Harry, Chelsy shared his excitement when he suggested they meet up in Botswana for a break before Sandhurst. She got permission to take time out from her studies and arranged to fly from Cape Town up to the tiny town of Maun, Botswana, where their romantic adventure could begin.

After arriving at Maun airport the couple planned to head off and explore the Okavango Delta, one of the world's best wildlife wildernesses. Harry had arranged for them to spend the first three days of their adventure on a horseback trek, sleeping under the stars and enjoying the remote beauty of the Moremi Game Reserve. Here, they spent their days looking for wildlife before setting up camp and enjoying cocktails and champagne as the sun set over the pools and dunes of the Delta.

In many ways this seemed like a dream for Harry: quality time in the wilderness with his first true love. Any anxiety he may have been feeling about starting his military career the following month, and being separated from Chelsy for the rest of the summer, faded away as they held hands, talked and forgot all about what was to come.

A source from one of the safari firms that helped organize the trip told me shortly afterwards: 'The one thing they wanted was to be alone, to be out in the wilderness and enjoy their time together. The Delta is the kind of place wealthy businessmen and even Hollywood stars come for their honeymoons. It's very basic and you really feel as though you are in the middle of nowhere. You can go for days out here without seeing a single person.

'If it's solitude you want, then this place ticks all the boxes. We are used to dealing with famous people in this part of Botswana. No one here cares who you are and that is part of the appeal. The trip that Harry organized had its splash of luxury, but anyone who comes on safari here has to be prepared to rough it. You are totally exposed to the elements. In the daytime temperatures often hit 40°C. And the cool evenings you have to be prepared for mosquito bites and the possible dangers of snakes, spiders and wild animals. In the heat you have to be prepared for the dust to stick to you and it can get quite uncomfortable.

'But that is all part of the draw for people. This is a safari experience like no other. Guests really feel like they are experiencing a taste of what it is like to be in the wild. It's not everyone's cup of tea, and Harry must know that his girlfriend is not precious about sleeping rough and coping without the luxuries of running water or nice cool showers.'

News of Harry's romantic pre-Sandhurst trip with Chelsy soon spread. Several newspapers were sent to Maun to report on the blossoming relationship. I arrived with a photographer at Maun's tiny airport, only for my heart to sink as I realized the scale of difficulties this choice of holiday destination posed. To the south of Maun was the vast Kalahari Desert, 900,000 square kilometres of remote savanna. The Moremi Game Reserve to the north may have been much smaller but with 5,000 square kilometres and only a handful of sandy tracks our chances of spotting a prince were next to zero.

We decided therefore to stay in Maun itself and wait for Harry and Chelsy to come to us. At the time I didn't feel at all easy with being sent thousands of miles to try and find the prince. It was quite clear that if – as I suspected – Harry didn't want to be found, we wouldn't stand a chance of getting a picture or story to send back to London. In these situations, as with Harry's trip to Bazaruto, the previous December, our presence there is little more than a 'watching brief'. The last thing we want to do is ruin the Royal's holiday, but at the same time the public had a right to know what was going on.

On the final day of his trip, Harry was photographed as he and Chelsy returned from safari. They were pictured in an open-top game jeep designed to give tourists the real-life experience of animals in the wild without fear of them being attacked by any of the deadly creatures that roamed the reserve. Harry looked every bit the adventurer with a pair of dark sunglasses and a blue bandana on his head.

The couple looked as though they had enjoyed the adventure even though the heat must have been unbearable. From that moment on there was no doubt that he had hit the jackpot in finding Chelsy. She may have been used to dressing up and partying in Cape Town, but Chelsy clearly had no issues with being in the wild, unwashed and without make-up. Not many of the women who would love to boast Prince Harry as a boyfriend would ever tolerate being in the wilderness for days at a time. There was no doubt these two shared a love of Africa and the outdoors, a bond that would only bring them closer together over the coming years.

In the back of the jeep was a trusted Royal protection officer. In the driver's seat, a Canadian-born and wild-looking safari guide who had been entrusted to take the VIP couple out into the reserve.

The night after the picture had been taken, a small group of us went for a meal in Maun's only sports bar. The air-conditioned saloon with its pool tables and freshly made pizzas was a rare oasis in an otherwise dust-ridden, sweltering town. This was one of the few places we could go to file our stories, eat a meal and relax with a much-needed cold beer. We also knew we could safely hang out there without fear of bumping into Harry and causing an issue. The odd mix of local drifters who earned their money guiding wealthy tourists through the reserve all knew each other. And we had made it clear to them we wanted to stay out of Harry's way.

However, that night as the small group of us enjoyed the relative sanctuary of the sports bar we were in for a shock. A much larger group of white locals stormed into the bar. These redneck drifters were clearly furious that Prince Harry had been pictured and they were out for revenge. Like the women I had met at Tonbridge station in the first week of my journalism career as I covered the fall-out from Diana's death, these guys saw us journalists as the enemy.

Wrongly assuming we had taken the pictures that day, they had slashed the tyres on our two rented 4x4s that were parked outside and stormed inside for a fight. One group, led by the Canadian guide who had been pictured with Harry, surrounded us at the bar and demanded to know who took the photograph.

At six foot four and the wrong side of seventeen stone I'm not easily intimidated. But there were at least a dozen of these guys and they all looked like South African rugby players. I had visions of being dragged out and dumped in the reserve with only my notepad to protect me from the lions that roamed the area at night.

Fortunately, one of our group was an attractive and streetwise female reporter from the *Daily Mail*. She smiled at them and suggested we buy them a drink. Within minutes she had expertly defused the tension and we were soon drinking beers and laughing about what we would have written if they had attacked us as planned.

I said: 'Prince Harry's Evil Henchmen would make a good front page, and if I survived the lions and the bruises I guess it would have been worth it.'

Once we had been given the chance to talk to the mob they realized we were not to blame and instead bombarded us with questions about what it was like to report on the Royal family all over the world.

I don't know how close we came to getting a Botswanan-style hiding that night, but we left the sports bar with new friends. They were very apologetic when we went outside to find our hired vehicles with slashed tyres and even decided it was the least they could do to drive us safely back to our hotel.

A few months later I was back in the sports bar and the same Canadian man came in to find me. It was quite ironic that this time he would storm into the bar, not to rip my head off, but to politely ask if I could send him the picture of him driving Harry and Chelsy that had caused all the fuss. He wanted it as a souvenir of the day he took Prince Harry on safari.

Harry said his goodbyes to Chelsy and flew back to England at the end of what must have been a very special adventure. More in love than ever the young Royal returned home ready to begin his toughest challenge yet, Sandhurst. This romantic trip to Botswana with Chelsy marked the end of Harry's whirlwind gap year, which had cemented his place in the public's mind.

Leaving school and heading straight into the Army may have been unthinkable for Harry. But there is no doubt it would have saved him from a lot of adverse attention. When he walked out of Eton Collage for the last time in June 2003 he was still off limits to the press. A young Royal still protected by the rules set up in the wake of his mother's death. But now, at the end of his two-year 'gap', as he prepared to walk into Sandhurst for the first time, Harry was one of the most talked-about Royals in his family.

Pictures of him cavorting at the Rugby World Cup in Australia, getting into a scuffle with photographers during a night out in London, and wearing THAT outfit had elevated Harry to front-page status. It was this two-year period that created the image of Prince Harry that we all know. He had inadvertently cemented himself a reputation as a boozy, party-loving young man.

Glimpses of his softer side had certainly come through as well. The documentary he had made while setting up his AIDS charity in Lesotho had shown a prince with his mother's magic touch. The image of him cuddling a little AIDS orphan and pledging to 'never forget' the children of the tiny African kingdom offered a glimpse of his potential. For the first time it appeared Harry was someone who could perhaps one day continue his mother's legacy. A prince who makes the front pages is a prince who can make a difference to those who need help the most. Whatever was going wrong in Princess Diana's life, she had an inbuilt ability to use her high profile to shed light on the plight of others.

For his part, there were signs that Harry could one day do the same. But there were other concerns about this young Royal, who had spent two years refusing to knuckle down and begin life outside of school. Every scrape he had found himself in during that period had inevitably been followed by commentators questioning whether he was out of control.

By far the most serious slip-up had been the Nazi outfit, but being accused of attacking a photographer also carried a high risk for anyone in the public gaze. It gifted those that were determined to criticize the Royal family a chance to lay into the Queen's grandson. And even the sight of Harry charging around the world to exotic locations flanked by police protection officers paid for by the taxpayer was enough to make the hairs on the back of palace advisers' heads stand on end. It laid him open to claims that he was enjoying the lifestyle of a jet-setting prince without paying the slightest bit of attention to the duty that comes with the role.

For many people in the public eye these examples would have been enough to cast a dark shadow over their reputations. A politician who punched a photographer would have done untold damage to his career. One who dressed as a Nazi, just when the world was remembering the plight of those killed in Hitler's concentration camps, would be lucky to keep his job. And a politician who stood accused of wasting taxpayers' money cavorting around the world with a beautiful new girlfriend would be forced to fall on his sword.

But Harry was not a politician. The other legacy of his wild 'gap year' was the Midas touch he enjoys. The net effect of all these scrapes was simple – they made him even more popular.

By the time Harry started at Sandhurst in May 2005, he was the unlikely darling of the British public. Here was a Royal with a rock and roll quality. After all, what would the nation really want from a 20-year-old prince? Would they want him to hide away on the family estates admiring their stamp collections and studying the classics? Or would they prefer a prince who wore his heart on his sleeve, enjoyed being out with friends and had that glint in his eye that suggested the loveable rascal beneath?

The more Harry subjected himself to pompous criticism, the more the general public sided with him. This was not a media strategy, more an inevitable consequence of his natural way with the public beginning to shine through.

By the time Harry started at Sandhurst he was also deeply in love. His roller-coaster relationship with Chelsy had given him strength to cope with his critics. In her Harry had found a soulmate, interested in him for who he was. She had helped him deal with some of the anger issues that lingered from his mother's death. She had given him the confidence to be himself even when others were accusing him of being a cheat. Above all, in Chelsy he had found someone who shared his sense of humour, love of Africa and desire never to take life too seriously.

It was going to be a tough challenge getting through Sandhurst and reaching the standards required to become an officer in the British Army but this challenge was to be made all the more difficult as he pined for Chelsy and had to knuckle down without her for weeks at a time.

A Sandhurst source, speaking on the eve of Harry's first day, explained: 'Cadets often start Sandhurst in long-term relationships. Very few pass out the other side with the same person.'

CHAPTER 6

IRAQ BLOW

'WE HAVE CONSIDERED your story carefully and on this occasion we would really urge you not to run it,' said Paddy Harverson, the Prince of Wales's communications director.

It was an unusual request and proof that they were taking my call very seriously indeed. Very few times did the men in grey suits beg us not to run a story. If what we were proposing to write was inaccurate, then they would always put us right. It was far rarer, however, for the press office to come back with a request that we pull a story, especially when there was no public interest reason for them objecting.

Hours earlier I had 'put in the call' to Clarence House to tell them we were planning to run a story from a contact out in Iraq. The source had interviewed Abu Mujtaba, a senior commander of the Mahdi Army, who had issued a direct threat to Prince Harry.

The commander, loyal to the insurgent leader and radical cleric Muqtada al-Sadr, had told our man: 'One of our aims is to capture Harry. We have people inside the British bases to inform us on when he will arrive. We have a special unit that would work to track him down, with informants inside the bases.'

He added: 'Not only us, the Mahdi Army will try to capture him, but every person who hates the British and Americans will try to get him. All the Mujahideens in Iraq, the al-Qaeda, the Iranians, all will try to get him.'

What could have been dismissed as a bit of mischief-making or insurgent propaganda appeared to be a real and present threat.

It was April 2007. Harry's unit was just days away from being deployed to Basra in Iraq, where the Ministry of Defence had confirmed the 22-year-old officer would spend six months in the front line.

At the time we got the tip-off it was clear the insurgent offensive against the British had been dramatically stepped up. The use of roadside bombs against our boys' patrols had already claimed eleven lives in the past four weeks.

Mojtaba's comments simply could not be dismissed. There was evidence he had a number of men under his command as well as weaponry, including rockets and automatic rifles. The troops in Iraq had indeed come under sustained attack in the months leading up to Harry's deployment and this had caused deep concerns at the highest levels.

The then Chief of the General Staff, General Sir Richard Dannatt, had been in constant contact with Harry's private secretary, Jamie Lowther-Pinkerton, a former SAS major. Ever since Harry's outspoken remarks during his twenty-first birthday interview – when he had insisted he would not 'drag my sorry arse through Sandhurst' if he couldn't go to war – General Dannatt had been aware of how high the stakes were. If the young Royal had been banned from the front line there was every chance the hot-headed soldier would have quit the Army. And if that happened, the top brass would face a barrage of criticism. Why were commanders prepared to send normal soldiers to war to be killed, but not Harry?

Just two months earlier, in February 2007, General Dannatt had delighted Harry by agreeing to deploy him with the unit he had trained with since passing out of Sandhurst, the Household

Cavalry's Blues and Royals regiment. They had made the bold decision that he would head to the front line to command a unit of twelve men, in exactly the way Harry had been prepared.

When Lowther-Pinkerton gave Harry the news, he was elated. For nearly six months he had been busting a gut in the gruelling build-up training that always preceded a real deployment.

There is a common misconception among the general public about the way soldiers feel about being deployed to war. This is what they are trained to do. It is the reason they join the forces in the first place. And while every soldier's experience in a war is different, ultimately they are trained and willing to serve their country, no matter how dangerous their mission.

In a bid to end the months of will he, won't he speculation, the MoD and the palace made the unusual decision in February to release a joint statement insisting that Cornet Wales, as Harry was known in his regiment, would serve in Iraq. He was to carry out 'a normal troop commander's role' leading a troop of twelve men in four Scimitar armoured reconnaissance vehicles, each with a crew of three.

News of the decision was even accompanied by praise from the then Prime Minister Tony Blair, who described Harry as a 'brave and determined young man' with 'a very special character'.

It meant that Harry would become the first senior Royal to serve his Queen and country in the theatre of war since his uncle Prince Andrew had served with distinction in the Falklands, way back in 1982.

A senior Royal source recalled Harry's reaction to being allowed to fight in the front line: 'This was all Harry had dreamed of since being a boy. Even as a young child he had a fascination with soldiers, tanks and all things military. But from the day he set foot at Sandhurst he knew that his dream of serving his country could be put under threat for political reasons.

'Despite the doubts, throughout the end of 2006 Harry had committed himself 100 per cent to the regiment's pre-deployment training. He had shown real determination to make the grade, even performing with distinction during exercises in Scotland and South Wales. So when his private secretary broke the news that he would be allowed to command his men, Harry punched the air in delight.

'The very last thing on his mind were the potential dangers in Iraq. As far as Harry was concerned he was a soldier and he wanted more than anything to serve his country, whatever the risks. Harry may have accepted he was a Royal, but as far as he was concerned his military career had nothing whatsoever to do with his accident of birth. Being a prince and being an officer in the British Army were, in Harry's mind, two totally separate entities. This was one of the main reasons a military career was so appealing to Harry. As an officer he could be normal. His grandmother may have been the head of the Armed Forces, but this didn't make a jot of difference in his mind. He was a soldier first and a Royal second.'

When I contacted Clarence House that day I had told them exactly what we were proposing to write. This was a serious subject and a story that we felt we were entitled to publish. It had been put at the top of the news list, which meant there was every chance it would feature on the front page of the following day's paper.

The problem was that Mujtaba's chilling threats posed a nightmare for General Dannatt and Clarence House. In his rant Mojtaba had added: 'For me he is just a British soldier and he should be killed if he comes to Iraq, but let's be realistic, we can kill hundreds of British soldiers before forcing them to withdraw. But Harry is a much bigger catch and we will force the British to come on their knees and talk to us.'

Even if these comments were nothing more than idle threats, the reality was they were rooted in truth. By putting the third in line to the British throne in Iraq there was at least an outside chance that he could be kidnapped or killed. Even if Harry himself completed the six-month deployment unscathed, what if his mere presence in Basra led to an increase in insurgent attacks? Could General Dannatt really risk the grieving mother or wife of one of Harry's fellow soldiers blaming the young Royal for their family's loss? Maybe the Mahdi commander's comments were just propaganda, but could they really take that risk?

By the time I received the return call from Paddy Harverson later that day, these were exactly the questions our proposed story had raised. General Dannatt himself had been informed, and the Ministry of Defence were preparing to stand by their decision to send Harry. A statement from the MoD's well-oiled media unit had been drafted and it would try to dismiss the comments as 'wild' and 'unfounded'.

From the *Sun*'s point of view, running that story the following day would spark a huge reaction and reopen the debate about Harry's deployment. But what we had to consider was the impact running it could have on Harry and his fellow soldiers weeks away from heading to Iraq. By begging us not to run the story, Clarence House was throwing the gauntlet down to the *Sun*.

We had a good relationship with Harry, and our readers were generally pro-Royal. More importantly we were without doubt the Forces' favourite newspaper, read by servicemen and women in their tens of thousands. How would they react if their paper of choice was seen to be spouting the propaganda of the insurgents who were killing our troops with chilling regularity? It was certainly not the job or policy of the *Sun* newspaper to gift the enemy of British troops a front-page platform to voice their hatred and threats.

The request from Clarence House was passed to the very top of the paper. The editor had to decide whether a good scoop was worth the possible negative reaction from readers.

As the Royal correspondent I was asked what I made of the situation. My advice was that the story was clearly legitimate, as the palace had not tried to claim it was inaccurate. But I was also of the view that publishing the story might well damage the paper's good relationship with Harry himself.

We would never pull a story as a favour to any member of the Royal family but on this occasion I knew full well that Harry would be furious that we had drawn attention to the rants of an insurgent and, in so doing, risked the plug being pulled on his deployment.

Ultimately the decision was made to spike the story. It was my job to pass this decision on to Paddy Harverson, but to make it clear that this was a goodwill gesture from a paper that supported both the military and Prince Harry.

We couldn't stop the story from getting out, however. All we could do was reassure the palace and the MoD that it would not appear in the *Sun*. The information had come from a respected freelance fixer who lived in Iraq. As soon as he was turned down by the *Sun* it was fairly inevitable that he would look to place the story elsewhere.

In the end that was exactly what happened. A few days later the whole story appeared in the *Guardian* newspaper. The palace had once again appealed for it to be shelved but the paper refused and ran it anyway.

It is always disappointing to see a story you have worked on appear in a different publication but to this day I believe we were right to pull it. Often reporting on the Royals is a little like covering a never-ending soap opera. Births, deaths, marriages and love affairs are the staple of Royal reporting but from time to time it is important to remember that you are writing about real people. If there was even the slightest chance that the threat to a British soldier could be increased by publishing a story, then in my view, the paper has a duty to use common sense.

It is worth remembering that the news about Harry's deployment reached the public domain in the first place via the statement issued by the Ministry of Defence and the palace. After that there was always a risk, if not an inevitability, that this high-profile deployment would be seized on by the insurgents trying to score a bit of propaganda. But the potential consequences of the story of the cleric's threat getting out there were the straw that broke the camel's back.

When the *Guardian* ran the story the Ministry of Defence did its best to stand firm. It issued the statement trying to dismiss the insurgent's comments as 'blatant propaganda from those who want to tear Iraq apart'.

However, one line in the carefully drafted statement did give us all a clue as to what was really going on behind the scenes. The decision to deploy Harry, it said, remained 'under constant review', a worrying hint that in spite of the official line there was a bit more to it than met the eye. In reality this meant that the decision was being looked at, and the MoD had to have a 'get out' plan if the generals and politicians were forced to make a U-turn. Sadly for Harry, this statement seemed to indicate that the writing was on the wall for his dreams of being deployed to Iraq.

It wasn't the running of the story itself that forced them to rethink the deployment. But once it had been published, the reality was that any insurgent in Iraq who hadn't already thought about targeting Harry would now be well aware of the bounty put on the head of the 'infidel prince'. By the time Harry and his unit would set foot in the war zone, just about every Iraqi fighter would be looking for him.

It was later claimed that pictures of Harry had been printed from the internet and were being handed around the streets of Basra. While these reports were never confirmed, they gave weight to the view that putting Harry into that theatre would be madness.

Behind the scenes British intelligence worked tirelessly to try and assess how 'credible' the threats being made against Harry really were. And within days they reported back with the verdict that was to devastate the prince – the threats were credible and the risk of sending Harry to Iraq was extremely high.

In the first week of May, General Dannatt himself visited Basra to meet troops and commanders on the ground. One of the reasons for this visit was to talk to his commanders and hear their honest feelings about the prince joining them on the ground.

One senior military source recalled: 'General Dannatt took the issue of Harry in Iraq as an almost personal mission. He was very keen to allow the prince his wish to serve in Basra. But when he visited the base he was told in no uncertain terms that Prince Harry's presence there would be more of a hindrance than a help.

'Senior figures on the ground took the view that it simply wasn't worth the risk of deploying the prince. They felt there was credence in the suggestion that the mere fact such a senior Royal was out there would increase attacks on British troops. Although this was not what General Dannatt wanted to hear, he had to listen to what his commanders were saying, and in fairness to him, that is exactly what he did.'

On 16 May 2007, it was announced that Harry would not be deployed to Iraq due to concerns about the number of 'specific threats' made against his life. General Dannatt was forced to accept that the risk to the prince and his men was 'unacceptable'. He said in a statement: 'There have been a number of specific threats – some reported and some not reported – which relate directly to Prince Harry as an individual. These threats expose not only him but also those around him to a degree of risk that I now deem unacceptable. I have to add that a contributing factor to this increase in threat to Prince Harry has been the widespread knowledge and discussion of his deployment.'

With this statement Prince Harry's dreams of serving his country in the front line appeared to be in tatters. It didn't matter how good he was as an officer, or how hard he trained to convince his superiors he was ready, it seemed he would never be allowed to fight because of who he was and what he represented.

This was a hammer blow for Harry. As a prince there were very few careers open to him. A life in the Army was all he had dreamed of as a young boy. One of the appeals of being a soldier was that it satisfied his yearning to be 'normal'. He had been told he could go and fight, but at the eleventh hour this had been ripped away from him for the very reason that he was anything but 'normal'.

In his lifetime Harry has had to cope with very low moments but the U-turn on his deployment to Iraq was one of the lowest. He wanted to prove himself and the reality was he was very good at his job. His men respected him as an officer, not as a Royal. Despite his lack of academic ability, he had mastered the more technical elements of leading men in an infantry unit. He lived and breathed the Army, and up until the point the plug was pulled on his tour he genuinely felt he had found his purpose in life.

When the news was announced, Clarence House were quick to try and defuse speculation that Harry might carry out his threat to quit if he could not go to war. A statement was issued accepting he was 'very disappointed' by the decision but that he would not quit as a result. 'He fully understands and accepts General Dannatt's difficult decision and remains committed to his Army career. Prince Harry's thoughts are with his troop and the rest of the battle group in Iraq.'

But it would later become clear that behind the scenes it was a different picture. Harry's mind was in turmoil. He was furious that all the hard work, all the effort he had put in, was wasted, and he was on the brink of resigning his commission and leaving the Army for good. Had it not been for the support of three people, there is little doubt the Iraq fiasco would have marked the end of Harry's military career.

The first person was Chelsy. Following the U-turn Harry turned to his long-term girlfriend for support. Sources close to the Zimbabwean revealed how the 22-year-old Royal confided in her. He was bitterly disappointed and angry, even telling Chelsy he was going to quit the Army as a result.

In reality, like most other halves Chelsy was relieved he would not be sent to Iraq. Six months is a very long time and if Harry had been sent to war the couple would not have seen each other for what might have seemed like forever.

Also, Chelsy was privately hoping Harry would be able to come to Cape Town in October that year when she was due to celebrate her twenty-first birthday. Had he been deployed, there was no way he would have been back in time for the party she was already planning.

A friend said: 'Often when soldiers go to war it is actually tougher on the loved ones they leave at home. Chelsy supported Harry but privately we all knew she was relieved his tour had been shelved. Harry was clearly very frustrated and angry, but Chelsy spent a long time calming him down and convincing him not to quit. Had it not been for her level-headed advice Harry's military career may have come to an end there and then.'

The second person Harry turned to following the U-turn was his brother William. At the time he was on a tank commander's course, having successfully followed in Harry's footsteps and passed out of Sandhurst.

But all was not well with William. His decision to invite Kate Middleton and her parents to his passing out parade at Sandhurst in December 2006 had caused a massive surge in speculation that he was about to get engaged. As a result Kate's London flat was besieged by photographers and William's heavy training schedule meant he was powerless to protect her.

In April 2007 things had got so bad that William and Kate had decided to separate. I had been aware that their relationship was in turmoil but I was amazed when the palace confirmed they had split. Clearly William had taken the view that his first real romance had run its course and he was willing to let his media team confirm the split.

When Harry confided in his brother that he was prepared to quit the Army, William was horrified. He knew more than anyone just how passionate Harry was about his military career. And until then it had been Harry who had spurred his older brother on at times when he was finding the training regime extremely tough.

Unlike Harry, William's military career was never really going to be more than window dressing. As heir to the throne William was never likely to serve in the front line. His desire to enter the forces was far more about being able to look servicemen in the eye. In 2005, while on tour in New Zealand with the British Lions rugby squad, William had told me about why he was determined to join the Army. He said: 'I feel it is important for me to under-stand the military and to be able to look soldiers in the eye with at least a tiny bit of knowledge of what they have gone through.'

Despite this motivation for becoming an officer, there was nothing easy about William's training at Sandhurst and his subse-quent tank commander's course in Dorset. He received no special treatment just because he would one day become the head of the Armed Forces. And in some ways there was even more pressure on him to reach the grade than any other cadet on his course.

When William faced challenges at Sandhurst, it was always Harry to whom he turned. His younger brother's support was rivalled only by Harry's genuine passion for all things military. He would often help William with advice and guidance to make sure his older brother would get through Sandhurst without being humiliated.

So when Harry confided in William it was time for him to repay some of this support. According to a Royal source, William told Harry in no uncertain terms that he should not quit the Army. He reminded him of why he had joined up and reassured Harry that there must be a way for him to be allowed to serve in the front line. At that time the wars in Iraq and Afghanistan meant that the Army was being pushed to its limits. A young, competent infantry officer like Harry would always have opportunities to put his training to good use.

The source added: 'William made it clear to Harry in no uncertain terms that he must not quit the Army. He reminded his brother of how hard he had worked to get through Sandhurst and complete his pre-deployment training with distinction. William was of the view that if Harry quit he would undo all that he had achieved as a young officer and send a very bad signal to everyone. He even went as far as to say quitting would look as though he was spoilt and truculent, and urged Harry to bite his lip and carry on.

'Harry and William are very similar in many ways, but there are also ways in which they are very different. Harry wears his heart on his sleeve whereas William is more considered and cautious. But William is one of the few people Harry will really listen to.'

The final person who helped Harry through the frustration of missing the deployment was his private secretary, Jamie Lowther-Pinkerton. Ever since Harry had passed out of Sandhurst, Lowther-Pinkerton had made it his personal mission to try and convince the top brass that he should be allowed to serve like any other soldier.

He had been brought into the household to act as a guide and mentor to both William and Harry. A softly-spoken, unassuming man, he instantly bonded with the boys. His serious nature coupled with a genuine loyalty and respect for the Royal family made him an excellent choice.

But Lowther-Pinkerton's greatest quality, as far as Harry was concerned, was his experience as a distinguished and decorated Army officer. He had served his country and risen to the rank of major within the legendary Special Air Service. His wiry and modest appearance disguises a far tougher interior, and among those who have worked within the palace walls he is someone both the boys have unlimited respect for. When Prince George was born, William wasted no time in asking Lowther-Pinkerton to be godfather. From the minute he arrived at Clarence House, he took on a role as guide and uncle figure to William and Harry.

So when Harry was forced to swallow the decision over Iraq, he knew that Lowther-Pinkerton shared his frustration. The pair had talked at length about serving in the front line and it had been largely due to Lowther-Pinkerton that General Dannatt had even considered allowing Harry to be deployed.

Harry was now told by his private secretary to keep calm over the U-turn and not make any decisions in haste. Lowther-Pinkerton promised him that he would try and find a way that would allow him to serve in the front line. He asked Harry to trust him and let him explore other ways.

It is true to say that Harry came very close to quitting the Army in 2007 but thanks to the three major influences in his life, the young Royal calmed down and agreed to play the long game. But there was a problem. How on earth could Lowther-Pinkerton deliver on his promise to get Harry to the front line? He was determined to try, but in reality the publicity surrounding Harry's pre-deployment training alone would only ever fuel the problems that had prevented him from going to Iraq in 2007. No matter how hard they tried, Clarence House could not think of a single way of getting the young Royal into the theatre of war.

In what must have been a sign of their desperation, I was contacted by Paddy Harverson less than a month later. Harry was back in his barracks in Windsor and his men were a month into their Iraq tour.

Harverson had a reputation as a frightening figure. Before working for the Prince of Wales, he had cut his teeth at Manchester United, managing their media operations and advising Alex Ferguson in all matters relating to the press. At times he could be very abrupt and often displayed a visible dislike and distrust of the media. Despite this he was fair, upfront and surprisingly approachable for someone who had to deal with the pressure of representing Prince Charles and his sons while maintaining a working relationship with the press.

To my surprise Harverson was trying to set up a meeting with me and the paper's respected defence editor, Tom Newton Dunn. He wanted us to have an off-the-record discussion about Harry's military career and more importantly hoped to bring Jamie Lowther-Pinkerton along as well. This was a very rare request. Lowther-Pinkerton was someone who simply didn't speak to the press. His interaction with the Royal pack was limited to a polite handshake on the few occasions he found himself in the same room as us.

To have the chance to sit down and have a full and frank discussion with the princes' private secretary was too good an opportunity to miss. It was agreed the four of us would meet at the Garrick Club in London's West End. The reason for the meeting was to sound us out on whether or not we thought it would ever be possible for Harry to go to the front line.

So, on 14 June 2007, we met in the elegant surroundings of one of London's foremost gentlemen's clubs to discuss an issue that was clearly bothering Harry's private secretary and Clarence House's foremost media adviser.

'We want to know if you think it will ever be possible for Harry to go to war,' said Harverson in his characteristically abrupt manner.

Clearly the two of them had only decided to meet with us on the instruction of Harry himself. The *Sun* was indeed the Forces paper at the time, and we had revealed our true colours by agreeing not to run the story about insurgent threats to Harry ahead of his scheduled deployment a few weeks earlier.

'Have you considered trying to get a media blackout on any future deployment?' asked Newton Dunn.

Tom was a respected defence editor who had reported from the front line in both Afghanistan and Iraq. He was well aware of the behind-the-scenes compromises that were made between journalists and the Ministry of Defence. In return for getting access to troops on the front line, journalists were happy to allow sensitive parts of their dispatches to be cut for security reasons. It was a customary feature of war reporting that in return for access to the troops on the front line, journalists would accept that there would be certain things they could not report.

The best example of this was when the legendary BBC reporter Brian Hanrahan sent a dispatch back to London at the height of the Falklands War. Referring to the Harrier jump jets that had taken off from the aircraft-carrier HMS *Hermes*, he famously said: 'I am not allowed to say how many planes joined the raid, but I counted them all out and I counted them all back.'

What we were suggesting was trying to get some kind of agreement where Harry could be deployed to the front line but the media would agree in advance to keep this a secret until after he was back home.

'Would that really work?' asked Lowther-Pinkerton.

I replied: 'Well, it seems to me that this is the only way Harry would ever be able to serve in the front line. If his deployment is publicized before the event, he will not be able to go. So perhaps this is the only option available.'

In reality neither I nor my colleague thought there was any chance of getting the British media to all agree to a blackout.

From my own point of view I remember thinking that at the time we probably wrote two stories a week about Harry. Surely our readers would smell a rat if for weeks on end we didn't carry a single story about him? Even if it was possible to forge an agreement with the media in Britain, it would be next to impossible to persuade foreign journalists to take part in what would only ever be a voluntary agreement.

If a media blackout was to be attempted, then the Ministry of Defence and the palace would effectively be asking the press to keep a secret that would be virtually impossible to keep. Despite this, Lowther-Pinkerton and Harverson seemed interested in the suggestion and left the Garrick Club that night with something to think about.

If ever proof was needed to show how close Harry came to quitting the Army in protest, there it was. His two senior advisers were contemplating trying to do an unprecedented deal with the British media. They would in effect be asking every major news outlet in Britain to keep a secret from their readers, viewers or listeners. By even considering this as an option, they were demonstrating the fact that as far as Harry's military career was concerned they really had no other. It was that or nothing.

It would simply never be possible to sneak Harry out to war without telling the media. The thousands of British troops out in Afghanistan and Iraq would all recognize the prince if he turned up at their base, and in turn they would be sure to tell their loved ones back home.

Following the meeting in June, Lowther-Pinkerton, Harverson and General Dannatt got to work on their bold plan and for weeks on end they met with editors and producers to sound them out on it.

Eventually we were all invited to the Ministry of Defence for a briefing. The great and the good from almost all national TV and newspaper outlets were there. Not everyone was in agreement, and in reality there probably wasn't a single person in the room who thought it would work. But the general consensus was that it was worth trying. If one newspaper or TV station decided to break ranks and report Harry's deployment, they would be taking a huge risk. Not only would they suffer the wrath of all of their competitors, but they would potentially be putting Harry and his comrades' lives in danger by drawing attention to the Royal's presence in the theatre of war.

Through the Society of Editors it was agreed that in return for their cooperation, the British media would be given pictures, footage and a series of pooled interviews with Harry out in the front line. This material would be handed over as and when he was safely back home at the end of any tour of duty.

It was a bold plan, and nothing quite like it had ever been attempted in a country with a free press. At last it seemed that Harry would be allowed to serve his country. If this plan didn't work, his military career would be all but over.

In late November, with the media blackout in place, Harry was finally preparing to go to war. Behind the scenes it was decided his first deployment would be to Afghanistan. To the delight of the young Royal, he was on the verge of putting all his training to use – the moment he had dreamed of since being a little boy was about to arrive.

CHAPTER 7

THE FLIGHT THAT CHANGED HIS LIFE

THE OPERATION TO remove Harry from the front line was as slick as it was carefully planned. So much effort had been put into forming a blueprint for getting the Royal warrior out of Afghanistan, whenever the time came, that nothing was left to chance.

Within minutes of the story breaking on the internet at the end of February 2008, a Chinook helicopter had left its base at Camp Bastion and was making its way across the Afghan desert to collect its precious cargo. On board were Harry's Met Police back-up protection officers, who had been living at the British base for the eight weeks their principal had been in action on the front line. They were joined by a team of heavily armed SAS soldiers, who would be first off the helicopter to ensure the loading area was secure.

In Afghanistan very few low-altitude flights were made during the day. The Taliban fighters knew that downing a Chinook would score a huge victory for their side. They were a premium target for the enemy and as a result all re-supply and non-essential sorties were carried out under cover of darkness.

While the insurgents were not thought to have ground-to-air weapons capability, as soon as a helicopter landed in the war zone, or flew below 1,000 feet, it was a sitting duck for machine-gun and rocket-propelled grenade fire. The only time these dangerous missions took place during daylight was when the medevac teams would land to collect badly injured troops.

There were countless occasions when the brave Chinook teams came under fire. Not long after Harry's stint in Afghanistan one British pilot was even shot in the head as he took off with a cargo of wounded soldiers. The machine-gun rounds pierced the glass in the cockpit and the only thing that saved the mission from disaster was the fact the bullet hit the pilot's metal bracket for his night vision goggles and ricocheted off.

On another occasion a rocket-propelled grenade hit a Sea King helicopter on the side. The missile went straight through and came out the other side while the troops inside looked on in horror. It was a miracle on that occasion that no one was killed.

These incidents revealed the sheer danger of landing in the daytime. But ultimately it had been decided that the mission to remove Harry was a risk that simply had to be taken. Once word reached the insurgents that the British prince was among the British fighting force, there was a real chance the Taliban campaign would be sent into overdrive.

Despite the urgency of removing Harry from the front line, military commanders were keen to reduce the risks to a minimum. When the Chinook took off from Camp Bastion it was joined by an Apache attack helicopter. If there was one thing that sent shivers down the spines of the Taliban fighters on the ground, it was the awesome sight of these £46 million flying fortresses. The mere sound of them overhead was usually enough to send any insurgents into hiding.

The Apache helicopter is equipped with state-of-the-art weapons technology that allows the pilot and his number two to scour the ground for any potential threats. When the Chinooks go in to land, the Apache hovers overhead, waiting for any possible attack. And if that happens the Apache is armed with a cannon as well as the deadly, laser-guided Hellfire missiles.

On the day Harry was removed from the front line the Apache team kept a constant menacing presence up above, with the co-pilot keeping his thumb over the trigger. Harry and his close protection officer were then waved towards the rear of the Chinook. Its large ramp was lowered and the passengers were told to run as fast as they could to get on board. Less than two minutes after it had landed, the Chinook took off and headed straight back to the relative safety of Camp Bastion, deep in the Helmand Province desert. The most dangerous part of the mission had been executed like clockwork, much to the relief of everyone involved.

Back home Clarence House press office and their counterparts at the Ministry of Defence were dealing with hundreds of calls from journalists the world over. News that Harry had been serving his country in Afghanistan was now breaking on TV and radio stations, websites and newsrooms across the planet.

One of the priorities for the team of press officers was to ensure the message that Harry was no longer on the front line got across loud and clear. The fear now was that British troops serving in the war zone might come under attack simply because of Harry's presence. So the quicker the palace and the Ministry of Defence could make it known Harry was already on his way home the better. True to their word, it was not long before the MoD gave the go-ahead for the media to start running the photographs and interviews that had been put together in return for the media blackout.

At the time Camp Bastion was a makeshift city and home for the British and American troops. Every day its vast runway saw as many flights as Manchester Airport. The sprawling desert base was considered a safe haven for servicemen and women. A place where they could buy fresh pizza, use the gym and catch up on some rest and recuperation, Bastion was nothing like the hostile conditions Harry had been experiencing out on the front line.

When Harry landed he went and had a shower and a change of clothes. Later he went with his protection officers to one of the base's many dining rooms for a hot meal, which must have seemed like the best thing he had eaten for weeks. But despite the relative luxury and safety of Bastion, nothing could lessen Harry's disappointment at what had happened. Any officer who is forced to leave behind the men he commands on the battlefield is never going to do so happily.

One former major who served in Afghanistan on two separate tours said: 'One minute Harry was on the front line with his men. The next he was having to wish them luck and say goodbye. The bond you form in that environment is unlike any other. You rely on the people around you to keep you alive. You get very close, and as an officer the feeling of being responsible for your own troops is even stronger.

'On a six-month tour everyone is given two week's R-and-R [rest and recuperation]. You are flown home to see your family and friends and to try and recharge the batteries. But in reality the two weeks are very tough. While it's amazing to see your loved ones the reality is you constantly think about the guys you've left behind. You hope and pray nothing happens to them while you are away and even feel guilty about watching TV or having a pint with your mates back home.

'It is very difficult for anyone who hasn't experienced this to understand the range of emotions you go through. When Harry was effectively ripped away from his men just two months into his tour it would have come as a hammer-blow. Even though everyone would know he had no say in the matter, Harry would have left Afghanistan feeling guilt, anger and desperation.

'In his case these feelings would have been magnified by the blaze of publicity surrounding his deployment. The last thing he would have wanted was to be hailed a hero when he arrived home. He would have felt very low and found it impossible to stop obsessing about the men he left behind.'

Meanwhile the media operation had gone into meltdown as journalists demanded to know when Harry would arrive home and what facilities would be laid on. News of Harry's war was on the front pages of all the daily papers before he had even left Afghanistan for the long journey home. But the Sunday papers were desperate to get their bite of the cherry with pictures and an interview as Harry's flight arrived back at Brize Norton air base.

It was customary for soldiers returning from a tour in Afghanistan not to fly straight back to the UK but to stop in Cyprus for a period of what was called 'decompression'. On the small Mediterranean island troops would chill out at the British base, drink a beer and be offered the opportunity to raise concerns or issues they might have. In Harry's case the Cyprus stopover gave the palace the perfect opportunity to draw breath. The collapse of the media blackout had happened even faster than they could have predicted. With Harry safely out of harm's way in Cyprus they were able to brief the world's press on how his arrival home was going to work.

While in Cyprus, Harry made it clear he didn't want to do anything public, but he was persuaded that the deal for a media blackout had come at a cost. He was told there was no choice but for him to be filmed and photographed as soon as he arrived back, and was even talked into doing a pooled interview before he left the base.

Harry later described how difficult it was to honour the agreement with the British media. He knew they had played ball and without their consent the eight weeks in Afghanistan could not have happened. But at the same time he was furious and disappointed the agreement had been destroyed by elements within the foreign media.

It was a mark of Harry's character that he agreed to play ball himself. The last thing he wanted to do was appear before the cameras on the day he arrived home. He was still seething with anger, but despite that he showed a willingness to dig deep.

Members of the Royal family are not used to being told they can't have their way, and that is hardly a surprise. Imagine what it must be like growing up without ever having to queue, with everyone you meet knowing your name and fawning over you. Somebody once joked that the Queen is so used to walking into rooms that have been hastily spruced up before she arrived that Her Majesty must just think the outside world smells of fresh paint.

When Harry was a boy he and William would be taken to pop concerts by their mother in a bid to make them feel normal. But unlike ordinary people they would be ushered everywhere as VIPs and afterwards they could expect to chat to the band members, who would bow and scrape out of respect.

You only have to look at young soccer megastars to see the corrupting effect fame and wealth can have. It is a credit to Harry that despite this utterly unique upbringing, he is far less precious or demanding than certain members of his family. And compared to many footballers his age, he is a positive saint.

In the twenty-four or so hours in Cyprus Harry felt low. All he could think about were the guys he had left behind. He knew that for the next four months he would have to helplessly sit behind a desk in his barracks, dreading bad news from the front line. When you are out in a war zone your adrenalin, training and comrades keep you sane. At home, when his men were still fighting without him, Harry would only be able to sit and worry.

In the late winter of 2008 the British commitment to the war in Afghanistan was increasing, with more than 7,000 British servicemen and women in Afghanistan. Every month more and more troops spilled into Helmand Province as the commitments in Iraq began to decrease. By the time Harry was waiting for his

RAF flight home from Cyprus to Brize Norton, he was surrounded by other servicemen and women returning home.

The troop carrier planes used at that time were a disgrace to the British military. The fleet of Tristar jets were once used by British Airways as passenger jets, but in 1976 they were retired and ended up in the hands of the Royal Air Force. Happily, since 2008 these decrepit old machines have been replaced. But back then the majority of our boys and girls returning from the rigours of Afghanistan had to put up with the sort of flights that made Ryanair look like Concorde. But it was because of this outdated mode of transport that Harry's journey home was about to mark a major turning point in his life.

The young Royal was dreading the media scrum he knew was waiting for him in the UK. But after he had taken his seat, ready for the five-hour flight home, something very significant happened.

Normally when Royals get on passenger flights they are the last on board and the first to leave. An army of British Airways staff and airport officials queue up with their yellow bibs and walkie talkies to whisk their VIP passengers off the flight before the riff-raff behind are even allowed to unfasten their seatbelts. But this was not the case that day. Harry was already in his seat when the final two passengers were brought on board. For once in his life, Harry was not the most important person on board. That day two other passengers took priority.

Like Harry, just a few hours earlier they had been serving their country on the front line. Their tour of Afghanistan, like his, had come to an abrupt end because of circumstances well beyond their control. But unlike Harry, on their return to the UK they would not be met with a fanfare of publicity and the inevitable cap-doffing hero's welcome that awaited the young prince.

These two men would be taken off the flight first, placed onto a military ambulance away from the cameras and driven straight to a British military hospital wing. These two men from the elite 40 Commando Royal Marines unit had both been critically injured when a Taliban bomb exploded next to them.

The worst injured, a young, athletic and popular Royal Marine named Ben McBean, had lost a leg and an arm after he trod on an Improvised Explosive Device (IED) while on a patrol the previous day. Up until that moment Ben had been a proud Bootneck (slang for Royal Marine), known to his mates for his big broad smile and kind nature. He was now gravely injured and there were serious doubts about whether the medics back in the UK would be able to save him.

There is no doubt that the sight of these two injured servicemen being loaded onto Harry's flight home in Cyprus was to have a profound effect on the young Royal. Although he had spent ten weeks in a war zone, this was the first time he came face to face with the true cost of war.

For those that are worst injured the planes were equipped with hospital beds and a team of highly trained medics who monitor their patients continuously. Throughout the flight the two casualties were unconscious, but their mere presence on board meant the atmosphere was sombre. For Harry this was without doubt a life-changing experience. He was already being hailed a hero back home, but for what – doing the job he was trained for?

Just because he was a Royal, because of an accident of birth, his image was splashed over every front page. As soon as the plane's wheels touched the tarmac at Brize Norton the TV cameras would be rolling, not because of the two men fighting for their lives, the latest victims of the war in Afghanistan, but because the third in line to the British throne was coming home.

Harry was well used to his life in the goldfish bowl of publicity, but this time the thought of facing the cameras made him feel sick to the stomach. He knew there was a very real possibility that some of the guys he had been forced to leave on the front line might be flown home in the same hospital beds.

As Harry's plane made its way towards the safety of home, the men he had been commanding were still in harm's way, with another three and a half months of their six-month tour to come. But he was now helpless to play any role in keeping them safe.

Waiting at the Oxfordshire RAF base were his father Prince Charles and brother William. They were to be photographed and interviewed as part of the media deal. Prince Charles, who had reluctantly agreed to be interviewed, spoke about the mixed emotions endured by the parents and loved ones of all soldiers returning home from war. But there was no sign of the families of the two wounded men, whose return home would inevitably mark the start, rather than the end of their battles.

That journey, and the sight of two unconscious and critically injured Royal Marines, is an experience Harry will never be able to forget.

Royals traditionally lead the country in paying tribute to the servicemen and women who have made the ultimate sacrifice for their country. Every year and on every foreign visit, members of the Royal family spend hours with their heads bowed next to war memorials. But by returning from Afghanistan on that flight, on that day in March 2008, Prince Harry became the first member of his family in recent history to witness first-hand the impact war can have on young lives.

No other Royal has made a journey like the one Harry made that day. And it explains why, all these years later, his commitment to those men and women who have been wounded in the line of duty is both sincere and affirming for him.

His work with children and the victims of AIDS and HIV is inspired by the values that his mother taught him as a child. But when it comes to Harry's work with the military and his commitment to the victims of conflict, the motivation comes from very real-life experiences, first-hand exposure to the costs of war.

When he finally stepped off the plane at Brize Norton, the images he had witnessed were buzzing around his head. The feelings of anger, frustration and helplessness were etched on his face. Ten weeks in the front line, and a journey home that he would never forget, marked a turning point in Harry's life. It was no surprise therefore that when he faced the cameras and took part in the short interview as agreed that day, his words would reflect the deep impact the Afghan experience was already starting to have.

When he spoke that day Harry's words came straight from the heart. Asked if he would describe himself as a hero, he stared straight at the reporter and said: 'I wouldn't say I'm a hero at all. I'm no more of a hero than anyone else. If you think about it there's thousands and thousands of troops out there.'

He then reflected on what he had witnessed on the flight home, the sight of the two critically wounded soldiers, and added: 'I was a bit shocked. It is a bit of a choke in your throat when you know that it's happening. There's a lot of time when you are actually in theatre [in the war zone] it isn't even mentioned that much. One of the soldiers lost a left arm and right leg while the other took a shrapnel hit in the neck. Both were unconscious throughout the flight from Afghanistan. Those are the heroes. Those were guys who had been blown up by a mine that they had no idea about, serving their country, doing a normal patrol.'

This was a Royal talking about the first-hand experience of fighting in the front line. And when asked about his own role in the war effort, Harry's response was equally matter-of-fact. Responding to a question about his job as a battlefield air controller calling in air strikes, patrolling in Helmand Province and firing on militants, he said: 'You do what you have to do, what's necessary to save your own guys. If you need to drop a bomb, worst case scenario, then you will, but then that's just the way it is. It's not nice to drop bombs, but to save lives that's what happens.'

Harry's admission that he had called in air strikes and his hint that he had no problem with killing insurgents meant that his security had to be stepped up after he arrived home. The warrior prince was now a prime target for terrorists, and even to this day the fact that he fought in Afghanistan means heightened security measures. But Harry is not in the least bit bothered by this aspect of his war legacy. Far more important is the fact that Afghanistan has given him an insight into the Armed Forces which it might be argued makes him unique within the Royal family.

There was little surprise therefore that less than two months after stepping off the flight at Brize Norton, Harry and William were making the journey to the military's rehabilitation hospital, Headley Court in Surrey.

Ben McBean had undergone surgery in the days that followed his return. By the middle of April 2008, he was well enough to be transferred from Selly Oak Hospital in Birmingham to the more comfortable surroundings of Headley Court.

On the day of his visit Harry and his brother William were taken upstairs to meet Ben, and the young Marine finally came face to face with the person he shared a flight home from war with. Although he had no memory of the flight, Ben had been made aware of how a twist of fate had brought him to the attention of the third in line to the throne. Harry admitted he was 'very moved' to have met Ben and was encouraged to hear that despite his devastating injuries he was determined to one day run a marathon.

Ben told the *Sun* after Harry's visit: 'I feel humbled that Harry said what he did. It feels good to be recognized. I don't see these injuries as any more than a blip in my career. In fact as soon as I get an artificial arm and leg I'm going to train for a marathon.'

Although Ben McBean is one of thousands of wounded soldiers Harry has met in his life, he has come to symbolize why the Royal is now dedicated to war veterans. The four hours Harry spent with a knot in his stomach watching from his plane seat as the medics battled to keep the young Marine alive are something he will never forget.

The wars in Iraq and Afghanistan may now be over, but few people are more aware than Harry of how many private battles are still being fought. The two conflicts have left a legacy of seriously injured men and women, and when Harry left the Army he was determined to do everything in his power to ensure the sacrifices made by so many in his generation are never forgotten.

Harry has since met his friend Ben on many occasions, and Ben recalls the prince instructing him to go and have a beer at the finish line of one of his many incredible fundraising challenges.

While it is true to say that Harry would have committed himself to the plight of wounded soldiers whatever he had witnessed in Afghanistan, his journey back from the conflict and his chance encounter with Ben McBean helped to shape his life.

Whatever Harry chooses to do with the rest of his life, he will always be at the very centre of the effort to ensure the wounded are not forgotten.

CHAPTER 8

HARRY'S R&R

THEY SAY ABSENCE makes the heart grow fonder, and as any soldier will tell you, never is this more true than when you are away at war while your sweetheart is thousands of miles away at home. Serving on the front line puts all relationships into perspective and the lack of things to do in the hours of downtime only makes you miss your loved one all the more.

During his ten weeks in Afghanistan Harry, like all soldiers, found he had a lot of time on his hands to ponder his friendship with Chelsy Davy and to dwell on where it might be heading.

The truth was that their whirlwind romance had been strained by the many weeks they had spent apart long before the Royal's dream of heading to war became a reality. Ever since the pair had met, their precious times together amounted to safaris in Botswana, river trips in Namibia or holidays with the Davy family off the coast of Mozambique. There was little, if any, of the 'normal' time in which relationships can slowly grow stronger.

In William and Kate's first few years together at St Andrews University, their love blossomed during quiet nights in, eating home-made spaghetti Bolognese and curling up on the sofa to watch films. By the time they went public, they were already on solid ground, which helped save their relationship when they briefly broke up in 2007. But Harry and Chelsy's romance had been a whirlwind from the word go. They had never experienced 'normal' life together to build a strong foundation.

A friend of Chelsy once put the first few years of their relationship in perspective when she said: 'They are madly in love but their times together are more honeymoon than normal life. They are either thousands of miles apart, or away together on holiday. It's feast or famine, and Chelsy in particular finds that very difficult.'

By September 2007, Chelsy had graduated from the University of Cape Town and applied successfully for a place on a postgraduate law degree course at Leeds University in the north of England. Much to Harry's delight, this meant his first true love would finally be living and studying in the same country, even if any journey to see her would mean at least a five-hour drive from London. While not ideal, it would be – Harry hoped – far better than the six thousand miles of separation the pair had been used to.

When Chelsy moved into her digs in a trendy student suburb of Leeds, the behind-the-scenes negotiations with the media aimed at getting Harry to war were in full swing. The reality was that Harry remained in limbo as his advisers battled to find a way of getting him to the front line in secret.

At the end of October that year the England rugby team had surprised everyone by making it into the World Cup final in Paris to play none other than Chelsy's South Africa. The young rugby-mad prince and his brother William had been invited to travel to the Stade de France to watch the showdown and the first person Harry asked to join him was Chelsy. But because of the demands of her new course she chose to stay in Leeds to continue her studies.

This was a blow for Harry because he had hoped that having his girlfriend much closer to home would mean they could spend weekends together. But Chelsy was very focused on her studies and made it clear the only way they could really be together was if he came to her.

Friends of the couple recalled Chelsy rowing on the phone with Harry during her first term at Leeds. One said: 'Chelsy was really frustrated with Harry. She was trying to work hard and he was at a loose end for much of her first term. Photographers would follow her to the main campus even though Harry was nowhere to be seen. This made her angry and she often talked about her frustration at not being able to study in peace like everyone else. There were definite cracks appearing in the relationship even then, and Harry found it hard to say anything without making her cross.'

As it turned out, throughout the entire first term at Leeds Harry only managed to visit Chelsy once, and even then it was at a friend's student house, which was far from ideal. One of the most telling signs of their problems came at the end of term when Chelsy made it clear she was heading straight back to South Africa after attending her final pre-Christmas lecture.

This meant that on the very day Harry was told he would be off to Afghanistan later that month, Chelsy was away on holiday with her brother and their friends in South Africa. There would be no prolonged goodbye for Harry, as he packed his kitbag and prepared to spend what was supposed to be six months on the front line. As the final day approached and he nervously set off for Brize Norton, his girlfriend was six thousand miles away, sipping cocktails and partying with her pals in Umhlanga Rocks, north of Durban.

It was disappointing for Harry because, like any soldier, he wanted to say a proper goodbye, knowing that it could well be as much as half a year apart. So he was left to fly out on tour with the growing relationship problems spinning around his head.

By the time Harry returned home ten weeks later he knew that it was make or break with Chelsy. The pair had spoken whenever possible during his ten weeks away. But now Harry's unexpected premature exit from Afghanistan meant he was determined to see Chelsy and try and work things out.

Chelsy had been pining for Harry and worrying about his safety all the time he had been in Afghanistan. When he arrived home on 1 March 2008, she travelled down to London to see him within hours. The time apart seemed to have reignited their romance and there was no way Harry was going to miss the chance to make the most of the situation.

After being given time off by his commanding officer, he hurriedly began to plan a week away and immediately knew there was only one place he wanted to take Chelsy. Within days of being back in the arms of his lover, Harry and Chelsy were on a tiny plane flying north from Johannesburg to Harry's beloved Botswana.

This was the place where Harry and Chelsy's romance had blossomed in their first year together. A place where they could spend quality time together talking through the months they had spent apart, and reflect on Harry's disappointment at being forced to leave the front line. For the first time since he climbed on board the Chinook that had flown him away from the front line, Harry was able to put the frustrations and concerns about his men to the back of his mind.

He and Chelsy decided to charter a rickety houseboat which would enable them to disappear into the Okavango Delta for six days of unadulterated time together. It was a world away from their troubles and the issues that had put strains on their relationship. The couple shared a two-man tent perched high on the roof of the houseboat, which kept them private from the police protection officers and skipper who slept below. Each morning they rose late, climbed down an aluminium ladder and on to the main deck, where they cooked their own breakfast on a small gas stove. The rest of the day would be spent lazily cruising along the crocodile-infested waterways, normally with a can of beer and a cigarette in hand.

The office had sent me with a photographer to report on Harry's trip, and after a few days of waiting near the Namibian border we watched them slowly sail past. They looked relaxed and at ease with each other and had no idea they had been photographed.

As soon as we had our pictures we drove the six hours back to the town of Maun, having been instructed not to intrude on their holiday. Once again we had to find the right balance, so that we could report what they were doing without disrupting their plans. We telephoned Clarence House and told the press office what we had done but agreed to hold the story for twenty-four hours to avoid other photographers rushing to Botswana.

It was good to see that the couple whose romance we had reported on for more than three years were back in each other's arms, but even then wondered how much longer they would last.

According to Chelsy's friends, she already knew there was not much chance of a long-term relationship. One said: 'Chelsy was still so keen on Harry, but the "prince issue" was still in the way. She and Harry shared a love of Africa and the outdoors but deep down she never wanted to be a Kate Middleton. Chelsy is a free spirit and had absolutely no interest in become a princess, with all the baggage that would come with that role.

'The sight of them together in Botswana was typical of Chelsy. She didn't care about five-star luxury hotels or being pampered by the pool. She is African to the core, happier sleeping under the stars and drinking beer from a can. In many ways the very thing that made Harry crazy about Chelsy was the very thing that would mean they never had a long-term future together.'

While those in Chelsy's circle knew the writing was on the wall for the relationship, for the present the trip to Botswana in March 2008 had the effect of bringing them much closer together.

The friend added: 'Spending quality time on her own with Harry made Chelsy realize how fond she still was of her prince. She loved the way he doted after her. In the eyes of the public Harry was a soldier and a prince but to Chelsy he was more like a love-struck puppy who adored every second they spent together. He was always so kind to her, making sure she was OK and entertaining her with his childish sense of fun.

'If that was how it could always have been, there is no doubt they would have maybe one day got married and settled down. But the reality was that these times together were the exception rather than the rule. Back home she was studying hard to make the grade as a lawyer while Harry was committed to his career in the Army and duties as a senior Royal.'

When Harry returned home from Botswana he was feeling good to have seen Chelsy, but the old issue of his Royal baggage remained. And if he needed any reminding that his position as a Royal came with its own unique difficulties, just a few days after he returned he was in for a shock. William and Harry were about to find themselves at the centre of a row which would make headlines for all the wrong reasons. This time it was a very odd decision made by William that was to land the brothers in hot water.

With Harry back from Afghanistan, he was free to attend his cousin Peter Phillip's stag do on the Isle of Wight. What better way to forget about his troubles than a booze-fuelled lads' weekend to celebrate Princess Anne's son's upcoming wedding?

Peter Phillips, the brother of Olympic equestrian star Zara and a former rugby player, has always been close to his cousins Wills and Harry. As children they often spent weekends and holidays together exploring the mazes of corridors and acres of gardens at the Queen's many residences.

Similar in age and united by their love of sport and the outdoors, Peter was close to William and Harry when they were all growing up under the shadow of Royalty. But although Peter is also one of the Queen's grandsons, his mother Princess Anne decided her children should not grow up as prince and princess. While he and his sister Zara remain high in the line of succession, they have lived relatively normal lives away from the scrutiny applied to William and Harry.

One of the most obvious differences between the cousins is the fact that Peter does not require round-the-clock protection from the police. Although security measures are in place, he is not accompanied by bodyguards everywhere he goes. The only time Peter appears in papers and on the TV is when he joins senior Royals at family events such as weddings and the annual Christmas get-together with the Queen.

So when William and Harry agreed to join him on the bachelor weekend, Peter was delighted. His twenty-five closest pals were taking him to the Isle of Wight for three days of drinking, cricket, sailing and more drinking. The friends who were organizing it had even gone to the trouble of having polo shirts printed for each of the special few sharing their pal's 'last weekend of freedom'. Among those expected to attend was Zara's boyfriend, now husband, World Cup rugby hero Mike Tindall.

The stag party were all booked into a cheap hotel in the famous sailing town of Cowes and were just a short walk away from the many bars and restaurants. Peter and his chums were due to arrive on the island at lunchtime on the Friday and had booked seats for the two-hour train journey down from London.

Details of the trip had been kept secret, not least because everyone going would be well aware of the potential press interest in the bachelor party of one of the Queen's grandsons.

However, the *Sun* had been tipped off about the weekend, and by the time the stag party arrived on the Isle of Wight we were in position, with two photographers, myself and another reporter. Our aim was to stay well back, let the lads have their fun but take pictures if and when an opportunity arose.

The island is connected to the south coast of England by ferries, and all those arriving by train simply have to walk from the platform to the jetty, where they can step aboard their boat.

As April days go, the weather was surprisingly good. The sun shone down on the ferry terminal in Cowes as the stag party climbed into a fleet of pre-ordered taxis waiting to take them to a nearby school. Every detail of the weekend events had clearly been carefully planned, and the organizers had booked the school's cricket pitch for that afternoon.

We kept our distance and watched as the group arrived at the school and started preparing for a game of cricket. As it got underway we could see Peter but there was no sign of his easily recognizable cousins William and Harry.

Nor were there any obvious signs of Royal protection officers and their vehicles. Clearly our information about the stag party was spot on, but where were William and Harry? While it is true that pictures of Peter Phillips enjoying a wild weekend away before his wedding would make the paper, the reality was that without William and Harry in tow it was unlikely to make front-page news. At the time William was busy learning to fly helicopters with the RAF, while Harry was obviously still very newsworthy because of his return from Afghanistan.

But there was another reason why the boys were of immense interest that weekend. After more than six months of exhaustive evidence in London's High Court, the inquest into their mother's death in 1997 had just returned its verdict.

It had found that Diana died as a result of a tragic accident which could have been avoided. One by one, the court had cleverly picked apart all the conspiracy theories about her death. In the decade since she died there were claims that Diana was murdered by the British government because of her relationship with the Muslim son of controversial Egyptian businessman Mohamed Al-Fayed. It had even been claimed that Diana's father-in-law, Prince Philip, had ordered her death in revenge for the damage caused to the Royal family following the break-up of her marriage to Prince Charles.

But the inquest had exposed these and other bizarre claims for exactly what they were. At last people could stop accusing the government and the Royals of being part of a crazy cover-up and the true events that led to Diana's tragic death had been laid bare.

Following the inquest verdict earlier that week, Clarence House had issued a brief statement on behalf of Diana's sons saying they accepted the findings and hoped their mother could now be left to rest in peace. I now began to think that maybe William and Harry had taken the decision not to attend the stag party because of the timing of the inquest result. Perhaps they had taken the view that it was best they stay out of the public eye while the media interest died down.

Despite our disappointment we took the view that we should avoid blowing our cover at the cricket match. If the stag party saw our photographers they would know that their secret was out and might have gone to lengths to tone down their busy schedule of drinking and letting their hair down on the Isle of Wight.

We decided to head back to Cowes and get in position ready for what we had been told was going to be a pub crawl through the town centre later that evening. To reach the centre of Cowes from where the cricket match was being played, we had to cross the estuary that cuts the sailing town in half. The quickest way of getting to the other side in a car was via a small chain ferry that holds no more than a dozen vehicles at a time as it slowly crosses the water.

Our car was first on board and my colleague was in his vehicle behind. As the ferry started to cross the estuary, I climbed out of the car and headed to speak to him. To my horror as I stood up, I instantly realized that I was being watched. The final few vehicles that had been loaded on behind us were the fleet of Royal protection officers' unmistakable Range Rovers. Sitting in the front passenger seat of the vehicle directly behind was Prince Harry. I had inadvertently blown our cover and could see the protection officers smiling back at me from inside their cars.

If William and Harry had planned to let their hair down that weekend, then the sight of the *Sun*'s Royal correspondent was surely enough to make them think twice. On the plus side, our information about them joining Peter on the island had been right all along. But now it was going to be far harder to get pictures because the boys would be on high alert for photographers.

Working on the Royal beat was so often a game of cat and mouse. We knew the boys accepted they would be pictured, but it was far easier if they were unaware of our presence. There we all were, trapped on a ferry, and the secret was out. All I could do now was to steer clear of the Royal party and hope that they would not decide to go home rather than risk being photographed by the *Sun*.

An hour later I was sitting outside a hotel with my colleague, dwelling on my mistake. I was even considering getting on the next ferry off the island and writing off the weekend as a waste of effort. But as we sat there I recognized a man who was walking up towards us. He was a friendly protection officer who I had known for several years. It was clear he had been sent to find us and to ask what we were planning to do during the weekend.

In these situations it is always better to just accept the game is up. There is no point in messing the protection officers about. I apologized for blowing my cover on the ferry and pointed out that the last thing we wanted to do was to stop William and Harry from being able to have a good time. As we chatted I became aware that someone else had walked over to listen to what we were saying. He was standing to my left just out of my line of sight. It was Prince William.

This was the very last thing I needed. Prince Charles's eldest son has a love-hate relationship with the press and can be very prickly. There is no doubt that if he was in the wrong mood, I was about to get a bollocking from the future king and be told in no uncertain terms my team was not welcome on the island.

But to my surprise William was very friendly. He said: 'Hello, Duncan, what brings you to the Isle of Wight? Let me guess – you are here on a fishing trip?'

Clearly William was in a cheerful mood and had decided to start his conversation with a light-hearted joke. Perhaps this wasn't going to be so bad after all, I thought.

'Well, let's just say I was as surprised as you were to see who was on the chain ferry earlier,' I said.

William had seen by my reaction that I was horrified to have blown my cover and clearly had been caught off guard by the fact his entire entourage had driven onto the ferry behind us. He added: 'What are you going to do? Will this be in tomorrow's paper?'

By now it was 6 p.m., and apart from a few pictures of Peter and the others playing cricket we had very little to put in the Saturday edition.

'If you print a story about me and Harry being here, you know as well as I do what will happen,' added William. 'By the time the paper drops tonight, photographers and reporters from everywhere will be rushing down to the Isle of Wight.'

William was, of course, exactly right. If we were, as I suspected, the only paper to know about the weekend, then a story for Saturday would simply tip off the world and his wife. By the time the stag party got out of bed the next day there could be at least fifty photographers waiting for them to emerge. If that happened, William and Harry would simply be forced to go home and they would understandably hold me responsible for ruining their weekend.

William asked: 'Is there any way I could ask you not to run anything in tomorrow's paper? You would still be able to print your story for Monday. Harry and I would be really grateful if you could do this for us, we've been looking forward to Peter's weekend for ages.'

This was a rare encounter. I would often chat to William or share a joke when we met on official setpiece events. We had a good working relationship and being asked as directly as this left me little option. I knew that it would be nearly impossible to keep the weekend a secret and the chances were that if I didn't put something in Saturday's paper, the stag party would be splashed all over our rival papers on the Sunday. But I agreed.

I said: 'OK, you have my word that we won't put anything in tomorrow's paper, but I can't guarantee we are the only paper that knows about it. So far I haven't seen anyone else I recognize, so with a bit of luck you will have a free run of it tomorrow and won't have to go home early. Is there anything else you want us to do, or avoid doing?'

William looked taken aback by my question. He seemed almost lost for words that I was offering more than to hold the story for Monday's paper. After thinking for a second he asked: 'Well, I think I know the answer if I ask you all to go home, but how about agreeing to keep your distance? We don't mind you taking pictures from a distance, but Harry and I hate it when photographers get in our faces and fire off the flash.'

I said: 'I don't have an issue with that. If you or any of the stag party are photographed up close this weekend then you have my word they will not be from the *Sun*. We will do our best to keep out of your way. If we bump into you during the weekend, we will pull off, you don't need to change your plans.'

William must have had his doubts about whether I would be good for my word, but he thanked me before shaking my hand and walking off. After he got a few yards away he turned round and with a big grin on his face shouted back: 'By the way, Duncan, you do know this isn't my stag weekend!'

It was very funny hearing William make a joke at his own expense about the constant speculation he and Kate were already engaged. In all my dealings with William back then before he was married, he always came across as very quick-witted and good fun. It seems sad that since he has settled down, had children and come to terms with the serious business of being a future king, we rarely see this light-hearted side of the heir to the throne.

Many people wrongly think that William is the serious prince and Harry the joker. While Harry's antics are the stuff of tabloid legend, his big brother is just as able to play the fool and make jokes at his own expense. The chief difference between William and Harry is that the elder son is less able to get that side of his character across in public.

It may well be a deliberate decision on William's part. He has far more responsibility on his shoulders and does feel the need to come across as serious when he is in front of the cameras. The only danger for him these days is that if he comes across as too serious it could turn the public against him.

And so the scene was set for a wild weekend to celebrate Peter Phillips' upcoming wedding. Little did William or I know, as we joked in the street that day, that the damage had already been done and within days he and Harry would find themselves splashed across the front pages again.

CHAPTER 9

A RIGHT ROYAL ROW

'YOU SAID I was dyslexic,' fumed Harry.

'OK, you've got me on that one, but are you saying that story was wrong then, Harry?' I replied.

'No, but why did you have to write that about me?'

Clearly he was very angry and the rigours of an all-day drinking session on his cousin's stag weekend meant I was slap-bang in the middle of the firing line. I had never seen the prince like this and to anyone looking on it must have seemed as though we were in the middle of a heated row.

In reality Harry was getting months of frustration with the press off his chest. He had been denied the chance to go to Iraq, details of the strains in his relationship with Chelsy had been published, the breakdown in the media blackout had forced him home from Afghanistan, and just three days earlier the results of his mother's inquest had made front pages all over the world.

Looking back, it was no wonder he was upset and had decided to take a rare opportunity to vent his spleen with a journalist. But at one point he was becoming so animated, as he bent my ear, that one of his Royal protection officers later admitted that he feared he would have to intervene to stop us from coming to blows.

It was a Saturday night in April 2008 and we were standing in the beer garden of a pub in Cowes, Isle of Wight. All day Harry had been with his cousin Peter Phillips as they celebrated the upcoming wedding.

The party had been out sailing on a yacht suitably loaded with beer, cider and spirits. True to our word, the *Sun* team covering the stag weekend had refrained from getting in the way and instead taken pictures of the antics on long lenses from the shore.

An hour or so earlier I had been with a colleague watching rugby on the TV of the same pub. We had let the photographers get their pictures and were staying well out of the way as agreed.

Following William's request, nothing about the stag weekend had appeared in that day's edition of the paper, and as a result the boys had been left alone to enjoy a right royal knees-up with Peter and his friends.

And we had been well rewarded for our agreement. When the stag party boarded their yacht they had forced Peter to dress up as a sailor, painted a moustache on his face and strapped a little plastic doll to his arm. Peter had been warned that if the doll went missing he would have to pay a drinking forfeit, so the Queen's grandson had carefully cradled it in his arms throughout the day. The pictures were great, and we knew the office would be more than happy with our result.

Yes, it was a gamble to have agreed to William's request, but as the evening rolled on it appeared the gamble had paid off. The only other photographer who had got wind of the stag do was a local sailing enthusiast and he was happy for us to buy his pictures off the market to ensure we had it to ourselves.

But when I spotted a protection officer arrive in the pub where I had been watching the rugby I knew it was time to leave. He was there as an advance party to make sure the coast was clear for the stag party to arrive. As soon as I spotted him I went over and explained we were happy to leave as per the agreement.

I said to the officer: 'It's OK. We've been watching the rugby but if you are all coming in we will go somewhere else.'

The protection officer thanked us and said he knew the boys were grateful we had stuck by our side of the bargain.

When we got outside, the street was filled with party-goers, all wearing their special blue polo shirts. I stood back as they walked in and then spotted the protection officer I had met the previous day when William had come over to talk. We chatted about the rugby match I had watched and once again I explained we were happy to leave the stag party to it.

That really should have been the end of the matter. William and Harry had enjoyed their weekend, and I knew we had a great set of exclusive pictures that would keep the office off my back. But just as I prepared to say goodbye to the officer, one of Peter's friends came back out of the pub.

He said: 'Are you Duncan?'

'Yes,' I replied. 'But it's OK, I'm just leaving.'

'No, you are coming with me,' he said. 'William is inside and he said it's OK for you to stay.'

It was hard to say who was more shocked by this statement, the protection officer or me.

I looked at the officer and said: 'What do you think? I was leaving but if I'm allowed in, I'm not going to say no.'

The officer just shrugged in surprise and before I'd had the chance to think about it, I was in the bar surrounded by all of Peter's friends. The big rugby-playing guy that had all but dragged me inside, then asked what I drank.

'I'd like a pint of cider if that's OK,' I said, still taken aback by what was unfolding. I added: 'Look, guys, I have agreed not to be in here so I hope you are not going to get me in trouble. Are you sure it's OK for me to be here?'

The guy smiled before handing me two full pints of cider, and then said: 'You can stay here as long as you down both of these. William is grateful that you have kept your distance but you can only stay in here if you are as drunk as us. We don't want you writing a story about being drunk unless we know you've caught up with us first.'

I was stunned by his demands, but if those were the terms I was more than happy to drink in the line of duty.

By now there were at least six of Peter's friends surrounding me, eagerly waiting for me to try and gulp down the drinks. I was pretty sure that what they were trying to do was make me drink so fast I would have to run to the toilet and be sick. If they managed that, then how could I write a story about their drunken high jinks? It was an alcohol-fuelled logic, but it did make a sort of sense.

I controlled my breathing and prepared to down the drinks. The first one went down in one, but I was already regretting asking for cider, which fizzed and bubbled in my stomach.

'Go on, drink the next one,' demanded one of the others. By now they were laughing as I put the second glass to my mouth and tried to call on all my experience as an ex-rugby player. With, dare I say it, a degree of pride, I gulped down the second pint before putting the empty glass back on the bar. There was a pause as my tormenters enthusiastically waited for me to run to the bathroom. However, by some miracle I was able to keep the fizzing cider inside and managed to hide my discomfort enough to say: 'OK, it's my round, what are you all drinking?'

My efforts were clearly enough to have broken the ice, and over the next half an hour I stood chatting with Peter's friends at the bar.

One of his friends then explained: 'Look, we know you work for the *Sun* but Peter is a really good bloke and we are just looking out for him. We wanted to make sure you are not going to write anything bad about him, because he is a top bloke and doesn't deserve nasty things being written about him.'

At last their plan to invite me in to drink with them began to make sense. They were defensive of their friend and were simply looking after his back. I felt a bit more comfortable now and assured them everything we'd write about the weekend would be done in the spirit of fun. Clearly Peter's friends were a bunch of down-to-earth guys he had known for years and I actually started to enjoy being in their company.

'So how has the weekend gone?' I asked.

One of them replied: 'It's been fantastic, great fun. William and Harry have been brilliant. They have been the life and soul since they arrived on Friday in their helicopter.'

A helicopter, I thought. So that was why they missed the cricket and why we never saw them arrive at the ferry port.

The guy added: 'Yes, they flew down here from London in a Chinook. William was at the controls and he picked Harry up in London.'

This was the first I had heard about the means of transport the princes used to get to the island. But before I'd had a chance to think about what I had been told, one of the guys changed the subject by asking: 'Have you seen Harry's funnel?'

I had no idea what he was talking about but he went on to explain that Harry had been going around with a plastic funnel attached to a small length of hose pipe.

He said: 'He's been making us drink out of the funnel, he is so funny.'

To this day I have no idea whether Harry had brought his makeshift drinking device with him on the stag weekend or whether he had spotted it with someone else and decided to take charge. But within seconds I was at the back of the pub on my knees with one end of the plastic hose in my mouth while one of the guys poured my entire pint of cider into the funnel.

By now I could barely face another drink, let alone one that shot into my mouth at high speed. Aided by the piece of hose, the cider shot into my stomach and it was all I could do to stop throwing up.

As the group all laughed at my expense, I saw Harry standing, cigarette in hand, looking on. Unlike his friends, he was not smiling. He looked decidedly unhappy that I was there and I felt bad that I was intruding on his weekend away. As I stood up, I asked Harry if he wanted me to go. He was very cross and I sensed that all was not well. Perhaps in my desire to appease Peter's friends, I had encroached on Harry's space. But with the alcohol now kicking in, I decided to confront the situation head-on. 'Sorry,' I said, 'but I was told it was OK to be here. I will leave if that's what you want.'

Standing next to Harry were his protection officers, by now the only sober people nearby. The pub was now very busy with locals who had heard the princes were in town and had rushed down to see. Many of them were shouting Harry's name from a distance and were trying to take pictures of him on their phones. I remember thinking that this is what it must be like for Harry every time he goes out for a drink. It must be really annoying to be recognized by everyone, especially when they think it is OK to shout his name from a distance.

'If you have a problem with me, Harry, then now's your chance. Tell me what is making you angry,' I said.

I could not have predicted what was about to happen and in all my years reporting on the Royals it was certainly going to be an hour that would stick in my mind for ever.

Harry's protection officers, worried by the sheer number of people who were now in the pub beer garden to gawp at their principal, ushered us to an area where we would be out of sight. It was a small gap between the pub's wall and a large van that was parked outside. From there the protection officers were able to stand guard and stop the increasingly excited locals from coming over.

As we stood in the makeshift alley, Harry said: 'You have written some bad stories about me recently.'

I was at a total loss to understand what he was talking about. Just a few weeks earlier we had carried a front page under the headline 'Harry the Hero'. Several pages inside marked his return from war with gushing compliments, praising him for his bravery and dignity in returning home early.

Surely, he must have been aware that it was in no small part thanks to the *Sun* that the concept of the media blackout on Afghanistan came into existence.

And as far as the cancellation of his Iraq trip was concerned, was Harry not aware that we had agreed to pull the story which was eventually run by another paper and contributed to the U-turn?

Yes, we had pictured him and Chelsy in Botswana, but we pulled out after one hit and informed the palace that we were being careful not to spoil his well-earned holiday. With all these things considered, it sounded to me like Harry was just being over-sensitive and more than a little unfair in aiming his anger at me and my paper.

Despite the effects of an entire day of drinking, Harry now started to list in great detail stories that had been written about him in the preceding weeks and months. I was astonished by how he was able to reel them off one by one as though he had been checking the cuts just minutes before meeting me that night.

Fortunately for me, each story he mentioned had been written by rivals. Every time he mentioned a story I was able to honestly argue that I was not the author, nor did those tales appear in the *Sun*. Until eventually he came to the story I had written about him being dyslexic.

A few months earlier Harry had been on a fishing trip with the former *Top Gear* presenter Jeremy Clarkson. They had met while on holiday in Barbados and agreed to spend the day together on a boat fishing off the coast of the Caribbean island. During the fishing trip Harry had told Clarkson about his dyslexia, perhaps forgetting that besides being a TV presenter he also worked as a columnist for the *Sun*. When Clarkson had returned from his holiday he wrote about his day out with Harry in his column, and I had been asked to write a news story in the same edition based on the dyslexia line.

To my relief Harry seemed reassured by my responses to his attack on the press. He even apologized for being angry and for taking it out on me. It seemed as though he felt better for having got a few things off his chest, and we continued to chat for what must have been a further half an hour. We talked about his mother's inquest result, his time away in Afghanistan and his hopes for the rest of his military career.

Much of what he said was too private to share, but it gave me an incredible insight into what made the young prince tick. It was clear that deep down he felt very trapped by his life as a senior Royal. He seemed torn between the demands placed on him as a Royal, and his desire to be a normal Army officer who enjoyed a drink and winning the respect of his men.

What I heard from him that evening enabled me to understand where he was coming from, and it also served as a reminder that when you write stories about a famous person, deep down they are just ordinary people living in a set of extraordinary circumstances. Harry may have learned to deal with a life lived in a goldfish bowl, but he remained incredibly sensitive about the things that were written about him, especially if they were inaccurate or unfair.

We shook hands and I thanked him for giving me the chance to defend myself. I then headed back to my hotel, still thinking about all the things he had said.

To this day I still respect the fact that Harry not only felt able to try and defend himself but was also man enough to accept where he was perhaps being a little harsh. That long conversation cleared the air and in no small part contributed to a far closer relationship between myself and the person whose job it was for me to write about.

The following day I told the office about our chat but deliberately held back the details in case they instructed me to write a story and betray Harry's trust. We wrote up our stories from the stag weekend and the editors were delighted with the pictures of Peter Phillips on the yacht and enjoying his 'last weekend of freedom'.

On the ferry on the way back to the mainland the next day I had a call from Harry's head of communications at Clarence House. He had heard about my 'pleasant chat' with the prince and was just checking that I had no intention of publishing the full extent of our conversation.

There are times when you have to try and play the long game as a specialist reporter. It is not my job to hold back information the public have a right to read, but at the same time it is important to balance this against the need to maintain a good relationship with the palace.

This balancing act was at the forefront of my mind when I reflected on everything I had seen and heard over the weekend. While it was, in my view, right to withhold details of my chat with Harry, it was going to be far more difficult to ignore the snippet of information I had heard when talking at the bar with Peter's friends.

There was no ignoring what they had said. William and Harry's arrival on the Isle of Wight in an RAF Chinook helicopter raised all kinds of serious questions. These vast machines cost thousands of pounds an hour to fly, and because they belong to the military the ultimate bill would fall to the taxpayer.

After putting a call into the Ministry of Defence, we were soon able to establish that it was absolutely true that both brothers had arrived on the island on Friday afternoon in a Chinook. William had left his RAF base and flown the chopper down to London to the barracks where Harry was working. The two princes then flew to a small airfield on the Isle of Wight, thus avoiding a journey of three or four hours by car and ferry.

Meanwhile the boys' protection officers had driven all the way down – again at taxpayer's expense – to ensure they were in position to collect William and Harry when the helicopter landed.

It was clear before we had even written a word of the story for the next day's paper that this was going to land both boys in a great deal of hot water. The last time Harry had climbed in and out of a Chinook, it had taken him away from the front line in Afghanistan. This time it had delivered him to his cousin's stag party and a weekend of boozing and high jinks.

It was a classic example of that balancing act you have to play as a journalist. We had no right to prevent the public from reading about the wasteful trip and I had to put my feelings about the weekend to one side. In the end we wrote the story very straight, and it was printed without much prominence at the bottom of an inside page. But the following day the 'outrage' of William and Harry's pleasure trip was splashed over the front pages of both the *Mirror* and the *Daily Mail*.

To make matters worse, it was then revealed that during his helicopter training with the RAF, William had made a number of flights which should have raised eyebrows. Although he was expected to spend a set number of hours flying Chinooks as part of his training at RAF Odiham in Hampshire, it emerged that he and his instructors had made some very bad decisions about where these sorties had taken him.

On one occasion William had flown over the Queen's private Sandringham Estate in Norfolk, and he had flown down to his father's home at Highgrove in Gloucestershire. Even more controversially, he had also landed in fields next to the Berkshire home of the parents of his then girlfriend Kate Middleton. On a final occasion William had even flown to a private wedding in

Northumberland in the north of England, laying himself open to claims he had treated his RAF training mission as a private helicopter taxi service.

In total it was estimated that the taxpayer had been slapped with a bill of more than £86,000 for the flights. As commentators slammed the prince for his choice of destinations, Clarence House were forced to issue an apology on William's behalf. And a few weeks later when details of the behind-the-scenes row over the 'pleasure flights' were made public it emerged that William's station commander had been kept in the dark about the 'true nature' of the Isle of Wight flight. Several senior officers were taken to task and William himself was forced to accept his part of the responsibility.

An MoD spokesman said in a statement: 'In retrospect there was a degree of naivety involved in the planning of these sorties but there is no question that anyone misled anyone.'

Clarence House said: 'Prince William accepts that the sorties were naive and accepts his share of the responsibility for what happened.'

It was one of the rare occasions when William found himself at the centre of a Royal row. The fact that he had inadvertently involved his brother in it by taking him to the stag do must have upset him.

A senior palace source reflected on the pleasure flights gaffe and told me: 'It was an unfortunate episode, a silly own goal that could and should have been avoided. It is unlike William to make such errors of judgement but it really did cause a fuss at the time. It was felt that any criticism of Harry was unfair and William was very sorry that his brother had been dragged into the row. The reality is the boys should have travelled to the stag weekend by road because the risk of the story getting out was too great. The episode was a learning curve for William and as he went on to earn his RAF wings it was a mistake he never repeated.'

It would be easy to say that William and Harry are able to shrug off these kinds of public rows. But as Harry demonstrated during his time on the Isle of Wight, the pair do take criticism very seriously.

It must sometimes feel that their public image takes one step forward and two back. Just days before going to the Isle of Wight, both boys had made the well-documented visit to Headley Court to visit wounded troops, including Ben McBean. But it serves as a reminder that if they make the slightest mistake they can find themselves on the front pages for all the wrong reasons. Life as a senior Royal may be marked by great privilege and position, but it can also come with huge costs if you are ever seen to step out of line.

Harry's role in the row was only minor on this occasion, but nonetheless he was very upset to find himself and William the focus of such widespread public criticism. In what should have been a period where he kept his head down after returning from Afghanistan early, Harry remained firmly on the front pages.

Not long after his trip to the Isle of Wight he was planning to use his Royal profile for good. With time on his hands, it was to his beloved AIDS charity that he turned his attention. He spent the following two months planning a trip that would help shed much-needed light on the plight of the forgotten children of Lesotho.

CHAPTER 10

LESOTHO

BEING A ROYAL correspondent inevitably means gaining access to members of a family whose faces and names are famous all over the world. Unlike pop stars, celebrities, politicians or wealthy businessmen, whose pictures fill the pages of magazines and newspapers at the height of their careers, Royalty is a lifelong sentence.

Public figures come and go. Most are born into obscurity, rise to fame, then their significance fades as they approach the grave. But from when Harry was a bump in his mother's tummy, to the day when he will be laid to rest, there will always be intense public interest in his life.

Inevitably working as a Royal journalist means meeting people who are fascinated to hear more about the person they admire as the 'bad boy' of the House of Windsor. When people think of Prince Harry they think of his slip-ups, his love of a party, his eye for the ladies and his refreshingly down-to-earth sense of humour. All of the above are indeed characteristics of the prince whose popularity as a Royal is eclipsed only by the Queen herself. His astonishing journey since leaving school has placed Harry in the hearts of millions of people all over the planet.

Gaffes litter Harry's CV like chocolate chips in a cookie. Chocolate chips because for most people they simply make him seem more delicious, a character with flaws but whose heart is firmly in the right place. The reality is that in these days of the cult of the celebrity we don't warm to people who are flawless. We like our famous people to slip up, to struggle with the things that we struggle with. It is only then that we can identify with the lives of those who dominate our newspapers and magazines.

I doubt Harry gets drunk anywhere near as often as most other young men. He probably attends fewer parties in the average year, and his list of ex-girlfriends would look very modest when placed next to that of the average Premiership footballer or reality TV star. So why does he have this reputation? Why does a simple Google search for 'Prince Harry booze' produce 628,000 hits?

Much of his hard-living reputation stems from the two years between leaving school and knuckling down to a military career. Yet these years, which he appeared to waste, also gave him an experience which has had one of the largest impacts in shaping his life.

For two months during his extended gap year, Harry lived in Lesotho, travelling across the tiny kingdom and coming face-to-face with the man-made epidemic that had wreaked disaster on one of the world's least known countries. Most of the trip took place well away from the cameras as Harry visited orphanages, medical centres and volunteers trying to cope with an AIDS epidemic which had claimed the lives of a third of Lesotho's population.

What was intended to be a low-key experience sandwiched into his gap year was to have a far more profound impact on the unsuspecting teenage prince. On that 2004 visit the young Harry would undergo a eureka moment which all these years later is still having an impact. He went to Lesotho as a fresh-faced 19-year-old keen to learn more about the lives of those whose accidents of birth were a million miles from his own. It turned into a visit and experience that was to change his life for ever. It was there that he made a lifelong commitment to use his Royal profile to highlight the plight of the 'forgotten children of Lesotho'.

If the young Harry needed to hear horror stories to prompt him into taking action, then sadly Lesotho had an abundance of case studies to shock the prince. A tiny, forgotten country landlocked by South Africa, Lesotho's beautiful hills and meandering rivers may at first glance seemed like Africa at its most idyllic. With its small villages and remote farmlands, it looked like the backdrop to a Hollywood film. But it was impossible for Harry to spend more than a few hours in the country before the reality of its dark secrets would be laid bare.

Ignorance of the HIV virus and AIDS had taken such a cruel grip on the country that the average person was not expected to live beyond their thirty-fourth birthday. A third of the population had the virus, making Lesotho one of the worst-affected countries on the planet. And with little or no awareness of the virus among its people, the prospects were likely to get even worse.

Harry was instantly struck by the 'missing generation' of people between the ages of eighteen and thirty-five. Children roamed the streets, many of them orphans, the epidemic having claimed the lives of their mothers and fathers.

The stark contrast between the beauty of the kingdom and the ugly realities of a killer virus that had spiralled out of control was immediately evident for Harry. On his first day in Lesotho he was driven deep into the countryside through the tiny villages and mud huts so many locals called home. While the larger villages may have boasted a makeshift grocery shop, a petrol station and police house, the one thing all of them had was a large undertakers surrounded by sprawling graveyards. The virus was so prevalent that funeral parlours were the only booming businesses away from the towns.

Harry joined volunteers based on the ground and was taken to meet some of the people worst affected by the swelling disaster. While he met many orphans on his visit, it was the experience of meeting two young children in particular that shocked him to the core.

The first was a 10-month-old baby girl who was being cared for by volunteer nurses in squalid conditions two hours from the country's capital, Maseru. One of the volunteers led him to a cot to see the little girl for the first time, and Harry listened in horror to the account of her life. Her emotionless eyes were fixed on the ceiling as he was told of her plight. She had been raped by her stepfather, so brutally abused that the doctors had already had to remove her tiny womb. The trauma of her ordeal was etched on a face that should have been bubbling like that of any other 10-month-old infant. Astonishingly, she had become the innocent victim of the epidemic because of the ignorant belief that one way a male could cure himself of AIDS was to have sex with a baby.

Later in his visit Harry decided to be filmed with the little girl in a bid to draw attention to just how hideously the children of Lesotho were suffering. Sitting on a bunk bed and cradling the infant in his arms, a visibly shaken Harry told ITV's Tom Bradbury about the first time he had seen her. 'She was just lying there, staring up at the ceiling, with just no expression whatsoever. She couldn't even cry. She could barely be fed. It was horrible, especially when we saw the footage the day after we were actually there and I saw her head in my arms – she couldn't move, had no expression, no smiling, nothing at all. She was completely emotionless. It was almost as though she knew what had happened. If I can, I would like to try and support her in her growing up.'

Another child who was to have a lasting impact on the prince was a 4-year-old boy called Mutsu. In the same interview near the end of his two-month visit, Harry recalled: 'The first day I met him, he came running up and just chucked a ball at me, and that was that, we had a laugh. Then at the photocall he was standing next to me and I asked him if he wanted to help plant a tree. With a bit of help from a translator he said yes. Ever since then he's been really sweet. He comes up and he's just a really sweet kid. He was the third youngest in the orphanage, with no father, no mother, a little devil at times, but we just had a really good laugh with him.'

For one day during Harry's visit the British press had been invited to Lesotho to see the prince at work with the volunteers. The publicity surrounding the official event had an instant impact on the relief work Harry had been shown. Pictures and footage of Mutsu, seen running about with Harry in a pair of shiny new blue wellies the prince had given him, got coverage back home and in neighbouring South Africa.

It was off the back of the success of this that Harry decided to go one step further. He invited the crew from ITV News to film a documentary on Lesotho, and in return he agreed to give a long interview. This was one of the first times Harry saw at first hand how his celebrity status could be used to help the plight of others. Until that trip the young prince had nothing but contempt for the media. He hated them. But now he realized how he could use them to the benefit of others.

What was so clear from the interviews Harry gave during that trip was just how shocked he had been to be confronted by the devastating effects of the out-of-control epidemic.

The media had shown no interest previously in reporting on a country most people had never even heard of, but they would fill their pages and bulletins with the plight of the forgotten children of Lesotho if Prince Harry was there.

Harry would have known how the Royals use their status to draw attention to good causes. His mother was the master of drawing attention to the needs of others by agreeing to be pictured and filmed on location. But when Harry spoke about his experiences in Lesotho that year, it was clear even he had been surprised by what could be achieved if he agreed to be used by the media.

In his documentary interview Harry recalled how within hours of posing for the cameras at an orphanage in Lesotho, good things began to happen. He revealed how the day after the photocall a South African farmer drove over the border to find the prince and offer his help. 'He pitched up and wanted to talk to me. So I spoke to him and he just basically said to me that the night before "I went home, turned on my television and there I saw a member of the British Royal family, and not just that, a 19-year-old who has come all the way over from England to Lesotho to make everybody aware of the problems."

'I mean there are all sorts of ways of getting around problems like this but I'm here merely to bring awareness to the problems. And he [the farmer] said he couldn't believe it took that much from someone from another Royal family thousands of miles away to come over just to do that when basically he was appalled and shocked by himself, the fact that Lesotho is on their back doorstep and they've got the means to help and they don't. He thanked us, and he said thank you for opening our eyes.'

Without realizing it, that unnamed farmer who tracked Harry down to offer help had inadvertently opened his to what his future might hold. Until that day Harry was an angry, slightly naive teenager with an understandable chip on his shoulder the size of one of his grandmother's palaces. But Lesotho offered him a purpose, a possible future where he could use his status for good.

He also gave a hint as to why in later life Harry would choose young people in particular as a focus for his Royal work. He said: 'I love children but that's probably because I've got an incredibly immature side to me. I love children back home but up here there's hundreds of children everywhere. There are 8-year-olds, 10-year-olds looking after cattle.

'The nicest thing out here is they don't know who I am. I'm just a normal guy to them, which is really, really nice. It's so special just to be one of them. OK, I'm very different, I've had a completely different growing up to them, but it's a case of being like them, having a laugh with them. You should see their faces. I've got my video camera, I've taken lots of pictures and they are all so happy.'

The trip he made at the young age of nineteen was to have such a profound effect on Harry that he spoke candidly about his mother's legacy and in so doing revealed for the first time what really makes him tick.

Asked whether he thought about his mother when he spent time with the children, he replied: 'Definitely. I've always wanted to do this. It is what she was doing. I'm only nineteen but there is a lot of me that wants to say, "OK, let's keep my mother's legacy going." But at the age of nineteen it's pretty hard work. I try and be as normal as I can, to try and have a normal life before it gets too hectic.

'She never came to Lesotho but she's worked around the same areas and I believe I've got a lot of my mother in me. And I just think she'd want us to do this, me and my brother. Obviously it's not as easy for William as it is for me. I think I've got more time on my hands to be able to help. We have both got our lives set out for us, but I think he's got his life really set out.

'Unfortunately it's been a long time now – not for me but for most people – a long time since she died. But it's just a shame that after all the good she's done, even this far on, people aren't bringing out the good in her. There's people who want to bring out the bad stuff because bad news sells. I'm not out here to try and change that, but I'm out here doing what I want to do and doing what she'd want me to do.'

Harry's words in that interview gave one of the best insights into how he thinks and where he sees himself as a Royal. He may have been speaking as a young man, but even today his words have a striking relevance. By using his Royal status to draw attention to issues close to his heart, he is continuing his mother's legacy.

He went on to sum up what it was like to be Prince Harry and looking back all these years later, his words read like a manifesto for his future life. 'I'm not normal,' he said. 'Much as I'd like to be normal, I'm not normal and my father reminds me of that the whole time. William and I can't be normal, but we grew up in the year 2000. We are part of the Royal family, but we've grown up surrounded by all our friends, it's completely different to what other generations have been like. I've tried, we've both tried to be as normal as we can. I think the British media and all sorts of other media try to focus on the fact that I am a playboy, I am a party prince, all that sort of stuff, which I'm not.

'I'm a teenager who goes out and has fun and no matter what time I come out of a club, they're going to write that it was four o'clock in the morning, there's nothing I can do about that. And recently in the papers after the press call the quote was "Nice try, Harry, but are you really converted?"

'But I'm not converted, I've always been like this, this is my side that no one gets to see. I'm not going to take a camera crew with me every time I go out and am trying to help out in different countries. I am who I am, and though I believe I'm no one special, I can do things like for instance the press. There I was at the orphanage and the fact that all the press came meant that we got £2,000, which meant that we paid for the whole fence, which was perfect because it meant that all the children were safe inside the orphanage.'

Asked to describe how he deals with the pressure of being in the constant media spotlight and whether he just lets it wash over him, he replied: 'Time after time it upsets me, but nobody will understand that other than my brother and myself. He and I are very close obviously because of our mother. But we both get the same kind of hassle, different times, different things, you know. It's hard. We've got friends of ours and we've got the British public saying "Good on them they're being normal", and then you've got the British media saying "Oh, but they can't be normal", or "This isn't normal, it's completely outrageous", that sort of thing.

'I'd love to let it wash over me but unfortunately I can't, I don't think anyone can. It's hard but I'm not out here for a sympathy vote. I'm not going to answer that question as a sympathy vote, I'm going to answer it completely honestly and say that William and I try to be normal, it's very difficult, but we are who we are.

'I'm coming to the age now where I can make the most of that. When I was young I was like, "Oh, I can't believe I've got to do this, got to do that." Ever since our mother died, everyone recognizes us around streets, you know, it's all a bit awkward, but as I get older I can use it like my mother did. She was just a normal woman who married my father and became this Queen of Hearts simply because she used her position basically and used her position in a good way, and that's what I want to do.'

It was on this trip that Harry made a famous pledge to highlight the plight of the children, one which he is still honouring with the passion that was sparked by his teenage experiences in Lesotho.

Shortly after returning from that visit Harry set about forming his charity Sentebale. Fittingly, its name means 'Forget Me Not' and in the years since his gap-year visit the charity has raised millions of pounds to help those whose plight Harry witnessed back in 2004. Two years later the fledgling charity was up and running after Harry teamed up with Prince Seeiso of Lesotho. Gala dinners, pop concerts and posh polo matches all over the world have helped the prince raise funds for Lesotho. Probably none of this would have happened had he not agreed to visit the kingdom in 2004.

While the charity has had many teething problems, it stands as a testament to the lifelong commitment Harry made as he returned home from Lesotho. The prince repeated his pledge in 2014, ten years after his first, life-changing visit to the tiny kingdom.

In an interview during a star-studded fundraising polo match in Abu Dhabi, Harry spoke about the setting up of Sentebale. 'It started really, really small … a very small group of us saying we're not going to use the funds for other people, it's going to be all for the kids and pretending we knew what we were doing. Ten years down the line we have made a couple of mistakes and in turn learned from our mistakes and now we know that actually, by speaking to the core problem, which in this case is the children themselves, you get a really good taste of whether you're achieving it or not. The great thing about Lesotho is that because it's so small, you know that if you're doing it wrong, it's highly visible. And if you're doing it right you start to see the change.'

He went on to admit his charity was a 'hard sell for a lot of people', but committed to continue the work, adding: 'It's a very small country that no one knows about, surrounded by South Africa, a landlocked country, and I think that combined with us thinking that we were doing right, it evolved and it changed for the better. We realized our mistakes and we were willing to change it by speaking to the kids on the ground.

'What I'd like to think is that Sentebale has brought everyone together to work for one great cause. It's been an emotional roller-coaster but we've come out on top and all I've ever wanted to do was raise enough money to make a difference for Lesotho.'

Harry has returned there many times and although he is now much older and more mature than on that first occasion, his feelings towards the people of Lesotho remain exactly the same. It was no surprise therefore that when Harry's tour of Afghanistan was cut short in 2008, he filled much of his time planning a trip to Lesotho with his men.

In July 2008 Harry's commanders with the Blues and Royals regiment agreed for him to take twenty of his men to Lesotho to help rebuild a school for disabled children as well as help with other projects supported by Sentebale. During the visit the media were invited to see the work they were doing and find out more about the charity's progress. There was nothing unusual about the invitation and most of the British papers and TV channels made the twelve-hour flight to South Africa and then the one-hour drive across the border into Lesotho. But this was not going to be an ordinary Royal photocall.

All senior Royals make foreign visits, carefully orchestrated to ensure the media get their slice of the cherry, while attention is drawn to the worthy causes in the spotlight. Touring with Prince Charles normally means visits to sustainable projects, rainforests or programmes to promote the built environment. The outspoken future king is often good value as he draws attention to the causes close to his heart. On these trips you rarely get any direct access to the Prince of Wales and are left to settle for photo opportunities and the occasional heartfelt speech.

But Harry being Harry, he was determined to put his own stamp on this visit. The night before the photocall at the school he had been helping rebuild, Harry's media team had arranged for the customary 'briefing' in a conference room of one of the few hotels in Lesotho's capital, Maseru. Usually these briefings are with the familiar faces of the palace press office and members of the organization in question. But as the door opened and we filed into the conference room that evening, to everyone's surprise the door was being held open for us by Harry himself. None of us were expecting him to be there in person, and after a long journey we thought we would simply be going through the usual planning session with the palace. Even some of the more seasoned Royal journalists were taken aback to be greeted at the door by Harry. It turned out that he had travelled more than an hour from where he was staying to greet us.

It was the first time I had seen Harry since our long chat in the beer garden of the pub on the Isle of Wight. He was in good spirits, laughing and joking with the media men he recognized and shaking hands with members of the local media, who were wide-eyed with delight.

Harry's ability to charm and put people at ease is a sight to behold. And because we had all been caught off guard by him being at the briefing everyone knuckled down to the matter in hand, taking more notes than usual and trying to out-do each other with clever questions about the following day's events.

After about forty minutes the briefing was over and we were all looking forward to getting some sleep ready for what was clearly going to be a long day ahead. But as we left the conference room Harry came over to us and said: 'Anyone fancy a beer?'

It was unheard-of for a Royal to join in a media briefing, let alone invite us upstairs to the hotel bar afterwards for a drink. Harry was very relaxed as he spoke to journalists and filled them in on the Sentebale projects he had been working with.

It was not long after his cousin Peter had married the Canadian Autumn Kelly. The couple had broken with Royal protocol and agreed to let their wedding be photographed and feature in a special edition of the celebrity magazine *Hello!* I asked Harry how the wedding had gone and about how he felt about the pages and pages of coverage it had attracted as part of the magazine deal.

Standing at the bar Harry recalled how one thing about the wedding reception had really stuck in his mind. He said: 'Someone had the bright idea to have a mirrored dance floor at the reception, can you imagine how crazy that was?'

After thinking through what he was saying the penny finally dropped. Anyone dancing at his cousin's wedding would be reflected by the dance floor.

I laughed and asked Harry: 'Oh dear, I bet you were worried about Chelsy dancing and everyone being able to see up her skirt?'

He quickly replied: 'Never mind Chelsy, it was my grandmother I was worried about.'

It was a hilarious exchange. Here was Harry joking about the Queen dancing on top of a mirror, and needless to say we all fell about laughing at what he had said.

This was typical Harry. Putting everyone at ease by making light of what could have been a most memorable family gaffe. This was Harry at his best, holding forth, pint in hand, and it would have been easy to forget he was a senior member of the Royal family, rather than just a guy who'd been to a family wedding and saw the funny side in what could – but thankfully didn't – happen.

He was in Lesotho for a serious reason, trying to keep public attention on a cause so close to his heart. But rather than fall into the trap of being aloof and too serious, he knew that by relaxing and putting people at ease he was far more likely to get the kind of coverage he was after. It was a refreshing experience for everyone there that night and made us all the more determined to ensure Sentebale got great coverage once the photocall had taken place.

As part of the media visit Harry had arranged for his men to take on the gentlemen of the press with a game of football. Following the photocall of Harry and his men pushing wheelbarrows of earth and working up a sweat as they repaired the small school, we were all invited to pull on a football shirt and have a kickabout on a nearby dusty pitch.

The only shirt that I had offered to me was far too small, and to the delight of Harry I looked terrible as I puffed about the pitch in the scorching heat. I've always loved football but never had the coordination or skill to play. So the sight of me running about chasing shadows as Harry and his team took us to the cleaners delighted the young Royal. As I ran to keep up, Harry started making hippo noises at my expense. This was a chance for him to humiliate me in front of the other members of the press pack and he was enjoying every minute.

At one point, as my frustrations continued, I tried to tackle Harry. But his soccer skills being so much better than my own, he spun around and expertly kicked the ball away before I'd got close. Then, in full view of the cameras, Harry faced me and put his hand up to his forehead before making an L-shape with his thumb and forefinger. 'Loser!' he shouted before running off. Once again Harry was playing the fool, but doing so at my expense. The photographers and cameramen along the side-line were laughing and started heckling me as I puffed about the pitch.

It was great fun, even if the joke was well and truly at my expense. But once again Harry knew exactly what he was doing. He was performing for the cameras, making sure that when the day's events were written up we all had lots to fill our pages for the following day's paper.

The ribbing I had taken only got worse when I phoned the office to tell them what had happened. 'Tell me you've got pictures,' demanded the very excited-sounding picture editor. Unfortunately for me, there were several pictures of Harry flicking the loser sign in my direction, and by now I was being ribbed by my colleagues six thousand miles away. The following day the picture of me and Harry filled a whole page, which simply meant the ribbing now also came from friends who had spotted the paper.

With my phone in meltdown with text messages adding to my humiliation, we were waiting for Harry to arrive at an orphanage for the final part of his photocall visit. When his car pulled up Harry gleefully jumped out and shouted in my direction: 'Have you seen your picture in the paper today – you look so stupid!'

He had clearly taken great delight in getting a bit of payback at my expense. But in so doing had ensured great coverage for Sentebale in the UK's biggest paper. For Harry it was mission accomplished and served yet again as a masterclass in how to use the press to his advantage.

It was very clear from that short visit in July 2008 that Harry's desire to do everything he could to help the children of Lesotho was stronger than ever. A pledge he made during the TV interview as a fresh-faced 19-year-old was being delivered in style. This was a prince on a mission to make sure the plight of those he had met during his gap-year visit was not going to be ignored.

Whatever people may say about Harry's antics, it is impossible to find fault with his determination to continue his mother's legacy. It is hard to think of any other member of his family who would be able to lark about in front of the cameras without making themselves look awkward. It was by no means the last time Harry would play the fool as he tried to get a far more serious point across. But his ability to do this with such sincerity and his natural sense of good fun may explain why he is the darling of the Royal family in so many people's eyes.

This was a prince who was already well on his way to soaring popularity. A Royal who could truly break the mould – and carry it off without looking stupid.

CHAPTER 11

STEALING AWAY

'IF THIS IS stolen then we might as well take this taxi straight to Belmarsh prison,' I said, and I was deadly serious. 'Make no mistake, guys, you will not get away with it,' I added.

The memory stick I was holding in my hand was dynamite. If the pictures it contained were sold on the open market they would be worth a small fortune. Once they had been published in the *Sun*, newspapers and magazines all over the world would be bidding for the rights to publish them. There was little doubt in my mind that they would be worth upwards of £250,000.

No doubt it was this very fact that stopped the two strangers I had met an hour earlier from seeing sense and taking my advice, even after I added: 'If you guys had anything to do with stealing this, or if they turn out to be stolen, the police will be all over you.' It was no good. My new acquaintances were determined to make some money and there was nothing I could say to make them see sense.

I was well qualified to offer advice. Just five months earlier, in spring 2008, I had appeared at the Old Bailey as a lead prosecution witness for the Metropolitan Police. They were prosecuting two guys who had contacted the *Sun* more than a year earlier.

That time the men were trying to sell video footage of a man who worked for one of the Royal family. He was taking drugs and bad-mouthing his employer. I was sent to meet one of the men I would eventually testify against in the Central Criminal Court. Fortunately, I took the view that he was far too dodgy to deal with and left it at that. However, I later discovered that the man and his accomplice had gone to other newspapers and after being knocked back several times had decided to try and blackmail the Royal in question by exposing his drug-taking employee. As a result, they were arrested in a police sting and were found guilty and sent to prison.

The experience had taught me that when it comes to the Royal family, the police take any suggestion of criminality extremely seriously. And more importantly, a jury are far more likely to side with the establishment than offer the benefit of the doubt to the defendant.

Five months on, I once again found myself meeting strangers who seemed blissfully unaware of the forces they were about to come up against. Now we were on our way in a black cab from Paddington to the office, where the news and pictures editors were awaiting our arrival.

Earlier that day a member of the newsdesk had come over to me in the office and said: 'I've just taken a call from a guy who claims to have a memory stick full of pictures of William and Kate on holiday. Here is the bloke's number. I want you to give him a call and arrange to meet him to see if it checks out.'

It was September 2008 and I was well aware that the future king and his stunning girlfriend had just returned from the island of Mustique in the Caribbean. As my finger hovered over the office landline, I thought to myself that if these pictures were taken by a friend of William and Kate, or another holidaymaker on the island, then maybe, just maybe, they were useable.

But as soon as I heard the voice on the end of the phone my heart sank. The 'source' who had phoned the *Sun* didn't exactly sound like one of William's old Eton chums. He spoke with a broad south London accent and seemed mainly interested in finding out what his pictures would be worth. I arranged to meet the man once he had finished work that day, but even as I left the office I had some serious reservations.

Working as a *Sun* reporter I had dealt with all kinds of people. I knew several of William and Harry's close friends but was also well used to getting information from ordinary punters.

I decided to take a photographer with me, not least because if there were pictures of Wills and Kate, and they did turn out to be stolen, I would need him to take discreet shots of the person trying to sell stolen goods.

I had at least two hours to kill while waiting for the 'source' to turn up. Arrangements like this were fairly common at the *Sun*. Often the person who rang in would get cold feet, sometimes they were just on a wind-up and enjoyed wasting your time, but from time to time they were genuine. But as I sat waiting in Paddington I kept thinking about what we were being offered. How could a set of holiday pictures that could not have been more than a few days old get into the hands of the person I had arranged to meet?

One thing was absolutely clear to me. If they were – as I suspected – stolen, the paper wouldn't run them in a month of Sundays. And if I was about to meet a thief and offer them money for stolen goods, surely I was putting myself at risk of being arrested.

As these thoughts span around my head I decided to make a call. I contacted the Clarence House press office and luckily spoke to one of the more friendly press officers with whom I had a good working relationship.

I said: 'Look, the paper has been offered some pictures of William and Kate on their recent holiday in Mustique. I'm not sure whether this is a wind-up, but perhaps in the meantime you may want to make a few calls and check nothing has gone missing, if you know what I mean.'

The press officer knew exactly what I meant. She was well aware that I was concerned about how these pictures, if indeed they existed, had come into our caller's possession. At the same time I knew that if the pictures had been obtained legitimately, then there was little the palace press office could do to stop us publishing them.

Eventually my phone rang and the source told me where to meet. The photographer then got out one of his longest lenses and found a position from where he could take pictures of me meeting the source without being spotted.

A few minutes later a white van pulled up at the agreed place. Two young guys got out and it was clear they were workmen of some kind. Even if their clothes hadn't given them away, a bigger clue was the name and company logo splashed across their van.

They claimed that earlier that day they had been doing a job in Chelsea and had found a memory stick in the gutter. They had then bought a digital camera so that they could view the pictures contained on the memory stick and couldn't believe their eyes when they realized the pictures showed Kate and William together on holiday.

The story sounded highly implausible, and it was extremely naive of them to think we would simply stick them in the paper without doing any checks. But from what I had seen I knew I had to get the guys to agree to come to the office to show them to my bosses. They were after money, and the kind of money they were hoping for was well beyond my pay grade.

I took the opportunity to call my office and tell them what I had seen, but insisted to the pair that the only way we could do a deal was if they came into the office in person to meet with executives. After a few minutes they agreed to get in a taxi and to come with me to our office in Wapping.

When we arrived at the office the source and his friend were still very excited to be doing a deal with the *Sun*. As far as they were concerned we would simply hand over the cash without asking questions.

The news editor had already prepared a conference room and a computer for us to look at the pictures together. The picture editor had been briefed and the associate editor was also on standby, ready to view what we were being offered.

'Oh my God,' said the picture editor as the first of what must have been fifty pictures flashed up on the computer screen. The pin-sharp images showed William and Kate enjoying their holiday on the exclusive Caribbean island from where they had just returned.

But they were no ordinary snaps. One after another, they showed the future king and queen enjoying their time together in paradise. There were shots of William in the villa they had rented, dressed in a white outfit and pulling funny faces for the camera. Others showed the couple drinking and relaxing as they holidayed in one of the world's most exclusive resorts. And the most stunning pictures showed Kate in a tiny bikini doing what looked like a yoga session on the beach. In one of the snaps she was smiling back at the camera while holding her head between her legs.

'How on earth did you get hold of these pictures?' asked the associate editor.

Sensing that all their Christmases had come at once, the two men repeated their story about finding them in a gutter earlier that day.

After we had seen all the pictures the guys agreed to hand over the memory stick on condition that we would not run them until we had agreed a figure. They even agreed to fill in a contract with their names and addresses, on the understanding that we could do business with them.

After showing them out of the office I returned to the conference room to discuss the situation with my superiors. In chorus we all agreed that they must have been stolen and there was no

way we could ever run them in the paper. Even though they represented the most intimate set of photographs any of us were ever
likely to see of Wills and Kate, there was only one option open to
us. The news editor decided that we would wait to hear back
from Clarence House before making any decisions, but we all
knew what was coming.

That night I drove home and met my wife and some friends at
a restaurant near our home. A few minutes after I arrived my
phone rang and I rushed outside to take the call. It was the woman
from the palace I'd spoken to several hours earlier.

She said: 'Hello, Duncan. Thank you for your call earlier. If it
is OK you are about to get a call from the Met Police. They want
to talk to you about the memory card but I wanted to fill you in
before they rang, out of courtesy.'

Less than a minute later my phone rang again. 'Hello, I was
hoping to speak to Duncan Larcombe,' said the voice at the other
end.

'Speaking,' I replied.

'Hello, Duncan, it is Sergeant Richard Head here from Chelsea
and Westminster Police. I understand that you met with someone
earlier today in relation to a memory stick. I would like to talk to
you about that if that's OK. Earlier today a car belonging to Pippa
Middleton was broken into. A handbag was stolen and it
contained a digital camera on which were stored a series of
pictures.'

I said I needed to call my office to inform them of the update
and would ring the officer back within the next few minutes. The
Sun's head of legal agreed that I should cooperate fully with the
police, and so when I returned Sergeant Head's call I was able to
give him all the information I had. He was pleased to hear that
we had the memory stick in our possession, and even more
delighted to learn that we had the names and addresses of the two
men who had tried to sell the pictures to us.

The following morning the source's house was raided and he was arrested. In the end the two of them pleaded guilty to stealing the handbag from Pippa Middleton's car and their early plea spared them a custodial sentence. The memory stick was handed back and the *Sun* never ran the pictures.

Whatever people may say about the British press, the reality is we do not operate outside the law. We will always protect our sources, but on this occasion the individuals trying to sell what they had stolen were fully informed of the risks. We could not join a criminal conspiracy by withholding their details and, as it transpired, they were guilty of breaking into a car and trying to benefit from what they had found.

The day after the two men were arrested I was at home with my wife watching a documentary about the anniversary of the death of Princess Diana. The programme showed the young princes with their heads bowed behind their mother's coffin. As I sat there watching, my phone rang and the number calling was one with which I was not familiar.

It was Prince William's private secretary Jamie Lowther-Pinkerton. He had taken the very unusual step of ringing me to say he had been asked to call and say thank you for what had happened. It turned out that William had taken the incident so seriously that one of his trusted protection officers had joined his Met Police colleagues for the raid the previous day. The fact that Lowther-Pinkerton was calling was an indication that William himself had asked him to make the call.

Although Harry hadn't been involved with the events that weekend, he was well aware of what had happened and the role the *Sun* had played in making sure the precious holiday pictures had been returned and the thieves arrested.

* * *

150

IT WAS AN odd time for Harry. With his Afghan tour cut short, he had been left twiddling his thumbs for several months. The visit to Lesotho with his men had provided a focus, but by the late summer of 2008 he had been left pondering where his military career was heading.

The media blackout had at least enabled the prince to have ten weeks in the front line, but following the breakdown of the agreement Harry was told in no uncertain terms it would never be repeated. The blackout had come in for a lot of criticism in some areas of the media, and the ethics of deliberately withholding information from the public had been questioned. For some media purists, agreeing not to report something as fundamental as the third in line to the throne fighting the Taliban was simply a bridge too far. While the blackout had worked to a certain extent, it was never going to be more than a one-off.

So for Harry his dream of fighting with his regiment seemed to have been and gone. He therefore faced a huge dilemma. Did he carry on with a military career which would amount to little more than sitting behind a desk? Or did he quit the Army and embark on something new?

Harry's feeling was that he was not ready to leave the Army and become a full-time working Royal. Yes, his charity Sentebale was something that gave him a sense of purpose and the satisfaction of doing something useful with his Royal status. But he felt that he was simply too young to resign himself to a lifetime of promoting good causes and carrying out Royal duties.

The solution was as brilliant as it was unsuspected. Harry had always had a keen desire to fly helicopters just like his father and his uncle Prince Andrew before him. And while in Afghanistan he had noticed the role that the Army played in providing top cover support and even embarking on missions with their fleet of Apache and Lynx helicopters. By the time it was made clear to him that he would never be likely to see active service in

Afghanistan as a troop commander on the ground, he had already begun to consider what might happen if he could make the grade as an Army pilot.

Although most people assume that the job of flying is only for members of the Royal Air Force, Harry was aware that it might just be possible for him to fly helicopters while remaining an officer in the British Army. In the early summer of 2008 he began to explore the possibility of switching regiments from the Blues and Royals and joining the Army Air Corps.

One military source close to the prince recalled: 'There was no way Harry would be allowed to serve in Afghanistan for a second time as a member of the Blues and Royals. However, he had seen the role played by the Army Air Corps during his ten weeks in the war zone. Harry raised the idea of transferring with his private secretary Jamie Lowther-Pinkerton. Returning to Afghanistan in secret was impossible. Serving in the front line on the ground was also seen as impossible, given what happened before he was supposed to have been deployed to Iraq. So the notion of a "third way" began to take shape in the summer of 2008.'

The beauty of serving as a pilot with the Army Air Corps was that Harry could, in theory, complete a tour of duty without increasing the threat level to any of his fellow soldiers.

The Apache and Lynx fleet in Afghanistan were based in the relative safety of Camp Bastion and its sprawling air base. The only time they went outside the wire would be during missions. The Apaches, in particular, never landed outside the wire. They were deemed far too valuable to risk them ever going below a certain altitude and thus becoming a target for rocket-propelled grenades and automatic weapons on the ground.

On the other hand there would still be a risk if Harry were to serve as a pilot. What would happen if his helicopter malfunctioned and was forced to land behind enemy lines?

Harry showed a love for helicopters from an early age. He's pictured here at the controls of a Sea King flying from Highgrove to HMS *Invincible* in July 1997.

The tragic image so deeply associated with Harry, his head bowed as the coffin of his mother Diana, Princess of Wales, is placed into a hearse at Westminster Abbey on 6 September 1997.

Even as a child Harry was known for the cheeky glint in his eye. Pictured here on his first day in his distinctive Eton College uniform.

Harry plants a fruit tree with four-year-old Mutsu during a visit to the kingdom of Lesotho. The visit, during his extended gap year in 2004, had a profound impact on the teenage prince.

The young princes join their father Charles for a photo call during the annual ski trip to Klosters, Switzerland, in April 2005. Prince Charles was accidentally caught on camera making his feelings towards the media known.

A Granny's pride. The Queen beamed with delight as she inspected Harry during the Sovereign's Parade to mark his passing out of Sandhurst in April 2006.

The look of love. Harry shares a laugh with Chelsy Davy, his first serious girlfriend, as they watch the England rugby team play South Africa at Twickenham in November 2008.

The front page of the *Sun*, when news of Harry's secret deployment to Afghanistan leaked out in February 2008.

Harry the easy rider. The prince messed about on an abandoned motorbike during his stint on the front line in Helmand Province, Afghanistan, in February 2008.

A smile that hides the real job of war. Harry mans a 50mm machine gun on the observation post of JTAC Hill in Helmand Province during his deployment to the war zone.

The following day Harry flicks a mocking 'loser' sign with his hands at Duncan Larcombe as the prince took on the press in a football match in Lesotho. Harry knew the light-hearted photo opportunity would help highlight the work of Sentebale, the charity he set up to help the forgotten AIDS victims in the tiny African kingdom.

Harry talks to Duncan Larcombe during a July 2008 visit to Lesotho.

Brothers in arms. William and Harry enjoyed six months together while training to become helicopter pilots at RAF Shawbury in 2009.

Harry larks about with Usain Bolt, the fastest man on earth, during his first solo overseas tour in 2012. Harry beat Usain – by cheating.

The warrior prince returned to Afghanistan for a second time in 2014, this time as an Apache attack helicopter pilot.

Harry's second romance. The prince enjoyed an 18-month romance with the stunning socialite Cressida Bonas.

Harry supports his brother William as best man on his wedding day on 29 April 2011, in front of two billion people.

The sight of Harry flanked by Kate's younger sister Pippa Middleton at the royal wedding set tongues wagging, but a romance was never on the cards.

Harry's commitment to wounded servicemen lies at the heart of
his future life. Pictured here during a seated volleyball game
at the launch of the Invictus Games in 2014.

A bearded Harry steps out
with his family during the
annual celebrations on
Christmas Day 2016.

'The One.' Harry's fiancée,
Suits actress Meghan Markle.

And the other potentially major obstacle to Harry's plan to be a helicopter pilot was the fact that only the elite make the grade. To qualify as a pilot for the Army Air Corps, he would have to reach some of the highest standards in the military. Flying helicopters is something that requires unusual natural ability and aptitude; even some of the most promising recruits never make it through the tough training regime.

But the war in Afghanistan was intensifying month by month. The Taliban were claiming more British lives than ever before, and for Harry to stay in the Army without being deployed was looking increasingly difficult.

The source added: 'At first the idea of Harry becoming a pilot with the Army Air Corps was dismissed. But the more that senior members of the military thought about it, the more it seemed that this was Harry's only remaining option. The view was taken that they may as well let Harry try to earn his wings because there was nothing left to lose. If he made the grade, then fantastic. If he failed to make the grade, then that was still a better option than Harry simply resigning his commission and leaving the Army.'

Once again it fell to Harry's private secretary, Jamie Lowther-Pinkerton, to enter into negotiations with the chief of the general staff and head of the Army.

Meanwhile Harry had to find something to occupy himself. Since leaving Afghanistan he had been left in limbo, unsure what the future held. So while he waited to hear back from the Ministry of Defence, he and William decided to make the most of their time.

By chance a charity that organized an annual motorbike trek in Africa called the Enduro had agreed to donate funds from their event to Sentebale. And when Harry heard about this he persuaded William to take part in the 2008 ride. Both the boys are keen bikers, having been taught to ride by their Met Police bodyguards. But it's not just their love of speed and the unique adrenalin rush of charging about on two wheels that appeals to the princes. Out on the open road, with crash helmets covering their faces, they get the added benefit of the anonymity they long for.

For Harry in particular, getting on his bike is literally the best way of feeling normal. No one ever recognizes him and with his protection officers in plain clothes riding along behind, no one even bats an eyelid. Ever since Harry passed his motorbike test he has regularly put his troubles to one side and gone out for long rides.

On one occasion he decided to ride down to Kent for the day to eat fish and chips by the seaside. But as he charged down the M2 motorway towards Canterbury with his protection officers in pursuit, Harry had an experience familiar to many riders. He was pulled over by the local police, who had clocked him breaking the speed limit. In fact Harry's protection officers had also been 'tugged' and were forced to pull over onto the hard shoulder.

His two protection officers pulled out their Met Police badges, hoping this would be enough to convince the local bobbies to let them go about their business. But the zealous uniformed officers were having none of it. They continued in their aim of issuing fixed penalty notices to the three riders they had caught. That was when Harry finally lifted his visor to smile at the officers. As soon as they saw Harry's face they laughed and miraculously had a sudden change of heart. This time a verbal warning would – in their view – suffice.

So as Harry's application to the Army Air Corps was being processed, he and William set off for a 1,000-mile adventure from Durban on South Africa's famous Wild Coast to Port Elizabeth. Their participation in the event in October 2008 had been kept secret, but the boys agreed to invite the media to see them set off for what would be eight days of gruelling riding through South Africa.

The charity was delighted with the extra publicity the princes drew to their annual event. And for their part William and Harry embraced the ride and insisted on being treated like any of the other eighty enthusiasts who took part.

Once again the Royal press corps was dispatched to South Africa to cover the event and take part in the scheduled photocall on the first day of the trek. It was by accident that as I travelled to South Africa I witnessed first-hand the impact Harry can have on ordinary people doing their ordinary jobs.

I was booked into an economy seat on the overnight Virgin flight that would take us to Johannesburg. As one of the last passengers getting onto the sold-out flight I was horrified to realize I had mislaid my boarding pass. Somehow I must have dropped my pass between having it checked at the gate and walking down the passageway onto the flight.

The efficient-looking air steward waiting to check my pass as I stepped onto the plane looked agitated as I checked and double-checked my pockets to no avail. After a few seconds, as a queue of frustrated-looking passengers formed behind me, the steward gruffly told me to stand to one side. I was starting to get worried. I knew that if I wasn't allowed on this flight I wouldn't get to South Africa in time for the photocall.

Journalists, being journalists, would have enjoyed relaying the story of how I was ejected from a flight because I'd stupidly managed to lose my boarding pass.

But it was no good, I couldn't find it anywhere. When the increasingly agitated steward came back over to me as I stood at the bottom of the steps that took the lucky few passengers up to Upper Class, he seemed to be getting in a flap. As I tried to explain that I was sorry and that my boarding pass had vanished, he almost went into a panic. He said: 'Look, for goodness sake, I'm going to need you to stand to one side because Prince Harry is about to get on board.'

Up until that point I had no idea Harry was on the same flight as me. The Royals always get escorted onto the plane last and are taken off first. But on this occasion I decided to have a little fun with the steward, who was clearly now in a panic at the silly passenger who was holding up a prince.

I said to him: 'Well, I'm not getting out of the way for Prince Harry, he can wait for me.'

The blood drained out of the steward's face. I could see that he was thinking, 'Why does this have to happen to me?' If he had had time, I'm sure he would have had me thrown off the flight before his VIP passenger arrived.

But by then it was too late. Behind the steward stepping onto the plane was one of Harry's most trusted protection officers. And, true to form, the next person to step on board was Harry himself. As the steward held his breath, Harry looked over to me and said: 'Hello, Duncan, guess you're travelling in Economy.'

Then as Harry began to climb the hallowed steps to the Upper Class cabin, he paused and with that familiar cheeky smile said: 'I hope you enjoy your flight, we've managed to blag an upgrade.'

I looked back at Harry and replied: 'Well, I wonder how you managed to do that, Harry, must have been the air miles.'

With that the Royal passenger disappeared upstairs, still laughing at my expense. It was then that I remembered the steward, who had been standing there all along.

'Oh my God, you really do know Harry,' he said, barely able to hide his excitement at getting that close to the prince. 'I thought you were just being difficult, I didn't know what to do.'

We laughed at what had happened and then I joked: 'Well, is knowing Harry enough for me to get an upgrade as well?'

Sadly it wasn't, but it did appear to be enough for my new friend to turn a blind eye to the fact I had no boarding pass. He very kindly showed me to my seat in cattle class and promised to bring me some champagne as soon as we had taken off as an apology for no upgrade.

Looking back at that flight, I was surprised at just how starstruck the cabin crew were to have Harry on board. Surely an experienced purser like my new friend must have welcomed hundreds of famous people on board. But he really was over the moon to have seen Harry in the flesh and, when he delivered me the glass of bubbles as promised, spent ages asking about my job covering the prince. He said: 'I love Prince Harry, he's the best celebrity I've ever met at work.'

The following evening the press were invited to a barbecue with all the riders taking part in the trek. A small group of us were invited into a room to be told about the charities it was supporting and to meet the organizers.

To my surprise, William and Harry were standing there next to a big urn of boiling water. William then poured us all a cup of hot tea and Harry went around with a plate of biscuits. They were in good spirits, and once again it was a surreal experience, even for those of us who had been on many royal tours. I remember thinking how jealous the Virgin steward would be if he knew I was having tea poured for me by the future king while munching on Jammie Dodgers served up by his favourite 'celebrity'. I told Harry how he had made the man's day the previous evening, and joked that if things didn't work out with Chelsy he could always look up the air steward.

All in all it was good to see both the princes relaxing with us as they prepared to set off on their latest adventure. I sensed even then that Harry seemed excited about the next chapter in his military career. Trying to make the grade as a helicopter pilot was going to test him to the limit. But if he could pull it off he would one day surely be able to return to Afghanistan and finish what he had started.

CHAPTER 12

HARRY THE PILOT

'YOU'VE DONE WHAT?' I asked the freelance photographer. 'Are you seriously trying to sell me a picture of Prince William's penis?' It was perhaps one of the more unusual conversations I'd ever had at work.

It never ceases to amaze me what some people think we would want to publish. But this was far-fetched, even by the *Sun*'s standards. The photo – which I hasten to add I have never seen – was taken of Prince William as he relieved himself during a brief break in his motorbike trek.

The photographer in question was a South African freelance who had covered the princes' 1,000-mile trek to Port Elizabeth. She had sneaked into the bushes to try and get a good spot from where to photograph the princes riding past. But then she had found herself in the wrong place at the wrong time when the group pulled over for a snack and the future king was caught short. Apparently if William had wandered any further into the undergrowth he might well have actually peed on the camera. But with her exclusive shot safely in the bag, she was now trying to see if any of the British papers would be interested in running it.

This was an occasion when I didn't even need to put in a call to the office to tell them what I had been offered. I thanked the photographer for coming to me first but suggested the best thing she could do was delete the image from her camera and forget it had ever been taken.

Oddly enough, it wasn't the first time I had been offered a picture of a member of the Royal family urinating. A couple of years earlier we had been sent a picture of Prince Philip using a urinal during a dinner he had attended as guest of honour. It too never saw the light of day.

But there was one memorable occasion when a photographer took a picture of Prince Harry weeing in the back of a horsebox during a polo event in which he was playing. Even though the picture only showed Harry from behind, the palace were furious when we published it under the headline 'Harry's Royal Wee'.

After that I had learned my lesson, and I was at a loss as to how the photographer in William's case had ever got so close.

The reality was that after the photocall on day one of William and Harry's motorbike ride through the Wild Coast, several freelance photographers had tracked the route and spent eight days trying to get more pictures. It must have been frustrating for the princes who, after all, had only agreed to invite the press along on the understanding that they would leave them alone for the rest of the trip.

This was often the trade-off for official and semi-official Royal events. But with Harry and William riding for up to ten hours a day on the back of 200hp motorbikes across dangerous terrain, there was no way any of the Royal corps that had flown all that way for the photocall were going to simply head home.

We were put on what was called a 'watching brief'. This meant staying a healthy distance away from the princes and not getting in the way of their trek, while keeping an eye on what was going on. If either of the boys had crashed or been involved in a serious incident, we would need to make sure we were somewhere relatively nearby.

In the event, the boys completed the journey without a scratch, although Harry did suffer with a bad stomach shortly after passing the halfway mark. But the so-called 'watching brief' was one of the perks of doing the Royal job. It effectively meant that we would often find ourselves in exotic locations under instructions from the office to steer clear of the princes but stay somewhere nearby.

The most bizarre of these occasions happened when William and Kate made another visit to the private island of Mustique in the Caribbean. A reader had rung the office to say they had just flown to Barbados on the same flight as the Royal lovebirds. In what was more of a knee-jerk reaction than common sense, the newsdesk called me and instructed me to take the next flight out to Barbados. I was to travel with a photographer and try to find out where Wills and Kate were going on holiday.

By the time I arrived in Barbados we had established that the couple had taken a shuttle flight to their paradise hideaway on Mustique, and, after a few checks, that there was no way we could follow them there. The island is private and it even has its own police force. Any journalist who flew there would be sent back and could even face the prospect of being locked up while waiting for the next flight.

I relayed this to the office, who said under no circumstances should we try and get onto Mustique. They told us to stay put and see if we could get a picture at the end of the holiday when the William and Kate would have to return to Barbados to fly back to London.

I came off the phone and told the photographer we had been put on a watching brief and were to stay put in Barbados. He was more than a little surprised and asked when they would be flying home. A moment later he shook his head in disbelief as the penny dropped. We were to stay in Barbados, the famous holiday isle, with nothing to do until the couple returned home.

He asked again: 'Well, how long are they on Mustique for?'

I replied: 'You had better get your suntan lotion out – they are not flying home for seventeen days.'

Needless to say, we obediently found a nice hotel and grabbed two sun loungers next to a pool – then spent nearly three weeks wondering where it had all gone wrong.

The Royal job would often throw up nice surprises like that. When we were waiting for William and Harry to finish their motorbike trek we decided to take advantage of an offer from the South African tourist board. They booked us into an exclusive safari lodge not too far from where the boys were due to complete their journey in two days' time. Once again it was tough looking at elephants and lions while we waited for the Royals to finish their boy's own adventure.

HARRY RETURNED FROM South Africa at the end of October 2008 safe in the knowledge that his military career was about to change.

His only real chance of returning to Afghanistan rested on his making the grade as a pilot with the Army Air Corps. Even if he succeeded, Harry was committing to several years' intensive training before he would be allowed anywhere near a combat role. And if he failed at any stage of this training, the reality was that his military career would be in tatters. He would have to accept the fact that he would never be able to serve in the front line again.

There is little doubt that failing with the Army Air Corps would spell the end of his military career. He would never have been satisfied with doing a desk job or confined to ceremonial duties with the Household Cavalry. Harry was in the Army because he wanted to be a warrior. He wanted to serve his country and lead men without favour or privilege. Returning home from South

Africa, his head was full of these thoughts. But what else did he have to lose?

He knew that his life was in many ways already mapped out for him and the longer he could stay in the Army, the longer he could delay the inevitable life as a full-time working royal, shaking hands and supporting good causes.

In view of this, and given that Harry is not someone who does things by halves, it was perhaps surprising that when he submitted his application to be considered for a place on the Army Air Corps flying grading course, it was more than a little half-hearted. It was written by hand on a sheet of A4 paper; to explain why he wanted to become a pilot, he simply said he had always been interested in flying and he was keen to follow in the footsteps of other members of his family; and as for the section asking candidates to list their other interests and hobbies, Harry left it blank. Even his handwriting made the document appear rushed and scribbled.

At this initial stage it was clear that Harry knew full well that his application would be accepted purely on the basis of who he was. The Army Air Corps is a famously proud regiment and there is no doubt that top brass would jump at the chance of adding a prince to their number. At the very least having Harry on board would represent a major coup in the unit's ongoing rivalry with the RAF. In military circles the Army Air Corps is dubbed Teeny-Weeny Airways – a reference to the relatively small number of pilots compared to the rotary wing section of the far larger Royal Air Force.

Harry clearly knew that it didn't matter a jot if his application was half-hearted and appeared rushed. No one within the Army Air Corps was going to hold that against him. The hard bit for him was not getting on the course, it was getting through the course. Many years ago Harry's uncle Prince Edward won a place on the Royal Marines All Arms Commando course, regarded as one of toughest in the military. As the Queen's third son, Edward was never likely to have his application turned down – but he famously flunked the course.

In November 2008 Harry arrived at the regiment's headquarters at Middle Wallop, in Hampshire, for what was going to be a career-defining month of intensive flying grading. The primary goal of the course was to test applicants' natural instincts and abilities in the air. The grading is not a physical test that would require Harry to dig deep and push his way through the pain barrier. This was a test of whether he possessed an aptitude for flying. The basics he could learn, but if he did not demonstrate a natural affinity with the aircraft Harry faced being bumped off the course at any moment.

The drop-out rate in flying grading is very high. Even people who have dreamed of being a pilot since childhood often find themselves unable to demonstrate the natural instincts required.

One former Army Air Corps pilot recalled: 'As soon as you arrive at Middle Wallop you have a sense of how elitist it is. It doesn't matter how good you think you are, there is nowhere to hide when you are at the controls with your every move being assessed. It is extremely expensive to train someone to fly helicopters in the military. What the instructors are looking for is people who take to flying straight away. Flying is sometimes compared to being able to rub your belly and pat your head at the same time. Some people can do it naturally, others can't. Even if Harry's application was a given, his chances of passing the initial flying grading were anything but.

'For a month you live, eat and sleep flying. All people talk about in the officers' mess is flying and you never know if the person you are talking to one night over dinner will still be on the course the following day. It really is that intense. Everyone is focused and it is a totally different atmosphere from other officers' mess environments. The course is split between spending hour after hour in the classroom learning about the principles of flying and the pre-, post- and in-flight checks you have to learn off by heart, and the hours you spend in the cockpit. There is no easy way to get through the course, you have to just knuckle down and hope your name is going to make it onto the final list.'

While at Middle Wallop Harry began flying in a fixed-wing training aircraft known as a Slingsby T67. The tiny plane is used by the Army Air Corps to test the flying skills of aspiring pilots who will only ever progress to helicopters once they have proved they can handle a fixed-wing aircraft. The Slingsby's cockpit is covered by a glass bubble to give recruits a panoramic view of what is around them. Many fail because they focus too much on the controls inside the cockpit rather than having a wider perspective of what is above, below and to the sides.

We had a tip that Harry was about to take the controls and make his first flight of the grading course. The first picture of him taking the controls of an aircraft would be great for the paper, even if it meant intruding on Harry's course.

We drove down to Middle Wallop to see if there was a place from which we could get a picture without falling foul of the Ministry of Defence police or Harry's protection officers. And as luck would have it the base had its own museum of flying and an observation area where members of the public could watch planes take off and land. Within minutes of the two photographers getting out their long lenses we were spotted by the protection officers, who were sitting having a cup of tea in the museum's café. They were relaxed as usual, but it was clear that if Harry didn't want to be pictured we would be wasting our time.

One of the officers was willing to go and check with Harry to see if there was a way we could get a picture if we then left straight after. He came back and told us this was agreed. It was a compromise but I felt it was worth it as the best way of getting our picture without winding Harry up.

True to his word, after about an hour the bright yellow Slingsby began taxiing towards the runway only a few yards from where we were waiting. The aircraft's large glass cockpit which served the rookie pilots well also gave us the advantage of being able to take a good picture of the prince as he passed by. The small plane rolled towards us, and straight away we could see it was Harry at the controls. He had even decided to help us by lowering his face mask so that we could get a clear shot. I remember thinking that was good of Harry. It showed he was playing the game and holding up his side of the bargain.

With the photographs in the bag, Harry's plane continued past as it made its way to the runway for take-off. The *Sun* photographer checked he had what he needed by looking at the small digital screen on the back of his camera and gave me the thumbs-up.

It was clear we were not the only paper to have had the same tip that today was the day Harry would make his first flight. The photographer from a rival paper had got similar shots, thanks to the agreement that we had made with the protection officers.

Now, as we packed up and prepared to leave the base as agreed, the other photographer stood his ground. Although he had a shot of Harry in the cockpit, he was determined to stay and try to improve on the picture. In fairness, the shot he had hoped to bag was of Harry in his full flying gear walking towards the plane in a scene that might resemble Tom Cruise in the famous Eighties film *Top Gun*. But it was immediately clear that there was no way of capturing Harry in such a pose from the only vantage point available. By the time he either climbed in or out of the cockpit he would be a long way from view and inside one of the base's many huge hangars.

Despite this the photographer refused to budge. I can remember feeling quite angry that the agreement I had made with Harry was going to be broken by one of our rivals. The Royal job is often about playing the long game. Harry had done his bit, but now it would look as though I was breaking my side of the bargain.

When the protection officers came over to ask why we had not yet left, I explained what had happened. The officer who had brokered the deal said: 'Harry's not going to like this. He was under the impression that as soon as you had your picture you would pull off and leave him alone to continue his training.'

It was frustrating because I had no authority to tell another paper's photographer to leave the base. Yet if he continued to refuse, Harry would hold me responsible for going back on my word. That meant that in future he would be less likely to agree to gifting us a picture, and why should he? A deal is a deal. With Harry's plane now safely up in the skies above, I had no choice but to engage in what you might call a 'heated discussion' with the reluctant snapper. After a few angry moments he finally saw sense and agreed to pull off. By the time Harry was back on the ground we had all moved away and the pictures of him making his first flight made a strong page lead in the following day's paper.

It was by no means the first time I had struggled to persuade other photographers to play the game and ensure we got what we wanted without upsetting Harry too much.

In April 2007 Harry had joined Chelsy and her friends in the Caribbean to watch England take part in the cricket World Cup. When the national side arrived in Barbados for their group game against the West Indies, the prince had found he was a sitting duck for photographers.

Barbados is famous for the fact that all its beaches are public. The government made the rule many years ago to stop the rich and famous from buying up large swathes of coastline and erecting barbed wire fences. As a result, Barbados has become known as the paparazzi paradise, ideal for bounty-hunting photographers hoping to bag a picture of bikini-clad celebrities on holiday.

In reality, famous faces who want to avoid being pictured steer well clear of Barbados. If you ever see a picture in a newspaper or magazine of a pop or reality TV star splashing about in Barbados, it has probably been set up by their publicity-hungry agent.

Because of the lack of privacy, when Harry and Chelsy tried to visit the island during the cricket they found themselves pinned inside their hotel, unable to even drive anywhere without being followed by photographers on motorbikes. At one point Harry felt so hounded he sent one of his trusted protection officers down to my hotel to try and strike a deal. The prince was offering to let himself be pictured on the beach in return for us leaving him alone. Although it was very tempting to agree to the deal and get the pictures in the bag, I had to explain that I had no control over the freelance photographers who successfully plied their trade on the island. The reality was if Harry posed for pictures on the beach, the following day there would be even more photographers camped outside his hotel trying to get a shot.

It was ironic, therefore, that in the end Harry and Chelsy were pictured jet-skiing further up the coast by the local paparazzi, who had been tipped off by their network of barmen. While we all stayed well clear to give Harry the space, these bounty hunters filled their memory cards with fantastic shots of the prince. It was very frustrating, but part and parcel of being a Royal reporter. If your face is one of the few Harry recognizes, you are going to get the blame if he is pictured.

Back in Middle Wallop we were happy that we had the pictures we needed. After all there are only so many times you can publish the same kind of photograph of Harry in the same outfit flying the same plane.

For the rest of his grading course Harry was left well alone. And in that vacuum he was able to knuckle down to his training.

There have been many turning points in Harry's military career but his performance on the course ranks up there as one of the most significant. Had he failed, the chances are he would have quit the Army. But not only did he pass the grading course in the required time, he did so with flying colours.

As an Army Air Corps source said at the time: 'Harry is a natural pilot. He breezed through the course and was genuinely one of the most gifted candidates in his intake. There was a great deal of pressure on him to pass, but he was able to put that to the back of his mind and focus on the job in hand. He showed he was more than capable of handling an aircraft and quickly mastered the basics. He still has a long way to go before making it as an Army Air Corps pilot, but he now has the green light to continue with his training.'

His success at Middle Wallop was a breakthrough for the young Royal desperate to forge a future in the military. It meant he successfully made it onto the Army Air Corps course which would turn him into a fully-fledged helicopter pilot. And after many months of uncertainty about his future, Harry now knew what the next two and a half years would involve.

He was posted to the Army Air Corps to begin his training for real. And when Clarence House announced his successful completion of the grading course they even made a reference to the fact that Harry could eventually be heading back to Afghanistan. In the statement his spokesman said: 'If Prince Harry qualifies as an Army Air Corps pilot, he will, like any officer, be available for operational service wherever the AAC flies.' In short, Harry's plan to get back to the front line by any means, initially dismissed as unworkable, was now beginning to take shape. The warrior prince was on track to reinvent his military career and return to finish the job he had started in the war zone. His success caused a huge sigh of relief for his private secretary, Jamie Lowther-Pinkerton. The young officer who had threatened to leave the

Army was now excitedly preparing to embark on the next phase of his military career. Harry the soldier was preparing to become Harry the pilot.

While the work was only just about to begin for Harry, his determination to become a pilot had given him a new focus. A year after he had been pulled out of the front line he would be entering his first few weeks on the Pilot's Course. It seemed that all the anger and disappointment of being pulled out of Afghanistan had been consigned to the past. Harry now had a new mission, and it was a mission which ultimately would indeed see him return to war.

This turning point for Harry was to have a profound effect on his life, not least because it meant he would have a focus for the coming months and years. But also it gave him a reason for staying in the Army and continuing with a career that, despite everything, he still loved.

CHAPTER 13

THE 'PAKI' ROW

WHAT A DIFFERENCE a year makes! It was Christmas 2008 and Prince Harry strolled beside his brother William as they joined their grandmother the Queen for the traditional Royal get-together at her Sandringham estate in Norfolk.

Just twelve months earlier Harry was in Helmand Province, Afghanistan. The press knew he was there, but under the black-out agreement, the general public had no idea. Even the thousands of flag-waving Royalists who make the Christmas Day pilgrimage to Sandringham every year to watch the Windsors hadn't seemed to notice when Harry was missing from his family's number in 2007. While the Royals were tucking into a festive feast, the third in line to the throne was about to be treated to a curried goat made by the Gurkha soldiers he was serving with in the war zone.

Now, a year on, the crowds outside St Mary Magdalene Church at Sandringham whooped with delight as they saw one of their favourite Royals stroll past. At these set-piece family occasions Harry is always one of the major attractions. As soon as he comes into view they shout his name in the hope of catching his eye and receiving a wave or a cheeky smile. At times when you are an observer it can almost feel quite embarrassing seeing how Harry's popularity eclipses that of his fellow Royals.

By 2008 his popularity with the British public had soared. He was the rock and roll prince who wore his heart on his sleeve and the public couldn't get enough of him. Crass outfits, drunken escapades and a seemingly turbulent love life did nothing to diminish the public's adoration of Diana's youngest son.

And in 2008 there was even more reason for the crowds to shout Harry's name. By then they were all aware of how he had served his country in the front line. The fact he had missed the previous year because of his role as a soldier was not lost on the gushing members of the public. As ever Harry played to the crowd, waving and smiling and poking fun at his brother William, who was sporting a beard for the first time. This was Harry at his best. This was the cheeky young prince that of all those who travel to Norfolk on Christmas Day out of a sense of patriotic zeal had come to see.

For his part, Harry had reason to feel good. He had passed his flying grading and was just weeks away from embarking on a new chapter in his life as a trainee military helicopter pilot. But as is so often the case with the Royals, he was blissfully unaware that in less than three weeks' time he would be splashed all over the front pages again. TV and radio stations all over the world would be dragging out the old questions about his judgement and suitability as a senior Royal.

For once Harry could be forgiven for not seeing this coming. The storm that was about to engulf him would stem from something stupid he had done more than three years earlier. He could hardly have predicted that a long-forgotten piece of carelessness was about to come back and bite him firmly in the proverbial backside.

On 10 January 2009, with the New Year less than two weeks old, Harry received a late night call. It was from Miguel Head, the PR adviser Harry and William had poached from the communications office of the Ministry of Defence.

'Mig' – as he was affectionately known – was a likeable and professional press officer who had got to know Harry at the height of the media blackout arrangements covering his trip to Afghanistan. For several years the boys had been desperate to have their own press officer, someone with whom they could work and get to know and trust. Up until Mig's appointment in the autumn of 2008, the media affairs of Wills and Harry had been dealt with by Prince Charles's team at Clarence House. This arrangement had worked well while the post-Diana media agreement was still in place, but there had been a number of problems in later years, after the princes had stopped being protected by the fact they were in full-time education.

Harry, in particular, was unhappy with the advice and guidance he was given by the men in grey suits who were, after all, employed by and answerable to his father. He felt that both he and William should have their own press secretary, to whom they could turn in a crisis and whose advice would be helpful the rest of the time.

Mig's appointment was a genius move by the princes. He had a far more approachable manner than some of the Prince of Wales's media team at Clarence House. He was also far closer to the boys in age, which must have come as a breath of fresh air after years of dealing with people more than twice as old.

And Mig had a proven track record. He had worked for the Ministry of Defence for long enough to build up good working relationships with journalists and was seen as someone the media could work with, rather than battle against.

In reality Prince Charles's team had developed a reputation for being confrontational with the media. They were not willing to forge close relationships with journalists and, like Prince Charles, appeared to see the press as the enemy. When trouble arose, they were aggressive rather than conciliatory. A call to the palace press office could often result in a call back from one of the Prince of Wales's cut-throat media lawyers. And this was an atmosphere which had not gone unnoticed among Fleet Street editors, who objected to being told what they could and could not print by what they saw as 'jumped-up' civil servants funded by the taxpayer.

The last straw was the handling of the fall-out from Princess Diana's inquest verdict. William and Harry felt let down by the fact they were told what to say and how to react to a verdict which covered an issue so close to their hearts. A month later the job of press secretary to William and Harry was advertised, but insiders already knew it was going to Mig. With both the princes pursuing military careers at the time, he was the natural choice given his experience working with top brass and the defence media corps.

His first media event was the motorbike trek in South Africa and it had passed off without any negative press. Recently he had gleefully released the announcement that Harry had passed his flying grading and he was on message when it came to the young Royal's desire to one day return to the front line.

But Mig's first real test was to come out of blue sky. Late on a Saturday evening he received a call from the *News of the World*, Britain's biggest-selling Sunday tabloid. They had bought a video which appeared to have been filmed by Harry himself. Although it was old and dated back to Harry's final days at Sandhurst in 2006, there was no denying the seriousness of what it contained.

As the cadets waited to catch a flight to Cyprus for their final training exercise, Harry had wandered around the room filming his fellow cadets and offering his own running commentary. At one stage, as Harry panned around the room, he spotted a fellow member of his Sandhurst platoon and uttered the words: 'And here is our Paki friend.'

To the horror of his new press secretary, Harry was clearly making a reference to a fellow cadet who had joined Sandhurst on attachment from the Pakistani military. There was no denying the voice was Harry's. Nor was there any chance of suggesting the video was anything but genuine.

To make matters worse, the *News of the World* had also obtained a clip in which Harry then refers to one of his fellow white cadets as 'looking like a rag head' – a derogatory term used to refer to people wearing turbans.

This call was certainly going to be a baptism of fire for Mig, who had only been in his new role for a matter of weeks. He telephoned Harry straight away to break the bad news that this video was going to make the front page of the following day's *News of the World*. A close source to Harry revealed how his initial response was to confirm that he had made the video but to insist that it was so old it didn't matter. However, Mig was well aware that this excuse would not wash with the tabloid or the millions of people who would get to hear about it the following morning.

Mig's advice was to issue an immediate apology for the 'Paki' comment. For many years it was an unacceptable term which had come to mean a racist and derogatory way of describing people of Pakistani origin. He knew that while many would dismiss Harry's careless use of language as harmless, there would be just as many people who would take great offence. Once again the Nazi outfit gaffe would be dragged up and questions would inevitably be asked about the young Royal's attitude towards ethnic minorities. This was a story that could not simply be brushed off as old and not relevant.

Having agreed a statement with Harry, Mig returned the call to the *News of the World*. In so doing he confirmed the story but bought himself an opportunity to get Harry's defence in at the earliest possible stage. The paper was briefed about how Harry was a good friend of the Pakistani cadet in question. In fact the two were still in contact, having spent forty-four weeks together serving in the same Sandhurst platoon. Mig insisted that the comments were not meant in a derogatory fashion and that it was a nickname that originated from the cadet himself.

As for the 'rag head' comment, Mig steered the *News of the World* to the fact that this term was actually very commonly used in the military. Rather than mean someone who wore a turban for religious reasons, it was common Army slang for a Taliban insurgent fighting in Afghanistan.

For their part the *News of the World* agreed to include the statement and the guidance which could be written up as coming from a 'senior source'. But when the paper hit the doormats of more than three million homes the following day, the front page carried a picture of Harry in uniform next to the headline: 'Harry's Racist Video Shame'.

Within hours the story was leading the news bulletins across Britain, and had been picked up in America, Australia, Canada and all over the world. Once again Harry was at the centre of a huge storm. The situation was not helped by the fact that Pakistan was itself a Commonwealth country, and Harry's grandmother the head of the Commonwealth.

The *News of the World* made painful reading for the Royals that day. The Queen, who was still on her break at Sandringham, had been made aware of the story the previous night. Prince Charles was similarly horrified by the news, although he too felt it was a low blow given the number of years that had passed since his son had made the video.

When these situations arise, the Royals and their advisers go into a sort of lockdown mentality. The media teams are instructed not to do or say anything that might fuel the situation, and Harry himself was told to keep a low profile for the foreseeable future. Royal stories spread like wildfire but they always die down over time. The best strategy for Mig and his principal was to let the story run its course and hope that it went away quickly.

As the prince was a serving officer, the military had a role to play in the fall-out from the 'Paki row' story. He was summoned to what is known in the Army as 'an interview without coffee'. The Ministry of Defence let it be known that the Royal officer would be given 'awareness' training as a result of the video.

As for the Pakistani cadet, who was now a serving officer in his native country, he refused, despite the best efforts of the media, to say anything negative about his old Sandhurst chum.

What was interesting about this Royal row was once again the way that the public reacted to it. While segments of the media were portraying Harry as public enemy number one, the over-whelming majority of ordinary people seemed to shrug it off, as if to say 'So what?' People took the view that there was little difference between calling a Pakistani a Paki and calling a Scotsman a Scot.

Of course this view is a matter of debate and there is no doubt that the term had its origins in the racist abuse suffered by Pakistani immigrants who came to work in Britain in the Fifties and Sixties. But once again the public were reluctant to use the gaffe as a stick with which to beat Harry. He was popular, he had served his country, and it was after all a three-year-old piece of footage. Politicians and public figures who have found their careers destroyed by similar indiscretions must have wished the British masses could have shown the same level of forgiveness in their situation.

Again Harry had escaped relatively unscathed. The public knew he was not a racist, in the same way as they were happy to accept he was no Nazi. This was a prince making a mistake which angered the politically correct brigade but did little to annoy the ordinary man on the street. Harry's popularity defies political correctness. He is seen as a prince of the people and once again his public were in no mood to hang him from the rafters.

Miguel Head had survived his first real test. The 'Paki' row had erupted on his watch, but had done little to damage the reputation of a Royal who was fast becoming the most popular member of his family.

Dickie Arbiter, the famous former press secretary to the Queen, gave several interviews in the wake of the story. He summed up the situation well when he told the BBC: 'These comments were made three years ago. Anyone who knows Harry knows that he is a very different person than the young cadet who passed out of Sandhurst.' Dickie was spot on. Since Harry made the video he had been to war, served his country and grown as a man. There was no way the public would allow a row like this to damage the standing the prince had earned in their eyes.

Once again the public reaction to Harry's gaffe had told us more than the gaffe itself. The masses do not expect Harry to behave flawlessly, and if there is the odd hiccup along the way it's a characteristic they rather like.

COVERING THE ROYAL beat so often means being asked about Harry. For some reason he sparks the public imagination in a way other members of the family could only dream of.

But there is one over-riding misconception about him, and one question which constantly arises when people ask about the prince they all wish they knew: 'Well, is he?' When I hear the words I know exactly what they are eluding to.

After Harry's locks of ginger hair became visible as a child, an unpleasant and in many ways cruel rumour began to spread. It was not long after Harry was born that details of Diana's extra-marital relationship with the Cavalry officer James Hewitt became public.

It has never ceased to amaze me how many people to this day want to know if there is indeed any truth in this thirty-year-old rumour. Often it is the very first question people ask when they realize I have covered Harry's life for such a long time. Even all these years after Diana's death the Royal rumour mill continues, thanks to an affair she had when her marriage to Prince Charles was already in tatters.

My friend and Diana's former police bodyguard Ken Wharfe recalls in his memoirs that Diana herself was greatly angered by the nudge-nudge, wink-wink, and I can only imagine how Harry must feel when he reads the conspiracy theories about his paternity repeated time and time again.

Ken tackles the issue head-on when he writes: 'A simple comparison of dates proves it is impossible for Hewitt to be Harry's father.

'Only once did I ever discuss it with her, and Diana was in tears about it. She didn't usually care what lies Charles's friends told about her, but if anyone turned on her sons it wounded her deeply.

'The nonsense should be scotched here and now. For one thing, the dates do not add up. Harry was born on 15 September 1984, which means he was conceived around Christmas 1983, when his brother, William, was 18 months old.

'Diana did not meet James Hewitt until the summer of 1986.

'The red hair that gossips so love to cite as "proof" is, of course, a Spencer trait, as anyone who has ever seen a photograph of Diana's sister, Jane, for example, as a young woman will be able to testify.

'The one person who knew beyond doubt the identity of Harry's father was Diana, and she told me: "I don't know how my husband and I did have Harry, because by then he had gone back to his lady, but one thing that is certain is that we did."'

Although no one has ever confirmed this, I have little doubt that the children born so high up in the Royal blood line would undergo DNA testing as infants. But even if that is not the case, Ken Wharfe's assertions are right on the money.

Harry and his family have to cope with urban myths being spread about them as if they were fact. In this case I hope that the real facts speak for themselves and people will realize there is absolutely no truth in the rumour that has dogged him throughout his life.

THE DUST SOON settled on the 'Paki row' story and Harry was able to focus on his next step, trying to make the grade on his pilot's training.

Having got through the first grading, in January 2009 the prince headed off to RAF Shawbury, Shropshire, where he began his demanding course learning the basics of how to fly helicopters rather than fixed-wing aircraft.

The secluded base in the West Midlands took Harry well out of sight of the London-based photographers and gave him a period to focus entirely on the job in hand. For the next nine months he would rack up forty hours of flying, during which he needed to master take-off, basic helicopter handling, landing and various emergency drills.

But there was added benefit of being based at RAF Shawbury. For the first time since they briefly shared a term at Sandhurst, Harry and William would live in the same place. William had by then left the Army and joined the RAF. He went to the same school of rotary flying as his brother in a bid to become a search and rescue pilot.

William had successfully passed out of Sandhurst two terms after Harry. But his Army career was never going to be more than a fleeting glimpse of what it was like to serve in the military. William went to RAF Shawbury knowing that he needed to complete the course if his hopes of becoming a search and rescue pilot were to be realized.

But for Harry the stakes were far higher. If he completed the course he would progress to learning to fly one of the Army Air Corps's helicopters. Ultimately this was his only realistic chance of getting back to the front line, even if it meant a long period of learning new skills.

The Shawbury base itself was nothing special, and after only a few weeks there the princes decided to find somewhere they could both live while coming to terms with the gruelling training schedules. As luck would have it, they found a place less than three miles from the base, near the small village of Clive. It was the converted stable block of a stately home, and large enough for their protection officers to stay without getting in the way.

The year 2009 may have started badly for Harry when the video emerged but now he was to enjoy several months in the relative normality of a life away from the cameras and the drag of official Royal duties. He had a chance to spend time with his brother as they argued about who would do the dishes and how bad William's cooking really was.

Surrounded by rolling hills and beautiful countryside, William and Harry's digs quickly became a home from home and there is little doubt that the low-key time they spent together helped their bond as brothers to grow even stronger.

William and Harry are very close, not least because of their shared experiences as children. After their mother's death the boys shared a mutual need for support. They became far closer than normal siblings and the luck of being posted together marked a golden few months for the Royal brothers.

It was during this time of sharing a home together away from London that they were also able to share their feelings about being princes in long-term relationships. Although William and Kate had had their ups and downs, they were by now entering the next stage of their relationship. Wedding bells may not have quite been on the cards at that stage, but it was already clear that Wills and Kate were going to go the distance.

For Harry, however, it was becoming increasingly clear that while his brother was heading for the altar, his romance with Chelsy was heading in a very different direction.

CHAPTER 14

CHELSY SPLIT

'RELATIONSHIP: NOT IN one,' read Chelsy Davy's updated Facebook profile. These four words confirmed the rumours that Harry's first real romance was over. After months of heated rows, long times apart and the distraction of two careers heading in radically different directions, it seemed there really had been trouble in paradise for the young lovers.

Of course the profile could be fake. Or maybe it was an attempt to hoodwink the media and buy the couple some desperately needed space away from the spotlight. But with a quick call to one of the fiery Zimbabwean's close friends it was immediately obvious that the Harry and Chelsy show had come to an end.

The timing of the post was also a giveaway. It was the end of January 2009 and the prince was just two weeks into his pilot's course at RAF Shawbury. Ahead of him were months of intensive training which would prevent him from spending more than the occasional weekend with the first girl who had won his heart.

Chelsy meanwhile was in her final few months at Leeds University and was studying hard to become a lawyer. Any spare time she had would have to be spent finishing essays and preparing for tough law exams. Even if Harry had the time to spare, his girlfriend was far too busy to be whisked away for the usual exotic trip and a chance for them to patch things up.

After five years we now knew that, try as they might, the two who had met in the carefree days of Harry's gap year simply couldn't make their relationship work. Sources insisted they still 'love each other to bits', it was just that all good things have to come to an end. But for Harry the split from Chelsy came as a bitter blow, even if in his heart of hearts he couldn't have claimed it was a surprise.

The couple's problems had been with them from the start. They lived thousands of miles apart, and any time they spent together seemed more like a honeymoon than a real life relationship. Paddling down the Orange River in Namibia, or sitting round a campfire on the safari planes of Botswana may have had an appeal in the early days but it was a far cry from a normal, stable relationship.

And then there was the 'Royal' elephant in the room. To Chelsy's credit, she never had an interest in becoming a princess. The thought of marrying into the Royal family filled her with dread. So, ironically, one of the major reasons Harry was so attracted to Chelsy in the first place, her independent spirit, was to become the central factor that tore their relationship apart.

According to more than one of her friends, the relationship had been doomed from the word go. While they were excited to see Chelsy so besotted with a man who adored her and treated her with the utmost respect, they could see how his status as a Royal, and all the baggage that entailed, terrified the free-spirited African.

The daughter of a wealthy landowner whose game reserve was twice the size of Surrey, Chelsy was born in Zimbabwe and grew up on her family's home near Bulawayo. Her early life could not have been more different from Harry's. Nor for that matter could it have been further away from the kind of life you might expect for a girl who would one day win the heart of a prince.

While the 'Chelsea Set' of trust fund girls were growing up playing princesses and enjoying life in the pampered world of their wealthy aristocratic families, Chelsy's upbringing must have seemed like it had landed from another planet. Rather than attending a posh pre-school surrounded by the sons and daughters of the wealthy elite, she spent her early days trying to stop the wild animals from interrupting her lessons.

In a rare interview with *The Times* aimed at promoting the jewellery line she set up in 2015, the then 30-year-old lifted the lid on just how unusual her early life experiences had been. She said: 'Ever since I was born I've been on a farm. Giraffes, lions, you take it for granted because when you're little it's just your life. I used to get so sad at the weekend because all my friends in towns were going to sleepovers and I was stuck with a bunch of impala – "this sucks". At my pre-school there were monkeys everywhere, stealing your crayons. All the kids ran around playing with warthogs. There's a video of me on a plastic toy motorbike in front of a herd of buffalo, just having a stare-off. One of the managers had a pet hyena, it was very sweet. Looking back now, I see it was a very crazy upbringing and I feel very lucky.'

Inevitably growing up in that sort of environment required Chelsy to be tough and aware of the natural dangers of living in southern Africa. On one occasion when she was out in the wild lands owned by her father a deadly boomslang snake, as long as a man, fell on her head. Another encounter saw her 'mock-charged' by a bull elephant, a creature that has claimed hundreds of lives of those inexperienced enough to try and run. Chelsy recalled: 'We both got a fright, but you can't run, you must stand.'

By the time she turned fourteen the situation in her native Zimbabwe had become so bleak that she persuaded her parents to allow her to go to boarding school in England. It was a life-changing decision which ultimately would lead to her being introduced to the teenage third-in-line to the throne.

Although Zimbabwe had enjoyed many years of relative peace and ethnic harmony under the regime of its despotic leader Robert

Mugabe, by the time Chelsy was in her teens the country was becoming increasingly hostile towards wealthy white farmers. Mugabe's infamous land reform programme saw dozens of white farmers thrown off their land and forced to flee. Even her father Charles, although well-connected, was forced to give up all of his arable land. Chelsy's grandparents' farm was forcibly seized and their home destroyed. 'It was really sad,' said Chelsy. 'They'd had that farm all of their lives. It got taken away overnight. It happened to everyone. It was a tough, tough time.'

With the political situation rapidly deteriorating, Chelsy's father Charles and mother Beverley agreed to her demand to study overseas. It was a huge culture change for a girl who had spent most of her life running around in bare feet.

With no family or friends in the UK, Chelsy and her parents flew to England to try and find a school that would suit her. But the school directory they had brought with them was so out of date that the first college they phoned had been closed for ten years.

Eventually they chose Cheltenham Ladies' College, but before long she moved to the more suitable Stowe School, in Buckinghamshire, a predominantly boys' school. Set in the magnificent surrounds of a stately home, Stowe must have seemed like a different world for the teenage Chelsy. As one of the most exclusive private schools in England, it boasts a list of famous alumni, including the multi-billionaire Richard Branson.

In her interview Chelsy revealed how it felt to arrive in the UK and how different she felt from everyone else. Recalling the culture shock she experienced on joining Cheltenham Ladies' College, she said she felt like Crocodile Dundee. 'You should have seen the way I looked. Very odd. I wore ridiculous things. I didn't know anything about fashion. Living in Zim, no one had many clothes, no one cared.

'The girls scared me a bit. Everyone was more grown up than me. I was this innocent, stunted child who'd been brought up in the bush, a little kid. I tell you, 14-year-olds in England are not little kids. I'd never worn make-up and suddenly everyone was in make-up. My eyes were like saucers: "Wow, this is bonkers." It was very exciting though. People were like: "Who is this weirdo from Zimbabwe?" But I made some fabulous friends.'

It is testament to Chelsy's character that the 'Weirdo from Zimbabwe' quickly fitted in at Stowe, where she was to rub shoulders with the children of some of the richest and most powerful people in the country. Chelsy was bright, and the fact that her parents and brother Shaun were so many miles away forced her to bond with others and make close friends quickly. Soon her sense of humour and her quirkiness had made Chelsy one of the most popular students. And if her schooling in Zimbabwe had left her behind the others academically, she soon caught up.

One former pupil, who was in the year above Chelsy, recalled: 'She was very different from the other students, but she used that to her advantage. When someone joins the year there is always an interest in the "new girl". But the fact that she spoke with a broad African accent, and seemed so different to everyone else, made her very popular. It helped that she was naturally very attractive. Many of the boys in her year fancied her and she was seen as a mysterious girl, even though she was a bit of a tomboy.'

Outsider or not, she enjoyed studying in England and passed her A levels with distinction. It was during her time in the lower sixth-form that she was introduced to Prince Harry through a mutual friend. Several of Chelsy's classmates had friends at Eton and they probably first met at a party or joint school event. Whenever it was, she clearly had made an impression on the prince, who, because of his 'accident of birth', has always felt like the odd one out.

In some ways that is exactly what he is, a prince among commoners. But growing up feeling different and being treated differently from everyone else had a profound impact on Harry. He yearned to be normal, hated being treated differently by classmates and people he met from other schools.

So while their upbringings had been poles apart, in Chelsy he found someone who shared his feelings of being different, standing out in their social environments. And it was no surprise that when the young prince visited Cape Town in April 2004 he decided to look Chelsy up and invite her out.

After finishing her A levels, Chelsy had earned a place studying Politics, Philosophy and Economics at Cape Town University in what was a far more familiar environment. By now she was part of a close-knit group of friends who made the most of studying in one of the great cities of the world. Her parents agreed to buy a house in the upmarket Cape Town suburb of Newlands, where she lived with her brother Shaun.

After Chelsy and Harry met at one of her favourite clubs in the city, the pair became very close, and within weeks the prince had invited her to join him for a polo trip to South America.

A friend recalled the whirlwind romance and said: 'Chelsy was living in Newlands when she started dating Harry. In the first few months their friendship had been kept secret and it wasn't until she flew to Argentina to spend some time with him that details of their relationship leaked out.

'They were very good together. They both shared a love for the outdoors and Africa. Because of her upbringing, Chelsy must have seemed like a breath of fresh air for Harry. She must have been very different from the usual girls that caught his eye. She was outgoing, funny and tough, and it was clear from very early on that Harry was mad about her.

'In the early days things seemed relatively normal. Of course Harry would come and see her at her house with his bodyguards in tow. But other than that he seemed like a normal, fun-loving guy and there's no doubt Chelsy fancied him rotten. But as soon as their friendship became public I think Chelsy was shocked by all the attention. For someone who is so attractive, she doesn't like being photographed and being the centre of attention is the last thing she wanted. She saw Harry as a vulnerable and slightly clumsy person with a good heart. She liked to mother him and he enjoyed spending time with her and her brother.'

It is not surprising that Harry found Chelsy's confidence and strength of character so appealing. And if there was any doubt about how tough she could be, Chelsy also revealed in her interview a horrifying moment that would have traumatized someone less strong.

After finishing a dissertation in her final year at the University of Cape Town, Chelsy and a female pal decided to go out and celebrate with a well-earned drink in a bar just up the road from her house. After a few minutes a gunman stormed in and raided the bar in what must have been a terrifying ordeal for everyone inside.

But recalling what happened that day, Chelsy revealed her steely side in the matter-of-fact way she spoke about it. 'Very few people in Cape Town escape a run-in with crime,' she said, and then she described the moment the gunman came up to the table where she and her friend were sitting: 'He put a gun to my head. They frog-marched us into the kitchen, made us all lie down, patted us for valuables, and said, "The first person to look up we're going to shoot." I was holding my friend's hand, we were both shaking.'

Being robbed at gunpoint and surviving the ordeal of having a weapon held up against her head seemed only to be a minor distraction for Chelsy. For most people the trauma of such an event could have scarred them for many years. But she is tough and clearly able to shrug off what happened as if it was just another life experience that she survived.

Sadly, though, the experience of being the focus of media attention, and the baggage that comes with dating a high-profile Royal, were things that Chelsy found impossible to shrug off with the same ease.

By the time she updated her Facebook profile and announced her split from Harry, Chelsy had decided that there was no future in her relationship with the prince. As soon as she arrived back in the UK after graduating from Cape Town the strains on their relationship were proving too great. And by the time Harry had started his pilot's course in January 2009 it seemed they would never be able to reconcile their differences.

There were many occasions when Chelsy found herself the centre of media attention purely because of her association with Harry. And this made her feel uneasy. She had never liked being the centre of attention, even as a child. Rumours that she once modelled were found to be untrue. Her friends revealed that she hated being photographed, despite her natural good looks and long blonde hair. Being followed by photographers and finding herself splashed over the pages of newspapers and magazines never sat comfortably with Chelsy.

She would often go to great lengths to avoid the media attention. For example, when Harry passed out of Sandhurst and the Queen came to watch his Sovereign's Parade, Chelsy opted to stay away. It was only after the press had left that she made the journey to the base and attended the Passing Out Ball with her lover.

This was in such sharp contrast to when William passed out of the academy a few months after his brother. Once again the Queen attended the parade, but this time Kate Middleton and her parents, Carole and Michael, arrived in full view of the waiting newsmen. The fact Kate was there was greeted as a sign that the couple might soon be getting engaged. The following month, when Kate celebrated her birthday, a scrum of photographers and TV crews gathered outside her London flat in scenes that were reminiscent of the days when Princess Diana's engagement to Prince Charles had been announced.

Unlike Kate, Chelsy never came to terms with being pictured and pursued. It made her feel like a hunted wild animal and at times it caused huge friction with Harry.

When Peter Phillips got married in 2008, he and his bride, Autumn Kelly, had taken the unusual step of allowing the celebrity magazine *Hello!* to cover the event. When the wedding edition came out the following week, Chelsy was horrified to see that several pages of the magazine had been devoted entirely to pictures of her and Harry. This was the last thing she wanted, and she was furious with her lover for allowing his cousin to lay them open to such a spectacle.

At Leeds University Chelsy had been followed and photographed on regular occasions, even though Harry was miles away. She pleaded with him to find some way of stopping the press from sitting outside her student house, but there was little Harry could do. He knew that this was simply part and parcel of dating a senior Royal.

Being the girlfriend of a prince did not entitle her to a Royal protection detail and this again put strain on the relationship. Harry was very frustrated by the fact there was nothing he could do, and when Chelsy got upset he often got the blame.

Chelsy's arrival in England to study at Leeds should have brought the couple closer together but in reality it quickly began to tear them apart. At university she made a new set of friends, many of whom had never met Harry and none of whom were in his trusted circle. This put Harry off from visiting Chelsy at university, meaning they saw less and less of each other. By the time he started the pilot's course in 2009 the relationship had nosedived, and eventually Chelsy decided to break things off.

It was fortunate for Harry that the break-up coincided with his time living and working at the same place as his brother William in the stable block of a stately home near their base at RAF

Shawbury. William was there for his brother and the demands of studying learning to fly helicopters proved a welcome distraction for Harry.

While Harry was determined not to let it end there, William convinced his brother to give Chelsy the time and space she needed. When William and Kate had split amid a fanfare of publicity, their time apart made them realize they were actually right together. Harry hoped the same might apply for him and Chelsy. Perhaps a break-off period was just what they needed to work things through.

In May that year the palace arranged for William and Harry to take part in a photocall to update the media on the training they were both undergoing at RAF Shawbury. In an interview with the BBC, Harry described how demanding the course had been in the first few weeks.

He said: 'On the helicopter course you start with something like four or five weeks of ground school and exams. Exams have never been my favourite and I always knew that I was going to find it harder than most people.'

The princes stood side by side during the interview inside one of the aircraft hangars at their base. As is so often the case when they do an interview together, Harry was quick to poke fun at his brother. Referring to what it was like to have finished the theory section and to finally be at the controls of a helicopter, he said: 'I'm through that now and have finally got hands on to a job that I absolutely adore. It's hard work but I'm better than William, which is all that matters.'

The jibe at his brother prompted a laugh from William, who took his chance to hit back when asked whether he had been helping Harry with the exams. William replied: 'I've helped him an awful lot, he needs a lot of help. It's the RAF way, you have to help the Army out quite a lot.'

The carefully set-up interview meant questions about Chelsy

were off limits. But despite this Harry gave an insight into where his mind was focused at the time.

Asked if his helicopter training was all about his return to the front line, Harry said: 'It is. I've always had a love of helicopters, I've always wanted to be a pilot, mainly of helicopters rather than fixed wing, even though I'm under the impression that fixed wings are slightly easier to fly than helicopters. I'm really enjoying it and as everyone knows it is my easiest way of getting back to the front line and maybe safer, maybe not safer, I don't know.

'There's a bit of pressure from certain places, which I'm sure you're aware of, for the reasons why I'm allowed back and if I do go back, apparently I can't do the same job as I had. So I'm looking somewhere different and the challenge of becoming a helicopter pilot.'

Harry was then asked if he was confident of getting back to the front line by this means, to which he replied: 'Massively so, unless they stop flying helicopters in Afghanistan, which hopefully they won't do. As I say, I'm just loving flying helicopters at the moment and I just hope I can be better than the best, that's what I always strive to be. To get out to Afghanistan again would be fantastic and my best chance is to be a helicopter pilot. I will fly whatever I'm told to fly and will go back there whenever I'm good enough, which could be in about five years' time.'

It was clear in the interview that Harry had committed himself to his career, and a sign perhaps that thoughts of Chelsy had been put on the back burner for the time being.

Finally, William and Harry were asked about what it was like living together while they trained at the same air base. Both the boys grinned before Harry joked: 'This is the first and last time we'll be living together.'

To which William said: 'It's been a fairly emotional experience. Bearing in mind I cook for him and feed him every day, I'd say he's done rather well. He does do a bit of the washing up then he leaves most of it in the sink and then it comes back in the morning and I have to do it.'

Harry insisted his brother was lying about their domestic arrangements as the pair shared a laugh. If the break-up with Chelsy had taken its toll on Harry, then there was no way he was going let on during the photocall. Clearly his sights were firmly set on getting back to Afghanistan and making the grade as a helicopter pilot.

Behind the scenes, though, William had been a huge support to Harry as he came to terms with the end of his five-year romance with Chelsy. The bond between the brothers – which was so obvious as they laughed and joked at each other's expense that day – was stronger than ever. With William by his side, Harry was able to forget about his relationship problems and focus on the job in hand.

CHAPTER 15

SANDHURST

'YOU'LL CALL ME "Sir", I'll call you "Sir", but the only difference is, you'll mean it,' barked the instructor.

If Harry had been expecting an easy ride as he embarked on his military career, then his first encounter with the non-commissioned officer (NCO) tasked with bashing the young Royal into shape would serve as a sharp reminder of the scale of the task ahead.

As the instructor's words echoed in his head, Harry nervously began to unpack his kit, carefully placing his standard issue boots and khaki greens in the small wooden cupboard by the side of his bed. One error, an item left out of place and Officer Cadet Wales, as he would now be known, knew he would face the wrath of his new masters.

For any cadet, the first day at the world famous Royal Military Academy Sandhurst is a nerve-wracking event. But if you are the third in line to the throne you know the next forty-four weeks represent a make-or-break moment in your life.

This was it, the 20-year-old must have thought, as he tried to remember the detailed instructions on how he was to unpack his kit. This was the real deal, the day he had been dreaming about since boyhood. For Harry the challenge of embarking on his training to become an officer in the British Army represented one of the biggest days of his life. If, like many of the 250 or so cadets who also arrived at the base that day, Harry couldn't make the grade, he knew he would be judged a failure for the rest of his life.

The choice of a military career was one of only a handful of roles available for someone in Harry's elevated position. And failure to reach the high physical, mental and emotional standards now expected of him at Sandhurst would be humiliating.

After all, if he dropped out, having failed to reach the required standards, this would reflect badly on his family and in particular his grandmother, and commander-in-chief, the Queen.

Just minutes earlier Harry, wearing a smartly pressed blue suit, matching tie and checked shirt, had stepped out of the car with his father, Prince Charles. As the cameras captured the occasion, he then said goodbye and nervously made his way up the steps of Old College, the building that would now be home for the rest of his training.

Of course, at school Harry had immersed himself in the Eton cadet force and was never happier than when he was in uniform, marching, shooting on the rifle range or camping out overnight on end-of-term mini-exercises. But Sandhurst was a mile away from the experience of playing soldiers and munching on canned meat as they spent a few hours under a hedge.

The academy course would test not just the cadets' ability to master the basics of infantry training. Here, they would have to cope with the entire range of skills expected of a young officer in the British Army. Harry would be pushed to the limit of his physical abilities. Even when his sodden feet were raw with blisters and his body weak and disorientated through lack of sleep, he would be expected to show leadership skills and the ability to work as part of a team.

Nothing he had ever experienced could have prepared him for what was ahead. But it was not the physical tests he would face that worried the young Royal. Harry was tough, he knew that even in the lowest moments of training he would find the resolve to continue. No, what terrified him as he arrived at Sandhurst that day were the demands that would be placed on his mental skills. Throughout the course he would be expected to write essays, and to attend lectures on military history, international relations and the political aspects of life as an Army officer. Worse, he would even have to pass vital exams that would test his skills in English and maths. Failure in any of these aspects of the course would mean that at best he would be bumped down a term and forced to join a new intake of recruits. At worst he could be kicked off the course altogether.

Sadly for Harry, he had good reason to worry. At Eton he came bottom in his first-year exams and was the only student in the sixth form who was allowed to take just two A levels. He achieved a B in art and a D in geography.

In order to win a place at the academy, he had already undergone the Regular Commissions Board selection. Part of this involved him taking what the would-be cadets call the 'intelligence test'. In this test of his suitability to become a commissioned officer he had to complete a series of multiple-choice questions. These computer tests are used to assess an individual's powers of reasoning, general knowledge and intelligence. Candidates also have to take part in a planning exercise, group discussions and give a short lecture to other members on the course.

One senior officer said: 'The raw intelligence test is exactly that. It is used to assess the potential of all soldiers from those who join the ranks to those who want to become officers. It gives the best indication of a candidate's IQ. We have seen people with very good degrees get very poor scores and those who have just scraped a few.'

A score of 10 out of 10 means you are a genius, while one or zero means you are barely functioning. Harry scored just 4 out of 10 – one of the lowest marks of his intake. So before he even started at Sandhurst, Harry knew that he was right on the border of the minimum academic standards demanded of him. This was pressure like he'd never known before.

Cadets at Sandhurst technically outrank their non-commissioned instructors. As such the very people who would guide, mentor and bully the cadets into shape were required to call their students 'Sir'. It is one of the peculiarities of becoming an officer but quickly becomes a normal part of daily life at the academy.

Sandhurst only selects the very best to the prestigious roles of becoming instructors. As a result the staff sergeants who guide the cadets are almost always experienced soldiers who have proved themselves in battle and have clocked up many years in the Army. The academy's regimental sergeant major is seen as having the most senior non-commissioned officer role within the British Army.

When Harry first encountered the colour sergeant assigned to his platoon, being barked at in this way would hardly have been a surprise. Nevertheless the third in line to the throne would have rarely been spoken to in this way. Only at home with his parents or at school, when the young prince had stepped out of line, would he ever have been told off. Outside of Eton, the nature of Harry's upbringing was such that people addressed him as 'Your Highness' and then as 'Sir'.

Oddly, after Harry recovered from the shock of being told in such a blunt way of how it would work, the encounter was a blessing. One of the things that attracted him to a life in the military was the fact that it was one of the few places where he would be treated like anyone else. The last thing he would have wanted, as he came to terms with his new regime as an officer cadet, was to be singled out because of his Royal status.

It would have been refreshing therefore that the second the wheels of his car passed the academy's guardroom that day, he was no longer Prince Harry. From that moment on he was merely

Cadet Wales, just a normal recruit facing the same level of treatment that any of his fellow hopefuls could expect.

If anything, the mountain he had to climb was even greater than those faced by his comrades. One former instructor who recalled Harry's first day told me: 'Before Harry arrived all of the instructors were called in for a briefing with the commandant. We were told in no uncertain terms that Harry was to be treated just like anyone else on his course. There were to be no "kid gloves" when it came to the training of Officer Cadet Wales. The commandant explained that Harry's protection officers would be living on the base and would always be present when we left for training elsewhere. But he said they would blend into the background and we were to quickly forget about the fact they were there.

'Most of the instructors were well used to meeting members of the Royal family. The link between the Royals and the Armed Forces is very strong, and to a man we had rubbed shoulders with them on several occasions throughout our military careers. But this was the first time we were to ignore the fact they were VIPs and we were warned that any of us caught giving Prince Harry any special treatment would face a dressing down.'

When the big day finally arrived and the instructors got to meet Harry, they were all surprised by their first impression. The former instructor added: 'My first memory of Harry was that he was very young. Cadets start at Sandhurst after finishing their degrees at university. There are those who go there straight from school, but they are the exception rather than the rule.

'Harry was only twenty and he seemed young at that. We had all read about his antics in the months that lead up to his first day at Sandhurst, the Nazi outfit, the girlfriend, the fracas with photographers. But when he arrived he seemed quite shy, very modest and totally down-to-earth. Some of us were perhaps expecting him to be full of himself and a bit arrogant, and we were looking forward to knocking him down a peg or two. But it was clear from day one that the young cadet had decided to try and keep a low profile and knuckle down.'

Anyone who has ever experienced officer training at Sandhurst will know what a shock to the system the first five weeks actually are.

After the longest gap year in history, Harry would now face being woken at the crack of dawn. Sleepy and disorientated, he would have to make sure his small single room was immaculately turned out, kit pressed and folded, boots polished ready for the daily 'Show Parade'. This is when Harry would have to stand to attention in the corridor outside his room, while the instructor made an inspection.

For the first five weeks the cadets were forced to comply with the strictest of rules. Creature comforts like posters or pictures of loved ones are not permitted in the rooms. For the entire five weeks they were not allowed off base, they faced a total booze ban, and the days were taken up with physical training, drills on the parade square and yomps around the base while being shouted at by the instructors. This is not a regime for the faint-hearted. More recruits drop out in the first five weeks than at any other stage of the forty-four-week course.

The former instructor added: 'The first five weeks are very tough for cadets, and that is for good reason. The idea is to break them down, to get them used to reaching the highest standards of personal admin and taking responsibility for themselves. Harry found this baptism very tough, but then in fairness, everyone does. There is no downtime. The only spare minutes in the evening are spent preparing kit, polishing boots or cleaning your rifles. It was clear from the start that Harry coped with the first five weeks by making friends, mucking in with fellow cadets and making sure he bonded with those around him.

'We were surprised at how this came to him naturally. Some of us had expected Harry to struggle to trust people around him or to make new friends quickly because of who he was. But he clearly had a natural way of getting on with people fast and within a few days he was one of the most popular cadets in his intake. Cadets who go into their shell, who fail to make friends and who keep themselves to themselves are the ones that struggle. Harry was the opposite of this. He made jokes, even played the fool when the instructors' backs were turned, and his fellow cadets warmed to him very quickly.

'As one of the youngest in his intake he was immature, and let's just say he didn't manage to keep a clean record with the instructors. He was a bit clumsy at first, perhaps because he lacked the confidence and composure you would expect from older recruits. There were a number of times when he got a dressing down, when you could hear the NCOs shouting at him. On several occasions he failed to make the grade at the show parades, meaning he got a telling-off and had to prepare his room all over again for an evening inspection. This is always difficult, because when you want to be getting prepared for the following day you have to make sure the room is ready for inspection. As a result there were several occasions when Harry had very little sleep.'

For five very long weeks Harry's baptism of fire saw him off the booze, confined to the base and, hardest of all, away from Chelsy. He was often overheard talking about his Zimbabwean girlfriend, telling fellow cadets how much he was missing her and how desperate he was to see her. Harry's devotion to Chelsy was full-on. He may have previously got used to being thousands of miles away from her, but they were in constant contact and barely a day would go by when they wouldn't talk.

When he had his first weekend off, Harry arranged for Chelsy to come and stay with him at St James's Palace. But for him, like all cadets, the chance of seeing family took second place behind a rare opportunity to catch up on some sleep. Unusually for the couple, they chose not to head out to party and instead just spent quality time together lounging around and talking about the ordeal of his first five weeks.

Once that initial stage of his training was over, things began to get a bit easier for Harry, not least because he and the other cadets would now get the chance to put some of their new skills into practice. There was a trip to the Brecon Beacons in Wales, where the cadets were expected to yomp across the hills using their map-reading skills to tick off checkpoints along the way.

But it was not until another exercise that Harry would be photographed for the first time in his Army fatigues. Just a few weeks into their training, the cadets made an hour-long journey in coaches for a three-day exercise in the Ashdown Forest in Sussex. The area, made famous as the setting for the Winnie the Pooh books, provided a perfect backdrop for Sandhurst training. Once again the cadets would have to find their way to check-points during long marches through the Sussex countryside.

Unfortunately for the instructors, this regular exercise took place on public land and in sight of dog walkers, cyclists and ramblers. But with Harry among the cadets' number this time, there was another group of people out in the Ashdown Forest that week. Dozens of photographers had arrived to try and get that first picture of Harry at Sandhurst.

There had been huge media interest in Harry's entry into the military, but nothing had been seen of the prince since his first day and the carefully arranged photocall with Prince Charles. Newspapers were desperate to get an image of Harry showing him getting down and dirty as he was put through his paces by the instructors. And, in their wisdom, the academy staff had refused to alter the rigid training programme, deciding to press ahead with the public yomp regardless. By the time they realized the area of heathland was crawling with photographers it was too late.

Harry was already out with his platoon in full sight of the public. It was inevitable that sooner or later he would be pictured.

This didn't bother his protection officers. They were well aware of the interest in Harry and, after all, they were not there to protect him from being pictured.

But the sudden realization that the photographers were waiting to pounce seemed to put the instructors into a frenzy. One photographer who was there that day recalled: 'It was a very surreal sight. There were dozens of soldiers in camouflage and carrying their assault rifles, but as soon as they spotted a couple of blokes with a camera they went into a frenzy.

'We all remember thinking how odd it was that battle-hardened, highly trained soldiers could be sent into a panic by something so simple as a person trying to take a picture. They started getting on their radios and frantically trying to get Harry off the hillside. They even tried to alter the route of the march, which plunged the whole exercise into chaos. It was hard to see how they could be so surprised. It wasn't as if Harry's arrival at Sandhurst had been kept secret, so what did they expect?'

For his part, Harry just took it in his stride. As the instructors continued to panic, he kept his head down and carried on with the exercise. At one point, when a reporter from the *Daily Mirror* approached Harry's platoon as they marched through the heath-land and tried to interview the Royal, he turned and angrily barked back: 'This isn't a joke, you know.'

The next day the papers were full of pictures of Harry with his new platoon, looking every bit the warrior prince. All these years later it seems funny that the Sandhurst staff got so cross about the pictures. Since then Harry must have been pictured in the course of his work as a soldier thousands of times. But following that incident they wrote to the editors of the national papers asking for them to show restraint and allow Harry's training to continue as planned.

Of course the whole thing could have been avoided in the first place, had the palace only had the foresight to release pictures of

Harry in training. As is so often the case, the media advisers arrogantly decided not to hand out any pictures until his training was complete. But all this did was to put a bounty on any photographs of the prince throughout the forty-four-week course. And there were many taken. Harry was photographed diving in a quarry in Devon, eating a McDonald's on the way back from an exercise, and one paper even claimed to have filmed him on the base itself in a scoop exposing slack security at Sandhurst.

The simple truth was that Harry was big news, and no stuffy colonel who fancied himself as a self-made press officer could do anything to stop him being pictured. Rightly or wrongly there was intense interest in every detail of Harry's training. When he went to Wales to undergo 'fixed bayonet' drills, the story appeared under the headline 'Killer Wales'; and when he was forced to miss an exercise because of infected blisters on his feet, the papers dubbed him 'Sick-note'.

In reality Harry's presence at Sandhurst was a huge coup for the Army and it certainly shed light on the world-leading training that officer cadets undergo while at the academy. After the Ashdown Forest episode, staff photographers did pull back and only took pictures from a distance to avoid disrupting the training. But there was another reason why Harry's training would benefit the Army.

The former instructor went on to say: 'Harry was seen as a dry run for when Prince William started at Sandhurst. In reality, the staff had no idea of the level of interest there would be when the boys arrived. A lot was written which wasn't true, but Clarence House were dealing with the press. By the time William arrived at Sandhurst the staff were much better equipped to know what to expect. Harry had cleared the way for when William arrived, two terms after his brother.'

When William started at Sandhurst Harry was entering his final term. By then he was well into his training and had impressed his instructors. Despite his fears about the academic side of the course, Harry had scraped through and was well on his way to making it to the end of the training.

To the huge relief of the prince's advisers Harry had proved his critics wrong. Despite some suggestions that he would be treated with kid gloves during the training, it was clear that Harry had had no special treatment. He may not have been top of the class, but instructors were privately very impressed by the leadership skills Harry had shown.

He was popular with the other cadets and the NCOs, who had been charmed by him throughout the course. Harry endeared himself to the instructors because he had a natural fascination for all things military. He would often spend downtime asking about the instructors' careers, where they had served and how they had made it to where they were. This was a young Royal whose enthusiasm for the Army was infectious, and his ability to laugh at himself made Harry one of the most popular cadets of his intake.

As far as the men in grey suits at the palace were concerned, they had good reason to feel pleased with how Harry's ten months at Sandhurst had panned out. But any celebrations would be short-lived. With less than a week to go before Harry would parade in front of his grandmother, the Queen, and in the eyes of the world, once again he would find himself at the centre of a storm.

It was a late night, even by the prince's standards. With their successful completion of the final exercise safely in the bag, Harry and a handful of fellow cadets from his platoon decided to let their hair down. At this stage in their training, the cadets were entitled to return to base whenever they liked. Gone were the strict rules about getting back to barracks before 10 p.m. The boys had earned the right to sink a few pints off base, safe in the knowledge that all they had left to do was prepare for the passing out parade. So they headed out to a bar just a short drive from Sandhurst.

In high spirits, the drinks flowed. One of the key aspects of becoming an officer is the bonding you go through with your fellow cadets. By now they were a trusted group of new friends for Harry. As far as they were concerned he was one of them, another young man about to become a junior officer in the British Army. Harry trusted each and every one of them, not least because of everything they had gone through since the difficult days after they arrived at the academy.

'It's still early, guys, let's go to a club,' suggested one of the cadets.

Harry looked at his watch and then at his protection officers, who tagged along with him whenever he was off the base. 'Where can we go around here at this time of night?' he asked.

It was not a pre-planned decision, but as the beers flowed and the fun continued, the cadets were not quite ready to hit the hay. It didn't take long for them to agree that there was still one place that would serve them drinks.

'Let's go to Spearmint Rhino,' suggested one. 'Come on, Harry, you in?'

There must be times in their lives when Harry's protection officers wish they had a bit more say over the decisions that are made. But they knew from his reaction that there was no point in even trying to talk Harry into going home instead. When he is drinking, and surrounded by people he trusts, Harry is the last person who would put a downer on the evening.

And so it was that shortly after 3 a.m. the group of cadets arrived at the doors of the notorious lap dancing club in central London and prepared to go in. Spearmint Rhino is considered one of the more upmarket strip clubs in the UK. The nimble dancing girls who gyrate as they strip off their clothes are well used to quite literally rubbing up against wealthy businessmen.

But there was little chance someone as famous as Harry would be able to melt into the dark without being recognized. Within seconds of their arrival, the girls had all been told by the door staff that Prince Harry was among that night's guests. Unsurprisingly, a buzz went around the strippers as they took it in turns to catch his eye. Within minutes one of the dancers made her move. Like many gentlemen's clubs, the girls are encouraged to ply for extra money by chatting to the punters in a bid to sell them a 'private dance'. For £10 they will peel off their tops and dance topless for the customer. And for £20 they will lead the client off to a private room for a full nude lap dance.

In a pair of skin-tight yellow hotpants and a matching bra, Mariella Butkute sidled over to Harry's table and jumped onto his lap. The unsuspecting prince began to blush and seemed to physically freeze as the glamorous Lithuanian began to whisper in his ear. What could Harry do? If he pushed her off she would almost certainly go to a newspaper and sell her story. And if he let her sit on his lap she would almost certainly go to a newspaper and sell her story. The fact was, it was already too late for Harry. It must have dawned on him by this point that simply by stepping into Spearmint Rhino that night he was walking onto the front pages of all the tabloid papers.

The next morning my phone rang. I was at home working on a feature about Harry passing out of Sandhurst when a voice I recognized came on the line.

'Hi Duncan, it's Merts here, you are not going to believe this one.' It was David Mertens, the longest-serving member of the newsdesk, whose appetite for a good story had remained unaffected by the years he had been taking calls from readers. 'We've just had a call to say that Prince Harry went to Spearmint Rhino last night,' he said. 'We think he may have even paid for a private dance.'

I could tell by the tone of David's voice that he was convinced the tip had some truth to it. All too often this kind of 'too-good-to-be-true' tip turns out to be a hoax. But I remember thinking surely this is a mistake. Harry wouldn't be that foolish, and anyway he must be busy preparing for the passing out parade. My instincts were wrong – my colleague's were not.

By the time I had phoned the palace to double-check the story, one of my colleagues had already been to the club, spoken to staff and stood the story up. Nor did I have to waste much time telling Prince Charles's director of communications why I was calling. Paddy Harverson had been expecting my call. He had already been asked to check out the tip for three other papers. The palace press office had no choice but to confirm the story, and although they declined to make any comment on Harry's behalf, they didn't warn us away from running a story.

Within minutes of the first editions of the next day's papers dropping that night, the 'sordid details' of Harry's 'night of shame' were being picked up by TV and radio stations across the world. Once again, Harry's reputation as a party-loving prince with an eye for the ladies was being cemented by commentators and 'experts' everywhere. Some people said he was stupid, others claimed Harry's actions were 'outrageous' and 'sexist'. Most were quick to point out the fact that by setting foot in Spearmint Rhino, Harry had become the first member of the Royal family to have ever visited a lap dancing bar.

Waves of criticism always follow Harry gaffes and this was no exception. It was claimed the following day that his antics had 'enraged' senior officers at Sandhurst who were preparing to welcome the Queen to the passing out parade. Harry and his co-accused were said to have been given a dressing down during an 'interview without coffee'.

However, the truth of what actually happened that night was a world away from how commentators were interpreting Harry's behaviour. When Mariella the dancer was interviewed about her famous customer she put a very different spin on what actually happened. Far from the young prince 'ogling' women and drinking heavily with his chums, she revealed that Harry had looked like a fish out of water.

She said: 'I couldn't believe I was sitting on a prince's lap. But he was the perfect gentleman He was definitely the most polite and well-spoken client I have ever had.' And despite her best efforts to lure Harry into paying for a private dance, he had flatly refused to enter into the spirit of the evening.

Mariella added: 'When I saw him I didn't know who he was, but one of the other girls said it was Prince Harry. I went straight over to him and kissed him on both cheeks. I asked him if he wanted a dance but he said he didn't because he had a girlfriend who he was really in love with. Harry said, "She's really beautiful. I wouldn't want to have a dance because that would be like cheating on her."'

Even when Mariella told him that Chelsy probably wouldn't care, Harry stuck to his guns. 'He was happy to talk away. He's a really handsome boy and was really nice to talk to. Soon after we started chatting he asked me why I was working there. He said, "Why don't you try to get a better job?" I told him I liked the club and earned a good living. I thought he was a really special person.'

Mariella said the prince talked a lot about his time at Sandhurst. 'He told me he was enjoying it but said he missed his girlfriend a lot. He told me the worst thing about being a prince was that he can't go anywhere without people looking at him. I told him, "Well that's how it goes, darling."'

Mariella's account demonstrates that Harry's decision to go to the club, while foolish, was motivated by curiosity rather than a desire to see naked women. He did little more than tag along with a few of his friends to experience what it must be like to be normal.

Harry may have been rightly criticized for entering a strip club, but he can't be accused of anything more than a minor error of judgement. In the grand scheme of things, the night in the lap dancing bar was an innocuous event. But there is no doubt it has, over the years, contributed to his hell-raising, partying reputation. Perhaps that is a little unfair on someone who sipped just a single beer, refused any private dance, and ended up questioning why someone would choose to earn a living by taking off their clothes for money.

Once again an otherwise unblemished year, in this case a year of knuckling down and training to become an officer, was overshadowed by a single event.

By the time Harry completed his training, there is little doubt he had changed. The experience of Sandhurst played a fundamental role in shaping the person Harry has become. He had started at the academy as an angry, naive and even immature young man. By the time he marched with his colleagues in front of the Old College at Sandhurst, and beamed with pride as his grandmother inspected his platoon during the passing out parade, he was a confident and self-assured junior officer in the British Army.

In 2016 Harry reflected on the impact Sandhurst had on his life when he was on a visit to a group of volunteer mentors. He told them: 'I was at a stage in my life when I was probably lacking a bit in guidance. I lost my mum when I was very young and suddenly I was surrounded by a huge number of men in the Army.'

Reflecting on the instructor who had mocked him on his very first day at the Academy, Harry added: 'He was someone who teased me at the right moments and gave me the confidence to look forward, to actually have that confidence in yourself to know who you are and to push forward and try to help others.'

CHAPTER 16

THE WARRIOR PRINCE

'IF THE INSURGENTS can get through two hundred Gurkhas to reach him [Prince Harry], then they've earned the right to cut his head off,' growled the colonel.

It had long been rumoured that when the soldier prince made it to the front line he would be joined there by an elite team of Special Forces, who would protect him from the enemy. But with these words the unnamed officer put pay to that suggestion once and for all.

Speaking as the press were briefed ahead of Harry's secret deployment to Afghanistan, the colonel revealed that he would be treated just like any member of the Armed Forces serving their country in the war zone. There was to be no sugar coating, Harry would lead men on the front line and execute the role he had been trained for. He would go there to do a job and that was that.

The deployment was to be the best-known secret in Fleet Street history. Every national media outlet in the UK would be told that Harry was off to war, and in return they would agree not to publish or broadcast the story until he was out of harm's way.

It was a compromise that sat uncomfortably with many, particularly some of the more left-leaning members of Her Majesty's media. But it was, in reality, the only way the prince would be able to serve his country without the lives of other soldiers being put at a greater risk.

It was agreed that if the Taliban fighters knew the third in line to the British throne was among the 9,000 British troops in Afghanistan then there was every chance they would step up their attacks. Even if they had no idea what Harry looked like, or where exactly he was serving, the risk of other troops being killed because the prince was out there was deemed too great.

Even those journalists who didn't like being asked to go along with the blackout were forced to accept the deal. If they blinked first, if it was their paper or show that revealed Harry was at war, they would face a huge backlash from their peers. They would risk being blamed for ruining Harry's chance of fighting or, worse, could even be seen as fuelling insurgent attacks on British troops.

It was an unprecedented agreement and one that is unlikely to ever be repeated. But remarkably the deal seemed to be working. Harry would head to Afghanistan in December 2007, and the British media would keep quiet – at least for now. In return for their cooperating, the palace and the Ministry of Defence would facilitate a series of embargoed reports from the front line that could be written and broadcast as and when news of his deployment was made public.

Sitting in the makeshift departure lounge at RAF Brize Norton in Oxfordshire, Harry had mixed feelings. This is what he had longed for. A chance to serve his country and to see action in the front line as a genuine soldier. The Royals have a very special place in the hearts of the Armed Forces. Barely a mess dinner goes by without the customary toast to the Queen. Each member of the family is colonel in chief of a series of regiments, and no one who has ever served in the forces is likely to have missed out on a chance to meet at least one member of the Royal family.

But Harry's task would set him apart from his family in a way that he had dreamed of as a little boy. He never wanted his fascination with the forces to stop at the ceremonial role mapped out for him. He wanted to be the Army, to serve alongside his men and earn his reputation as a good officer first and a popular member of the Royal family second.

The wait at Brize, sitting with his feet perched on his large kitbag, must have seemed like days rather than hours. The flight he would catch would be the same as everyone around him. After six hours there would be a refuelling stop in Cyprus, then it was straight to Kandahar airport in Afghanistan. From there he would climb aboard a Hercules troop carrier which, under the cover of darkness, would take Harry and his fellow troops to Camp Bastion, the British and American base in the heart of war-torn Helmand Province, southern Afghanistan.

As the plane started its descent, the signal went up for everyone on board to put on their body armour and helmets. This was it, thought Harry. This was the moment he had dreamed of since being a little boy and meeting soldiers during Royal visits as a child. All the blisters, sleepless nights and pressure of Sandhurst, all the pre-deployment training and the disappointment of missing out on his tour of Iraq – it had all been for this moment.

Like a footballer who had waited most of his life to finally pull on the kit for real and run onto the pitch, Harry felt this was what he had been preparing for, this was his destiny. The Taliban insurgents had little ground-to-air capability. But when the Hercules was low enough to make its landing into the vast air base in the middle of the Afghan desert, all those on board became sitting targets for rocket-propelled grenade attacks from the ground. For the first time in his life, Harry felt the real surge of adrenalin that only comes when you know there are people below who want you dead.

As any soldier does when arriving in a conflict zone for the first time, Harry felt a mix of excitement and fear as the plane approached the runway. He had been told his job was to serve on the front line as a forward air controller, a role that would bring him up close to the enemy. He would serve in a Forward Operating Base (FOB), a makeshift mud-walled compound in the heart of Helmand Province. There would be no luxuries while he was there. The FOBs were basic, to say the least. He would live off military ration packs and any other local supplies his men could find. It would be his task to man a radio, calling in air strikes on insurgent targets on the ground within a few hundred metres of where he was based.

When speaking over the airwaves he would no longer be Prince Harry. Instead he would be known as Widow Six Seven, a suitably warlike call sign that had already got Harry's heart racing. At just twenty-three and a junior officer in the Household Cavalry, this tour of duty would test the prince to the limit. And it would not be without its dangers. As their names suggest, the FOBs are outposts from where the allied troops took the battle to the enemy. Every day troops would leave the FOB to carry out foot patrols through the dusty and deserted tracks nearby. These essential missions were aimed at reassuring local Afghans and ensuring a signal was sent to the militant insurgents – the British troops were here to force you out.

In late 2007, when Harry set foot in Afghanistan for the first time, British forces were desperately overstretched because the war in Iraq was still in full swing. Only a year or so earlier the Taliban fighters, who had been resisting allied advances in their country since 2001, had begun to use a far more terrifying weapon. Outgunned and outnumbered, they had started using a new way of striking fear into the hearts of their enemy. Rather than risk engaging British troops in gun battles, they were increasingly using home-made bombs and booby traps to injure and kill.

These so-called Improvised Explosive Devices (IEDs) had already claimed the lives of dozens of British troops in the months leading up to Harry's deployment. In many cases the insurgents would use anti-tank mines left over from the bitter war with Russia to wreak havoc on British convoys, and the roadside bombs now posed an increasing threat.

No matter how well he was trained, Harry – like all soldiers fighting in Afghanistan – knew that the greatest threat came the second they stepped out of the FOBs. Each and every footstep could trigger a deadly explosion and the enemy would be way out of sight.

Less than twenty-four hours after he arrived at Camp Bastion, Harry was flown to the FOB he was to call home, a tiny base on the edge of Garmsir, then the southernmost corner of NATO control in Helmand. Harry joined a handful of Gurkhas manning the base which overlooked an area of 'no man's land' intended to form a buffer zone from where enemy attacks and ambushes could not be launched. Anyone spotted wandering into this area was deemed a threat and the soldiers took turns keeping 'stag', Army slang for lookout.

Meanwhile, back in the UK, the British media kept their side of the bargain. In the first few days, as Harry adjusted to life in his new makeshift quarters, his entry into Afghanistan had been kept secret.

On Christmas Day, when the Royal family took part in their traditional visit to St Mary Magdalene Church on the Sandringham Estate in Norfolk, the crowds of Royal well-wishers watching the family go past had no idea why Prince Harry was missing from their number.

Ever since he was born, Harry and his brother William had spent Christmas at Sandringham with their grandmother and the rest of the Royal family. It was a tradition which for many Brits was as much a part of Christmas as Brussels sprouts, opening presents and watching great-uncle Keith fall asleep in the armchair after his third glass of brandy.

But if the hundreds of Royal fanatics had failed to realize Harry was missing from that year's gathering, the empty chair at the Royals' Christmas lunch did not go without comment. Before they ate, the Queen said a prayer for her grandson and for his safe return from Afghanistan. Her family's concerns were shared by the families of thousands of British servicemen and women who would spend the festive season miles away from their loved ones while serving in the front line.

Strangely, however, Harry was in his element that day. The sense of release he felt at being able to spend Christmas without the tradition and duty was overwhelming. While of course he missed his family, and his girlfriend Chelsy, he had now found a new group of friends with whom he could toast the most important day on the Christian calendar.

Instead of dining at Sandringham, Harry joined a group of Gurkhas he had befriended in his new environment. One of the soldiers had been able to buy a goat from a local farmer and the plan was to make a tasty Nepalese curry over an open fire. A source who shared the feast with Harry that year revealed: 'It was bitterly cold, but everyone was in high spirits. One of the Gurkhas had somehow managed to get hold of a goat and the thought of having a day off eating from the rat [ration] packs filled everyone with joy.

'Prince Harry was fascinated by the Gurkhas. He had quickly made friends with them and was on first name terms with just about all of them. On Christmas morning they slaughtered the animal as Harry looked on. Even though we were in the middle of a war zone, no one really cared. It was a very special day and the curry was the best scran any of us had eaten since leaving home.

'Harry seemed to love the fact it was laid-back and totally different. It must have been the first time he'd ever been able to enjoy a Christmas without having to take part in the usual traditional surroundings of Sandringham. He spent hours chatting to the Gurkhas, asking them to tell him stories, and seemed genuinely fascinated by what they had to say.

'A lot of people struggle on Christmas Day, missing their families and wishing they were at home. But Harry seemed to be enjoying being out there more than anyone else. He made jokes and played the fool, which lifted everyone's spirits.'

Life on the front line was tough but clearly something the young prince was enjoying.

Apart from the men who served alongside Harry, very few people had any idea what life was really like for him as he realized his dream of seeing combat. The only insight came from the one print journalist who was tasked with making two separate visits to the front line while Harry was there, a Northern Irishman called John Bingham.

Bingham was a young and talented journalist working for the Press Association (PA) when the blackout deal with the British media was forged. It was agreed that a reporter and photographer from PA would make the trip to Afghanistan, take pictures and interview the prince. In return their pictures and copy would be shared with the British media as and when the blackout was lifted. It was a high-pressure assignment but one that Bingham jumped at. A year earlier he had embedded with British troops in Afghanistan and sent stories home for the PA from the front line. This made him the obvious choice when his news editor was tasked with finding one of his reporters for the job.

Bingham's account of what really happened during Harry's first tour in Afghanistan is the most reliable on record. By his own admission, the one thing many people assume about Harry's deployment is that he was kept well out of harm's way, that it was more of a PR stunt than a genuine stint serving his country.

When I spoke to Bingham, it was clear he still finds this misconception a frustration, having had first-hand experience of life in the front line with Harry. 'In the intervening years I have lost count of the number of people who remarked that, of course, Prince Harry was nowhere near danger,' he said.

In reality, the bases where Harry spent the bulk of his ten-week deployment came under regular attack. Barely a day went by when insurgents were not firing rockets and small arms fire in Harry's direction, Bingham told me. 'I was there as the sole print journalist along with a photographer from the Press Association, where I worked at the time, to see the prince at home in a setting as far removed from the nightclubs of London as it is possible to imagine.

'Then a 23-year-old Household Cavalry officer, he was serving as forward air controller, responsible for controlling military air movements from the ground and – on occasion – calling in air strikes such as the one that morning. To the pilots and air controllers in other parts of Afghanistan he spent hours speaking to over the radio, he was just another voice – known only by his call sign Widow Six Seven.

'It was early January 2008. The prince had already been serving in Afghanistan for about a fortnight as part of a deployment which had to be shrouded in secrecy for fear of putting his fellow soldiers in extra danger.

'By the time we arrived on our first visit he had already slipped the leash. We had been briefed that he would be based at a forward operating base in the middle of the desert, experiencing what were euphemistically called "austere" conditions, doing an important job but not exactly in harm's way. Instead he had wangled a transfer "forward".

'We first caught up with him at a base on the edge of Garmsir, then the southernmost corner of NATO control in Helmand. At the time Garmsir was a virtual ghost town, a handful of streets of empty shops and abandoned houses, complete with worthless banknotes blowing in the breeze. The base was even more austere, a ramshackle complex of half-ruined buildings, without doors, windows and – in some parts – roofs. It was chilling in the bitter Afghan winter when night-time temperatures regularly touched -10°C.

'He evidently loved it. When not at work, he spent his time hanging out with a company of Gurkhas manning the base. Some of the food, it has to be said, was sensational: scrawny cockerels, slaughtered with Gurkha kukri knives and transformed into Nepalese curries.'

And was Harry doing a real job in Afghanistan? Details of the role he played in engaging with the enemy have often been played down. But there is no doubt that he played a role in killing Taliban fighters that had tried to launch attacks on the base where he served. As Bingham recalled: 'The black-and-white footage was grainy but unforgettable: the silhouette of a man running for cover as a fighter jet swooped down ready to strike. Moments later the outlines of fields and mud-walled compounds vanished into a cloud of dust.'

It is probably not a term he would use to describe it, but this was Prince Harry's first 'kill'. Bingham continued: 'I watched it unfold like a surreal video game on a laptop screen a few miles away in a base in the far south of Helmand Province. With the Army's customary black humour, they called it "Taliban TV".'

If Harry's deployment had been nothing more than a PR charade, then that is not how it felt to Bingham. That night he and his photographer had been forced to take cover as insurgents launched missiles from a trench no more than 500 yards away from the FOB. It was, according to Bingham, a frightening experience but by no means unique for Harry. 'The base was under daily attack,' Bingham said. 'There was no way this was staged for our benefit. Harry was in the war zone and the dangers were all around. On the second day there, we went up a nearby hill, which had been turned into an observation point. Things got a bit hairy when a firefight broke out on the way down the hill. Harry was already back at the base when we returned and just laughed: "I see you got contacted."'

Even in the midst of battle Harry seems to have let his sense of humour shine through. He often talks publicly about his dislike for the press, which is understandable in many ways. But when Harry is with reporters he is surprisingly engaging, almost as though he enjoys the chance to tease them.

Bingham's brief encounter with Harry has left a lasting impression on him. 'I was quite surprised and impressed by how Harry seemed to be enjoying his time in Afghanistan,' Bingham told me. 'It was clear that he had made a point of learning everyone's name, from the cooks and the most junior soldiers, to the captains and officers of a more senior rank. He came across as very natural. There were no issues about him being a Royal and he acted as if he was just one of the men, doing a job in a difficult environment.'

The words and pictures gained by the Press Association on that trip would eventually fill the pages of newspapers all over the world. It was on their first visit that Harry was famously filmed firing a high calibre machine-gun from his base. At one point he is seen turning around and facing the camera with a large grin on his face. Because of this, many people – including myself – have always assumed this was staged for the media. However, Bingham revealed this was not the case.

Speaking about the moments leading up to when Harry opened fire, Bingham said: 'The footage of Harry firing the machine-gun may have looked staged, but it wasn't. We were with him at the base when the shout went out that there were insurgents spotted in the no man's land nearby. We could hear shots coming in from small arms. Harry immediately ran to his post and began to fire rounds back. He didn't even have time to put on his body armour and helmet. But the reason he was smiling was because he was pleased he'd managed to get to the machine-gun first and had beaten others to the post.'

The footage had to be shown to commanders at the MoD before they could be given the green light for release ready for when the blackout was lifted. When they saw the images of Harry without his protective gear they were worried about allowing the public to see the footage of him in nothing more than a brown T-shirt. In the end they relented, but it showed just how sensitive the top brass were when it came to making sure their VIP soldier's first encounter with battle went smoothly.

A great deal of planning had gone into Harry's deployment. The months dealing secretly with the media were just the tip of the iceberg. His private secretary, Jamie Lowther-Pinkerton had lobbied hard for him to be allowed to fight, and a careful plan had been put in place to ensure he was able to see action. However, as is so often the case in the heat of war, Harry's desire to get stuck in shone through when he was finally out on the ground.

Bingham noted that when he made his second visit to Afghanistan a few weeks later, the plan for Harry had altered. 'The next time we joined him, about five weeks later, he was back with his Household Cavalry comrades moving around in a convoy of tank-like Spartan armoured vehicles in the desert near Musa Qala further north.

'We were dropped off in the middle of the night from the back of a Chinook helicopter at a grid reference, with a consignment of mail and some boxes of supplies. As the helicopter's dust cloud receded, a familiar face emerged in the darkness nonchalantly welcoming us back, a souvenir kukri on his back.

'If comforts at Garmsir were basic, here they were non-existent. At night, like everyone else, he took his turn "on stag" from the turret of his Spartan, when not sleeping in a hand-dug trench. Again it seemed he had slipped the leash. When his battlegroup moved its headquarters to a base outside Musa Qala – then recently recaptured – he left Garmsir to join them. But within a week or two he had already negotiated permission to join a

"Mog" (Movement Operating Group) – a sort of nomadic armed convoy.

'On the night Prince Harry was flown home from Afghanistan I went to the MoD to interview General Sir Richard Dannatt, now Lord Dannatt, who was then head of the Army, about how the highly sensitive deployment had gone. When he referred to the base Prince Harry had been ostensibly deployed to, I mentioned in passing how much he had enjoyed roughing it in the desert. For just a moment, the general glanced up, looking genuinely puzzled.'

Even the head of the Army appeared not to have known just how far forward Harry had managed to get. There was never a plan for him to sleep outside of the relative safety of the FOBs. But it seems Harry's hunger for getting closer to the front line meant that he had managed to wangle his way onto different task forces.

Footage from the second time the press pool visited Harry in Afghanistan was memorable because he was filmed riding a rusty old motorbike in the desert. This baffled Royal-watchers, who had no idea what he was doing, or how he managed to get his hands on what was clearly not a military machine.

Bingham laughed as he recalled the back story. He said it happened as the troops Harry was with were waiting to push on into an area that had been held by the Taliban. They camped out in a trench under the stars while they waited for the command to advance. In the morning when the press pool woke up, they saw a group of British soldiers wheeling the motorbike about, trying to get it started. When dawn broke they had found it lying there just a few yards from where they had been camping.

To this day no one knows how it ended up there, but the best guess is that a local must have been riding it when they spotted the troops nearby. In a panic they must have abandoned the bike and disappeared into the night.

As soon as the soldiers had managed to get it running, Harry ran over and grabbed the handlebars. To the delight of his comrades, the young Royal wobbled away on a joyride as they looked on. The incident was caught on camera and became one of the lasting images of Harry in the front line. In at least one paper the pictures eventually appeared under the headline: 'Easy Rider'.

In spite of all the smiles, it would not be long before the media blackout was to crumble spectacularly. The PA team returned home and prepared their copy and pictures for when the Ministry of Defence and the palace would allow them to be printed. But then, just ten weeks into the deployment, an Australian magazine and a US website revealed the secret that journalists in the UK had been keeping from the readers for weeks.

Within hours Harry had been hoisted out of the front line and was back at Camp Bastion. There was no way he could stay on the front line now that his presence in Afghanistan was all over the internet.

It was only years later that Harry finally revealed just how hard it was for him leaving his men behind in Afghanistan. In an interview with *Good Morning America* in 2016, he said: 'I had done everything I could to get out there. All I wanted to do was prove that I had a certain set of skills. Literally being plucked out of my team, there was an element of me thinking, "I'm an officer, I'm leaving my soldiers and it's not my own decision."

'I was broken. I didn't know what was going to happen to them, and then, suddenly, I find myself on a plane that's delayed because a Danish soldier's coffin was being put onto the plane.'

No matter how frustrating it must have been for Harry to have his dream deployment cut short, the experience of serving in the front line remains one of the most important in his life. There is no better way of gaining an understanding of the military than to have served your country for real. There is no doubt that this ten-week period has helped shape the way he thinks about the men and women who risk their lives in the course of their jobs.

In reality Harry had no special protection in the front line and he did indeed put his own life in danger. The role he performed in that first tour of Afghanistan was typical of the work thousands of British troops have experienced, and this will always give him a special bond with his fellow servicemen and women. Being able to look them in the eye and have a mutual respect and understanding will prove invaluable now that Harry is a full-time working Royal. But the legacy of this tour runs far deeper than that.

The British media agreed to bend the rules of journalism to enable him to get to the front line, and although the blackout was broken, he did have a chance to live out a childhood ambition. It is impossible to understand what makes the Harry of today tick without grasping the impact those ten weeks had on his life.

Harry's passion to support the forces, particularly those who have been injured or the families of those killed, comes from a deep affinity with the risks taken by ordinary men and women who serve their country in war.

It is ironic that the ten weeks that we might expect to have been the most challenging and horrific of a young man's life were in fact the most special. The truth is, he suited life in the front line. Harry's wit and natural charm endeared him to all those he met while in Afghanistan. He was willing to muck in with everyone else, never complained about being away from his family and friends, and spent most of his brief deployment trying to get closer to the action.

If the Harry that set off from Brize Norton in the cold December morning of 2007 was naive and inexperienced, the young soldier who returned to the base from Afghanistan less than three months later had grown up.

The experiences gained would later prove invaluable when the prince would return to the war in a very different role. His knowledge of what it was like to be on the ground, yards from the enemy, gave him an insight that few of the Apache pilots he would serve alongside on his return would ever have.

The young warrior prince also learned more about himself in that short space of time than in all of his years at school.

CHAPTER 17

ROYAL WEDDING

'ARE YOU READY?' Harry asked his brother as the signal came through that it was time for them to leave St James's Palace. William looked nervous and as white as a sheet as he nodded back.

Fear manifests itself in many ways – cold sweats, butterflies in the stomach, a dry mouth and visible shaking to name but a few. Prince William was on the verge of experiencing at least one or two of these symptoms, so when he made his way up the steps of Westminster Abbey on the morning of 29 April 2011, he needed his younger brother more than ever.

Inevitably the future king had chosen Prince Harry to be at his side on what was always going to be one of the biggest days of his life. For his part Harry was delighted to accept his brother's request for him to be his best man on the day he would tie the knot with long-term girlfriend Kate Middleton.

But as they took in the grandeur of the abbey that day, William and Harry were both blown away by the magnitude of the occasion. Sure, they had both spent months carefully rehearsing this moment in their heads but nothing could have prepared them for the sheer scale of what was happening around them that morning.

Even before he had stepped into the building where Britain's most senior clergyman, the Archbishop of Canterbury, would pronounce them man and wife, William had been given a taste of what was to come. The streets along the Mall and throughout the route from St James's Palace to Westminster Abbey were crammed with tens of thousands of well-wishers, many of whom had camped out all night to ensure they got a view of the groom and his best man. As soon as William's limousine came into sight they cheered and waved Union Jack flags in excitement at what was to be one of the biggest public events in British history.

When it had been announced that the happy couple would marry on a Friday, the government had declared the day a national holiday, which meant that millions of Britons would be glued to their television sets to watch the events unfold. And as William and Harry approached the abbey, any thoughts that this event would be an all-British affair were quickly quashed. At the front of the abbey every available space had been crammed full of temporary stands from where television crews from all over the planet beamed coverage back to their respective countries. The bright lights of their legions of broadcast sets beamed down on the steps of Westminster Abbey like floodlights on a football pitch.

The bigger broadcasters had even forked out tens of thousands of pounds to rent the rooftops of buildings nearby to ensure a good view. This was a media event on a scale rarely seen before. Half of Green Park, next to Buckingham Palace, had been sealed off and transformed into a vast mobile broadcasting event, with dozens of satellite vans, make-up tents and crew marquees filling every square inch. One American broadcaster had flown in more than 120 staff to ensure that their coverage went well. And with this many mobile units in position it was clear that the global hunger for up-to-the-minute live coverage had reached fever pitch.

It was estimated that more than two billion people worldwide were glued to their sets to see the future king tie the knot. Even for William and Harry, who had been paraded in front of the cameras since the day they were born, the Royal wedding was on a different scale from anything they had experienced.

CHOOSING HIS WIFE was probably the most important judgement Prince William would ever have to make. No matter what events and challenges lay ahead for the eldest son of Prince Charles, the choice of bride was going to rank at the very top of the list of decisions for the young Royal.

It is true that because of his accident of birth, William's life was always going to be mapped out for him. He would never really own his destiny. Instead he would have to find a way to muddle through life bit by bit, hoping that somehow he would live up to the enormous expectations placed upon him. Unlike Harry, William would never have the freedom to play the field, to party his way through prospective suitors in a bid to find Princess Right. If Harry felt frustrated that his love life would be laid bare, like the plot of a soap opera, the pressures on his elder brother were in a different league.

Sure William had his flings. Over the years the heir to the throne was romantically linked to a host of glamorous young girls, most of them from wealthy, upper-class families. As soon as William entered his late teens he only had to look at a girl and the rumours that he had found his true love would begin to circulate. The rumours were never denied, because William's intensely private nature meant his advisers were denied the freedom to play down speculation. And for their part, the girls at the centre of the gossip almost always basked in their fifteen minutes of fame.

It was not unheard of for young women to target the same parties and social events William would be likely to attend in a deliberate attempt to catch the future king's eye. Everywhere he went, he would be aware that immaculately turned-out girls were looking in his direction, desperate for some way of breaking the ice. There is barely a teenage boy alive who wouldn't have dreamed about this kind of female attention. While the average 17-year-old would try to get noticed by splashing on his father's aftershave, pulling on his favourite pair of jeans and moulding his hair with his sister's hairspray before going to a party, William would be dreading the attention.

What would be a dream for most teenage lads was in fact a nightmare for William, given that the eyes of the world would one day focus on who he would fall in love with. The paradox was that in spite of being born with wealth, status and privilege, in many ways the young prince was trapped. Fortunately for William, however, he reached the end of his search for the right girl when he least expected to.

The story of how William and Kate's romance began is well known. But it is hardly surprising that when it came to choosing a bride, William took his time and ensured the only basis upon which he would marry was one of love. Courtiers and even his family knew better than to try and match-make.

He longed for the normal life, and he decided at a young age that when it came to the biggest decision of all he would follow his heart, not his head, and certainly not Royal protocol. And when a pretty brunette caught his eye at a charity fashion show in his first year at St Andrews University, William felt that knot in his stomach he had been waiting for. Kate was of course stunningly beautiful. But she was also a shy, understated girl who wasn't loud and brash like many of her fellow students.

The more he got to know Kate, the more William began to realize that she wasn't like the other women he'd met. Yes, she had been educated at one of the poshest private boarding schools in the country. But she'd never really fitted in and preferred playing hockey to sitting around chatting about boys.

Kate had a strong personality and a confidence that William increasingly adored.

But he was never going to rush. Even as their relationship got stronger and stronger, it seemed that William was determined to do exactly what he'd said to me in Klosters, and wait to marry until he was 'twenty-eight or maybe thirty'.

In 2007 it looked as though the fairy tale had ended. Before that, William had spent weeks away from his girlfriend and focused on his military training. By the end of 2006, when he passed out of Sandhurst, the eyes of the world were on the Royal couple as Kate and her parents were invited to watch the academy's historic parade with the Queen. That was seen as a sign the couple were on the verge of getting engaged, which sparked an intense media scrutiny.

But William felt it was too soon; he was reluctant to make such a big decision at such a young age. He dithered, spending more and more time away from Kate as he trained to become a young officer in the Household Cavalry. And by the end of March 2007 their relationship had changed.

They were no longer living as a normal couple far away from the public's gaze. Even a day at the Cheltenham races in March had seen them surrounded by photographers, so much so they could hardly get out of the racecourse car park at the end of the day. As William tried to drive through the scrum of photographers, frustration and anger were etched all over his face. In April, William and Kate had travelled to Zermatt with a group of friends, but sources later revealed that tensions in the Royal couple's relationship came to the surface during that trip, and it was said that Kate had tearful discussions with William.

They decided to spend some time apart and even went to the unusual lengths of allowing news of their split to be confirmed by Clarence House. It was this experience that taught William how to advise Harry when his relationship with Chelsy hit the rocks.

He suggested Harry take time out and focus on his flying training.

Less than two months after their very public split, Wills and Kate were back together. The time apart had taught William just how much she meant to him. He invited Kate to a summer ball at his base in Bovington, Dorset, and from that day on they never looked back. William and Kate agreed that they would stay together for ever, but only when the time was right would they make the ultimate commitment by tying the knot.

Kate patiently waited for her man to decide when he felt able to go down on one knee, and finally, three years after their split, the moment everyone had been waiting for arrived.

Harry had witnessed his brother's relationship grow and grow, and in some ways he envied the way William would talk about Kate with such tenderness. During their shared time together training to be helicopter pilots at RAF Shawbury, the brothers spent hours talking about their girlfriends.

Harry's romantic troubles at that time seemed different from those of his brother. Chelsy was worried about commitment, while Kate had seemed strained by William's lack of the very same thing. While Wills and Kate had worked through their troubles, Harry and Chelsy's romance was well and truly over by the time the future king was about to confide in his brother that 'it was time'.

In the late summer of 2010 William spoke to Harry, man to man. It was clear that he had something important to tell his brother and the excitement of what was about to come was written all over his face. That October William was planning to fly Kate to his favourite place on earth, the magnificent conservation reserve in Kenya where he had spent much of his gap year.

There was nothing too unusual about William's choice of holiday destinations. He and Kate had shared many vacations together, skiing in the Alps, sunbathing in the Caribbean, and watching wildlife on the African reserve owned by William's close friends, the Craig family. They had enjoyed at least three exotic holidays together each year as well as a host of romantic breaks on the Queen's Scottish estate Balmoral.

But Harry sensed this time was different. Royal sources revealed how Harry was the very first person to discover the news that would become one of the biggest Royal events for decades. 'William had decided he was going to pop the question to Kate when they visited Kenya in October that year,' one source told me. 'He had been dying to tell Harry about his plans and waited until the two of them were together and alone several weeks earlier.

'Indeed William was bursting with excitement when he confided in Harry. He said "It is time" and Harry instantly knew what his brother was talking about. The brothers hugged each other before William added: "And I want you to be my best man."'

With a youthful excitement, William described how he was going to take their late mother's priceless engagement ring with him to Kenya in his pocket. During the trip he had arranged for them to fly by helicopter to a remote lodge high in the foothills of Kenya's second highest peak. There they would stay in a simple log cabin to enjoy the views and the sounds of the wild animals roaming around.

Harry loved the plans, the source said, and was amazed at how much thought his brother had put into them. 'The only advice Harry gave to William was to try and sneak a bottle of champagne out to the lodge for when she said yes. He even joked that William might want to take a bottle of brandy as well for him to drink if she said no.'

It was vital to William that Kate knew nothing of his plans and Harry was naturally sworn to secrecy. The boys agreed that their own close circle of trusted friends would be kept in the dark. Even the Royal protection officers, famed for their discretion, were not to be told. They agreed that the only other people who would know in advance were the Queen, Prince Charles and Kate's father, Michael Middleton.

Telling the Queen was a no-brainer. Royal protocol dictates that the heir to the throne should gain permission from the monarch before proposing marriage. This tradition has been followed for generations and in any case William was desperate to inform his grandmother. He and the Queen are famously close and there is no one in the world whose advice William would have valued more. His opportunity to tell his grandmother came during the August break when she was staying at Balmoral. Apparently the conversation between them has always remained totally private. There is no doubt, however, that Her Majesty would have been delighted for her grandson.

For most people, telling your granny your happy news is a pleasant experience even if she may not be the very first relative to find out. For William it was essential that he spoke to the Queen before even popping the question to Kate. Fortunately, the monarch had grown very fond of William's only serious girlfriend in the years they had been dating. Kate had met the Queen many times and palace sources have always spoken of how fond they are of each other.

One source said: 'The Queen is very proud of all her grandchildren but she has a special bond with William. They may be very many years apart in age, but they share a common understanding of the roles they were both born into. When William made the big decision to marry Kate he met with the Queen in Balmoral long before he was planning to go down on one knee. Of course his grandmother was delighted and she gave him her full blessing and wished him luck for the proposal. In the Queen's view, Kate was a perfect match for William not least because their relationship had been given time to grow, get through its ups and downs. But most important of all, she knew how much they were in love.'

Before setting off for Kenya, William finally approached Kate's father, Michael, to ask for his permission. Although he was sworn to secrecy, Michael respected William's traditional approach of asking the bride's father in advance.

The engagement was announced in November to a storm of media interest. At the time William and Kate kept the public guessing about the details of when and where they would tie the knot, revealing only that it would be 'in the early summer' the following year.

Bookmakers had listed the Queen's home at Windsor Castle in Berkshire as a possible venue, as well as St Paul's Cathedral, where Charles and Diana had been married. But in the end Wills and Kate agreed the best venue would be Westminster Abbey, the central London site where one day he will be crowned king.

As an intensely private couple, they would probably have dreamed of a small-scale event in a traditional parish church surrounded only by close family and friends. And even as William approached the chosen venue, he and his bride may well have been fantasizing about being free to elope abroad with just two witnesses and a friendly hotel manager for company. But as is so often the case for the Royals, they were duty bound to share their day with the world, a public ceremony rarely seen anywhere across the globe.

As William and his brother stepped into the abbey, the noise of cheers and screams from outside contrasted sharply with the relative peace and serenity of inside. On either side of the vast abbey the couple had chosen rows of trees to help create an air of calm and beauty as they each approached the altar. But despite the stillness those trees delivered, it would have been impossible for William and Harry not to have spotted the lines of famous faces that flanked them on either side.

More than a thousand people had been invited to attend the service and watch as a chapter of British history was written.

They included stars of film, stage and sport as well as a host of people associated with Royal charities and William's work with the military. David and Victoria Beckham had found their seats on one of the many pews to the left of the abbey. Nearby, Elton John and David Furnish had also arrived early and were flicking through the Order of Service that had been laid out on every seat.

Dotted among the throngs were friends of the couple, many of whom were sitting alongside leaders from government, religious bodies and Royal dignitaries from all over the world. In one seat sat the Sultan of Brunei – one of the richest men on the planet. But like all those gathered as William and Harry slowly made their way to the front of the abbey, the Sultan was treated as an equal. His seat was just one of those temporarily laid out along with dozens of others; there were no thrones or special positions from which to view this event.

I was lucky enough to have been given an invitation and was among a handful of other journalists seated in Poets' Corner, a few rows away from the front. From this vantage point we were able to watch the vital role that Harry played that day. For a normal best man, the challenge is to smile at the guests, remember to wave at Great Aunt Maureen and, whatever you do, don't forget the rings. But Harry wasn't a normal best man. His biggest challenge that morning was to make sure his brother made it through the abbey without buckling under the enormous pressure.

The eyes of the world were quite literally on William as he arrived through the Great West Door to take his place at the front of the abbey. His every move was being analysed live by body language experts and even lip readers employed by media teams desperate to cover every cough and splutter. If Harry needed to turn to his brother to stop him flagging, this would be picked up and talked about all over the planet. William had to do his best to hold the line, to appear as though this was his dream day and the way it was being played out was exactly how he wanted it.

Nothing could really have been further from the truth, and who could blame a groom showing a few nerves on his wedding day – let alone a groom being analysed by two billion people. This wasn't the wedding William would ever have chosen, but he knew it was his duty to get through the ordeal and to make it look on the outside that it was exactly how he had planned it.

Fortunately for William, who was dressed in the dazzling colours of the Irish Guards colonel's uniform, his brother had already anticipated what he would be going through. The most nerve-wracking time for any groom is when he is waiting at the front of the church for the bride to arrive. This is the famous, no-going-back moment when the seconds spent waiting seem like minutes, and the minutes like hours. Harry knew this would be the most difficult part of the day for William. And being forced to stand at the front of Westminster Abbey with the television cameras rolling, it would have been almost impossible for him to have kept his calm. Again, any signs of nerves would have been instantly interpreted as a hint of doubt, even regret. A raised eyebrow, nervous cough or frown would have been subject to microscopic analysis.

With this in mind, Harry had arranged for the two of them to get to the front of the abbey and then disappear into a room adjoining Poets' Corner to their right. The plan was for Harry to get his brother down through the aisle, then take him out of view of the cameras while they waited for the signal that Kate had arrived.

And so it was that with just minutes to go before the wedding of the decade would get underway, Harry led his brother to the side room and closed the door behind him. We will never know what was said in the minutes the two brothers spent in that room but it was a perfect plan to give William a chance to take a deep breath and try to calm his nerves before composing himself and reappearing two or three minutes later.

From where I was sitting I had a ringside view of the Royal brothers heading into that room. I had never seen William looking so nervous. The dazzle of his bright red tunic did little, I thought, to mask the sheer white fear he was trying so hard to hide. Harry, who was also wearing the ceremonial colours of his regiment, the Army Air Corps, managed to throw his brother a reassuring smile as he led William into the room. There is no doubt that the sight of Harry, seemingly playing it cool, must have come as a lifeline to William. There is no one he would have wanted by his side more.

Westminster Abbey was of course the place where, some thirteen years earlier, the teenaged boys had stood side by side as they went through the agony of their mother's funeral. On that sad occasion in 1997, it was largely the fact they went through the ordeal together that enabled them to cope. Diana's death brought William and Harry together in a way that nothing else could. So it was in some ways fitting that all these years on they were once again relying on each other to get them through another difficult event.

We will never know what was said as they waited in that room for the signal that Kate was about to arrive and William had to take his place at the altar. But what is certain is that they would have gained strength from the knowledge that their mother would be watching. The paradox of being surrounded by more than a thousand people, being watched by hundreds of millions more that day, yet feeling a sense of isolation and loneliness would not have been lost on William.

By the time the princes emerged from the room to make the short walk to the front of the Abbey, William looked much more composed. From that point on he would rely on adrenalin to carry him through the wedding service, and of course, he would be joined in the limelight by his bride.

As William walked towards his position and past the Queen and other Royals, the vast abbey echoed to the sound of cheers and applause from outside. This was it. Kate had clearly arrived, and the wedding of the decade was all systems go. For everyone inside the abbey there was a very real sense that they were watching history being made. The pomp and ceremony of the occasion produced an atmosphere never witnessed before.

But as the congregation stood in anticipation of the arrival of the bride, there was perhaps just one person whose feelings must have been different. Clutching her Order of Service, Chelsy Davy stood as the magnitude of the occasion began to grip each and every guest. Harry's ex had been invited to attend the Royal Wedding, both because of her continued friendship with William and Kate and the fact she was still good friends with Harry. As a thousand pairs of eyes focused on the beautiful Royal bride, Chelsy must surely have been wondering 'what if?'

Her split from Harry stemmed in no small part from her inability to cope with all the baggage that comes with dating a prince. If ever Chelsy needed reminding of what she had given up, the sight of this occasion laid bare everything she dreaded about committing to Harry. The little barefoot tomboy who grew up surrounded by animals on her father's African ranch could never have imagined she would one day be watching a global spectacle like this.

As the guests waited for William to arrive not twenty minutes earlier, I had spotted Chelsy sitting in her seat three rows back from the front. She was alone and although immaculately dressed, didn't look at all comfortable. I noticed her fiddling with the Order of Service, almost awkwardly trying to focus on something as she waited.

Had things been different, had her relationship with Harry continued, she must have known it could have been her at the centre of such an occasion. By her own admission Chelsy hated being photographed. Despite her stunning looks, she had always felt awkward in the public gaze. By turning her back on Harry, she turned her back on the kind of limelight that she would never be able to cope with.

While Kate craves being normal with William, she has never struggled with the big occasion or the trappings of being a Royal girlfriend or wife. No one could ever get used to this level of attention, but from the start of their relationship dating a Royal never seemed to affect Kate in the way it had haunted Chelsy. Sure, there were things Kate hated about the baggage that came with her role. The focus on her family and friends, the photographers following her in the street and the constant stream of bitchiness fired at her through the pages of the gossip columns. But in the end Kate was willing to ride the worst aspects for the sake of being with the man she loved.

Chelsy, however, was unable to cope with what a life with Harry would entail. The sad thing about this impasse was that in a way her reluctance to date a prince made her a perfect match for Harry, who longed for a relationship with someone he could trust.

From her vantage point at the side of the abbey, Chelsy would have looked on with very mixed emotions. Everyone enjoys seeing two friends finally tie the knot. But for her, the significance of what she was seeing held a far deeper meaning, and according to one of her close friends Chelsy admitted after the wedding that it made her feel sick to the stomach.

'Chelsy will always hold a special place in her heart for Harry,' the friend said. 'But William and Kate's wedding day was a watershed for her. Seeing the scale and the magnitude of the day convinced Chelsy that she and Harry were right to separate. While Harry and Chelsy both share a love of Africa and the outdoors, the wedding really brought home the reality that they come from different worlds.

'Deep down Harry must have hoped his brother's wedding may have softened Chelsy. But it had the opposite effect. The last thing

Chelsy would ever want is to be thrust in front of the cameras in that way. She is a private person, she enjoys the simple things in life. This kind of circus would suffocate her soul.'

Of course in the end few commentators focused on Chelsy that day. Amid the excitement of the occasion most became side-tracked by another possible suitor for the handsome officer and eligible best man. That attention went, unfairly, to Kate's younger sister, Pippa. At the time she was single, and the image of her bending down to adjust her sister's dress on the steps of Westminster Abbey became a talking point all over the world.

Pippa the bridesmaid was, in line with tradition, walked back down the aisle by Harry, causing a frenzy of speculation that the two shared a chemistry. This was as much an embarrassment to Harry as it was to Kate's chief bridesmaid, but in the end it served as an unlikely if welcome diversion for Chelsy.

Pippa looked fabulous as she dutifully helped her sister through the big day. For many people this was the first time Kate's younger sister had been seen on the world stage. In Britain she was already well known, thanks to her good looks and the list of wealthy young men she classed as friends. But on the global stage, the wedding day helped elevate Pippa to instant stardom, and talk of Harry and Chelsy fell right off the agenda. It wouldn't be long before Chelsy was dating again and Harry began to try his luck elsewhere.

The wedding of William and Kate, memorable for so many reasons, will always mark the end for Harry and Chelsy. Without a sea-change in her life, Chelsy will remain convinced that she and Harry were not to be.

CHAPTER 18

HARRY'S OTHER WOMEN

WILLIAM AND KATE'S fabulous wedding day had once again focused the eyes of the world on the British Royal family. The fairy tale romance between the future king and his first serious girlfriend had viewers across the globe glued to their television sets. Proof, if it were needed, that the public's fascination with the British House of Windsor was as strong as ever.

The 'living museum' had a new exhibit, and the sight of the stunningly beautiful Kate walking down the aisle was enough to make even the most staunch republican wonder what other public ceremony could define a country so completely. It was a triumph for a family whose future role had not that many years before been called into doubt. Since the tragic death of Princess Diana, her sons had stepped up to the plate and the dark days of divorce and scandal were safely confined to the past.

But as her elder son tied the knot, guaranteeing the legacy would continue, the question many were beginning to ask was 'What about Harry?' When his relationship with Chelsy Davy was in full swing, the pair seemed inseparable, and they shared a love of Africa, the outdoors and wild parties that made them seem to the outside world a perfect match. But this romance had run its course by the time Kate had made an honest man of her prince. Harry was single, and the sight of him standing by his brother's side on that April day in 2011 had merely highlighted the fact. For most people who follow the ins and outs of the Royal soap opera, their fondness for Diana's youngest son was matched only by their desire to see him too find a soulmate.

Rumours about the supposed spark between the best man and chief bridesmaid that day were nothing more than wishful speculation. Pippa and Harry, although good friends, would never be an item. Even if their respective siblings had allowed it, they had very little in common beyond their ceremonial duties that day. So it was little surprise that when Kate and William set off for their first overseas tour together in June that year, their arrival in Canada would be overshadowed by events back home. Just a few weeks after the wedding day, red-blooded Harry had struck up a friendship with the ex-girlfriend of Formula One racing champ Jenson Button.

There was no need to explain what it was about the leggy lingerie model turned actress that had caught Harry's eye. Besides her stunning looks, Florence Brudenell-Bruce ticked just about every box when it came to finding a suitor for a prince. Educated at a posh private school and with a history of art degree to her name, Flee – as she was known to friends – was a 25-year-old society girl whose ancestors included James Thomas Brudenell, the Seventh Earl of Cardigan, one of Britain's most famous war heroes. Her wine merchant father Andrew was, like Harry, an Old Etonian, and the family were so well bred that she was actually a distant relative of her new boyfriend.

Unlike Chelsy, Flee seemingly had no problem with being in the limelight – in fact she appeared to enjoy it. During her fling with Button she had spoken openly about the romance and never seemed to complain about being splashed all over the pages of glossy magazines. Perhaps this is why news of their fledgling relationship was greeted with such high expectations among the seasoned Royal reporters. After years of a turbulent on-off relationship with Chelsy, had Harry finally found 'the one'?

It was the *Sun* that broke the story after Harry's black Audi A3 car was spotted outside Flee's £2.5million flat in London's trendy Notting Hill. The palace advisers made no attempt to deny the relationship – yet another clue that it was serious. From the outside looking in, it appeared that Harry and Flee were the perfect match, a beautiful couple who, it was hoped, would follow in the footsteps of William and Kate. But unfortunately this whirlwind romance was over before it had barely got off the ground. Only a few weeks after the widespread media speculation had raged, the couple had split, dashing hopes of a new fairy tale for the Royal family.

Harry's infatuation with art collector Flee may have been real, but after their split her friends revealed that she found it impossible to cope with Harry's flirting with other girls. Only weeks into the romance, Flee had questioned whether they had any future together, not least – claimed her friends – because of the level of female attention he received. A source close to Flee said: 'She felt he had a wandering eye all the time, and she wasn't really into not knowing who he was flirting with or talking to when they were apart. So she ended it. She didn't want to carry on in a relationship that wasn't going to go anywhere. Call it a summer fling. They both enjoyed themselves but Flee wasn't interested in taking things further.'

Things were said to have come to a head, according to the same source, when the couple went to the upmarket Kimberley music festival in Norfolk later that summer. 'At one point Harry was in an area of the festival known as the Tractor Shed, flirting with another pretty blonde. Flee saw he was chatting to her and got very jealous and disappointed.' Then Harry, who was twenty-six at the time, was spotted surrounded by bikini-clad girls after a friend's wedding on the Spanish isle of Majorca.

Another of Flee's friends thought the break-up was partly caused by what she called the 'Chelsy factor'. She said: 'Harry had been with Chelsy for a long time and although he made it clear to Flee that the relationship was over, it was obvious he still had feelings for her. From time to time Harry would talk about places where he would like to take Flee on holiday. Unfortunately, these were often the same places where he and Chelsy had enjoyed time together. She saw this as a bit of a warning sign and never felt too comfortable.'

Less than two years after the split with Harry, Flee would quash any chances of the affair being rekindled when she married multi-millionaire Henry St George in a lavish ceremony in the south of France. The public focus on the relationship between Harry and Flee slipped away almost as quickly as it had surfaced. But it did leave one lingering question. How would Harry ever find someone he could enjoy a serious relationship with after Chelsy?

When William and Kate first met they were both students at St Andrews in Scotland. Because he remained in full-time education, William was seen as 'off limits' to the press. It was in the context of this vacuum that their friendship was able to blossom. Sadly for Harry, the agreement to give the boys space in the wake of their mother's death had long since expired by the time he found himself in his late twenties and single. Trying to find love is hard enough at the best of times without having to accept the intense public interest in who you choose to date.

This subject has riveted the press just as much as it has frustrated Harry and his team of advisers. While he accepts that his position as a senior member of the British Royal family means there will always be a preoccupation with his love life, in reality it has made it even harder for Harry to hold down a long-term relationship.

It was several years after his split from Flee that Harry finally spoke out about the difficulties he faced in finding a girlfriend. In an interview marking the start of the Invictus games for wounded soldiers, Harry told an American TV station he was prioritizing his work over his love life until his nephew Prince George was old enough to make him look 'boring'. While accepting that the Royal family is 'completely aware that we are in a very privileged position,' he said the level of attention his love life received had made the job of finding a girlfriend harder.

He went on to admit feeling 'massive paranoia' about even talking to women, because of the attention. 'Even if I talk to a girl, that person is then suddenly my wife, and people go knocking on her door,' he said. 'If or when I do find a girlfriend, I will do my utmost to ensure that me and her can get to the point where we're comfortable before the massive invasion that is inevitably going to happen into her privacy,' he said.

'To be fair, I haven't had that many opportunities to get out there and meet people. At the moment, my focus is very much on work. But if someone slips into my life then that's absolutely fantastic. When people finish work in the City or wherever work is, if you want to have a bit of downtime, you might go to the pub with your mates,' he said. 'I do that less, because it's not downtime for me. I don't know who I'm going to bump into, I don't know if someone's going to try and grab a selfie. So there is very little private life.'

Whether or not people sympathize with Harry's frustration, the reality is that there is another, far more difficult force to control than the media. The advent of social media has made it even more difficult for Harry to have a girlfriend in the public eye. The press can, and often does, rein itself in when the view of the readers is that they have overstepped the mark. But this does nothing to stem the tide of social media trolls who can use the internet as a platform to make unkind, inaccurate and, at times, downright unpleasant remarks.

The first time this issue was really brought home to Harry was when he embarked on his next relationship following the fling with Flee.

Being part of a human caterpillar is perhaps not the most conventional way of gaining the attention of the British press. But then again, when the two legs in front of you inside the costume belong to a princess, it is perhaps not that surprising that you find yourself on the front pages of the national papers the following day.

It was April 2010, and the Duke of York's eldest daughter, Princess Beatrice, had agreed to take part in a world record attempt. She, along with twenty-eight other runners, would attempt the London Marathon and in so doing earn a place in *Guinness World Records* for 'the most people to complete the 26 mile run while tied together'. Behind Beatrice in the caterpillar was a model called Cressida Bonas, the daughter of four-times-married Lady Mary-Gaye Georgiana Lorna Curzon, famously one of the Sixties 'It' girls.

Even without the caterpillar suit, the stunning model's background, and her friendship with Harry's cousins, Beatrice and Eugenie, made a chance meeting with the Royal considered to be the most eligible bachelor in the world a dead cert. In May 2012 the inevitable finally happened when Cressy – as she is known – was introduced to Harry as she rubbed shoulders with the great and the good at the Valley festival on a friend's Hampshire estate.

Despite the famous falling-out between Princess Diana and Sarah, Duchess of York – the pair are said to have blanked each other in the year leading up to Diana's death – Harry has always had a soft spot for his cousins. Similar in age, they were playmates at numerous family get-togethers, and perhaps because he never had a sister, he formed a close bond with Bea and Eugenie which continues to this day.

The daughters of the Duke and Duchess of York are famed for their social life, mixing in the circles of the children of the wealthy elite and titled families alike. So it was no surprise that when

Harry noticed the pretty, slim blonde by his cousin's side he was captivated. Having been single for more than six months, he couldn't take his eyes off the mysterious, bohemian-looking girl next to Eugenie.

'Harry, this is Cressy, she was one of the caterpillars,' joked the princess, keen to play the role of cupid-in-chief for her close friends. After a few minutes of small talk, Eugenie slipped away, confident that her matchmaking powers were working. Of course Cressida knew all about her cousin's friend, his ups and downs, his life as a pilot and his taste for beautiful women. But she must have also known that when it came to catching the prince's eye, she ticked all the boxes. She too was blonde, well educated and from a family with historic ties to the Royals. Eugenie may well have been planning the chance encounter for a long time, knowing that Harry would not be able to resist the carefree nature of her beautiful friend.

Unlike many in the Royals' circle, Cressy was outgoing, enjoyed letting her hair down and was more than capable of giving Harry a run for his money. A model for fashion house Burberry, she had attended Stowe, Chelsy's old school, before moving to university in Leeds, where Harry's old flame had also studied. The couple had a great deal in common and their friendship quickly turned into romance. Unusually for Harry, within two weeks they even stepped out in public together at the premiere of the Batman film *The Dark Knight Rises*.

As seems always to be the case with Harry, he fell head over heels within days of meeting his latest squeeze. Every break he had from his helicopter training was spent rushing to be by Cressy's side. This was the first real relationship he had had since splitting with Chelsy and it gave him the warm feeling inside that he had craved for so long.

Within weeks Cressy was Harry's official plus one when he attended the birthday of Sam Branson, son of Virgin tycoon

Richard. They shared a room on the family island of Necker before Harry flew to Las Vegas with his mates. It is perhaps testament to how quickly their romance had blossomed that it survived the revelations that Harry had stripped naked during a game of pool in the suite he shared with his close friends. Even the sight of other women splashed all over the front pages was not enough to break the budding relationship.

When Harry returned to Afghanistan for his second tour of duty, this time as an Apache pilot, Cressy stayed dutifully at home waiting for his e-mails and texts to say he was OK. Their time apart simply brought them closer together, and when Harry returned from his four-month deployment, the relationship reached another level.

No doubt proud of their matchmaking skills, Princesses Beatrice and Eugenie invited Cressy and Harry to join them on a skiing trip with their parents, Andrew and Fergie. The annual pilgrimage to the exclusive Swiss resort of Verbier was something Fergie and her ex-husband rarely missed. Ever since their divorce more than two decades ago, the Duke and Duchess of York have remained close. Unlike many divorced couples, they regularly holiday together, and when she is in the UK the duchess is happy to stay at the family home in Windsor Great Park.

It may have been a tame night by Harry's standards, but when he and Cressy joined the Yorks for a meal to celebrate his uncle's fifty-second birthday the intensity of their feelings for each other was unmistakable. Sitting in the swanky Pot Luck Club restaurant as they swilled champagne and tucked into medium rare steaks, Harry and Cressy appeared oblivious to the other diners. At one point Cressy jumped onto his knee and the pair started kissing, looking to one witness 'like love-struck teenagers in the back row of a cinema'. It was only a few weeks after Harry had returned from his second tour of Afghanistan and the public show of affection was seen as proof of how close they had become.

Neither seemed in the slightest bit bothered that their canoodling was being watched by nearly all of the forty or so other people eating in the club that night. Nor did it seem to make the slightest bit of difference to the couple that they were on a table right next to where Harry's uncle was sipping mineral water with his ex-wife.

A fellow diner revealed afterwards: 'They were all in good spirits but by the end of the meal Harry's girlfriend seemed to have shed any inhibitions. She jumped onto his lap and the pair started kissing like love-struck teenagers in the back of the cinema. They were all over each other and it was tempting to shout out "Get a room". Clearly they are at that stage in the relationship where they simply can't keep their hands off each other. It was a rather surreal thing to witness, someone as famous as Prince Harry snogging in the side of a restaurant. They didn't seem to care that people were watching, not even Prince Andrew, who was sitting just a couple of feet away.'

Harry's public show of affection during that trip to the Alps didn't stop there. The following day as the couple waited for the rest of their group to step off a ski lift, he threw his arms around Cressy and they once again started to kiss. The romantic moment, which was caught by a French freelance photographer, filled the pages of newspapers back home. Once again it seemed Harry had fallen deeply in love and he didn't care who knew.

In reality the Royals rarely make such public gestures without knowing exactly how they will be interpreted. There is no way that Harry of all people would have publicly embraced his girlfriend on the busy Swiss slopes without expecting it to be reported. Verbier, like many of the posh Alpine resorts, is swarming with paparazzi who make a living out of selling their pictures of celebrities on the slopes. By making such a public show of affection towards Cressy that day, Harry knew he was making a statement. He was in love and felt as though he had finally banished the ghost of his old flame Chelsy. The pictures were similar to those taken of William and Kate when they ski'd together in Switzerland in 2008. Those pictures too had been seen as a statement, following reports that William had been pictured with a girl in a nightclub just a few weeks before.

There was no doubt that Harry's feelings for Cressy were both intense and genuine, as they spent the following weeks and months together whenever he was off-duty with the Army. The sight of Cressy by Harry's side began to fuel speculation that he might have met 'the one'. They were pictured watching an England rugby match at Twickenham, and the occasional photo of them emerged during nights out in London. But there was one event which really sparked the frenzy of speculation that, maybe, just maybe, an engagement was on the cards.

In March Harry persuaded his girlfriend to take the next leap in their relationship, inviting her to join him for the first time on an official engagement. In the Royal world, this gesture is always seen as a landmark for any boyfriend or girlfriend. When Kate attended William's passing out parade at Sandhurst, for example, it was greeted as a sign of what was to come.

So when Cressida arrived at Wembley Arena with her chums to watch her other half launch the young people's charity event, WE Day UK, it was like a red rag to a bull for the papers. To the delight of Royal watchers, Harry was even seen kissing his girlfriend at one point as they sat alongside 12,000 young people for a music concert. Surely, it seemed, with such an open display of affection during what was after all an official – if slightly unusual – engagement for the prince, the couple are trying to tell us something?

In the weeks that followed the papers in the UK and gossip sites across the Atlantic were full of predictions that the young lovebirds were on the verge of making an announcement. One paper even went as far as to claim Harry and Cressy were planning an 'engagement summit' with other senior Royals.

In July Harry was spotted with Cressy at the Glastonbury music festival, which did little to dispel the rumours. Yet Cressy's close friends had already begun to sense that behind the scenes things were not quite as rosy as they seemed. The reality was that the more Harry and Cressy got to know each other, the less they found they had in common. Harry is a man of simple pleasures, while there was much more to the party-loving Cressy than met the eye.

'In the early days of their relationship, Harry and Cressy were very physical and she certainly felt she had been swept off her feet,' explained one of Cressy's close friends. 'Harry was very attentive, was always checking she was OK and in many ways appeared perfect boyfriend material. But after a few months it became increasingly clear that they didn't actually have that much in common. On paper Cressy may have ticked all the right boxes, but in reality they were not actually that suited. They got on very well, but Cressy became increasingly frustrated that Harry seemed to show no interest in some of the things that were close to her heart.

'Cressy is very passionate about art and culture. She is an avid collector and has been brought up to appreciate art and culture, it is incredibly important to her. But Harry would never be able to understand this. He is a people person, great fun and very outgoing. There is a deeper side to Cressy. She is actually a very shy, gentle person and this just didn't click with Harry.

'As the papers speculated about their engagement, deep down Cressy knew that the relationship had run its course. Yes, there was the pressure of being in the spotlight which was a constant frustration to both of them. But it went further than that. They just didn't have enough in common to make the relationship last.'

The source said it was very hard for Cressy to break things off with Harry and revealed that she began to notice he was becoming needy. She added: 'When they went to Glastonbury together you could see how different they were. Harry wore a trilby hat and suede shoes, while Cressy relaxed in a pair of dungarees and a bright blue hat. She was in her element at the festival but, no matter how hard he tried, Harry just looked out of place.'

Within a month of their being seen together at the event in Wembley, an unnamed palace source confirmed the split: 'It is very sad that they have decided to split. It's very amicable but they have decided to go their separate ways.'

It has since been claimed that the pressure of being in the media spotlight put the final nail in the coffin for Harry and Cressy. The Royal author Ingrid Seward, who is also a long-term friend of Cressy's mother, revealed how the 25-year-old struggled to cope with being spotted in the street by strangers. Speaking at the Henley Literary Festival, Mrs Seward confirmed Miss Bonas told friends she split from the prince after two years having been faced with a barrage of negative comments whenever they went out.

'She just said it was awful because every time she walked down the street she could hear people criticizing her,' Mrs Seward said. 'They would whip out their phones and take photos of her. They'd say "Oh, look at her hair", "Oh, look at her clothes, look at her boots, she hasn't got her laces done up." I mean this is just a normal, pretty girl and she just couldn't take it. She just thought "Why are they getting at me?"'

According to Mrs Seward, Cressy was also deeply upset by some of the comments made about her on social media. For someone who is surprisingly timid by nature, the experience of being trolled is not easily ignored.

There was at least one occasion when Cressy became very frightened because she felt she was being followed. Driving alone, she was convinced someone was following her. By the time she managed to get home, Cressy was so upset she phoned Harry in tears, asking for his help. Although it was never entirely clear whether someone was on her tail, the incident enraged Harry, who felt helpless to keep her safe.

Once again it seemed the pressure of being in the spotlight had contributed to Harry's relationship failing. In an age when social media trolls feel they can write what they like about someone with impunity, the pressure on a high-profile Royal romance appears to be greater than ever. This would not be the first time the issue would frustrate Harry, but it does help to explain his reaction some years later when yet another relationship came out into the public eye.

CHAPTER 19

THE FIRST
SOLO TOUR

THEY WERE TWO of the most famous faces in the world, the rock and roll Royal in lane three and the fastest man on earth in lane five. This was to be a photocall with a difference and, for the pack of travelling Royal reporters, one they would never forget. As the unmistakable six-foot-five inch frame of Usain Bolt carefully unzipped his tracksuit top, his opponent seized his chance and made a dash for it.

Prince Harry didn't even bother trying to remove his gold, green and black outfit, so keen was he to pin his ears back and sprint to the finish line. By the time the Olympic champion realized he had been outsmarted, it was too late even for him to catch up. As the cameras rolled, Harry crossed the finish line first before jokingly pulling his opponent's famous lightning bolt pose.

It was a very amusing, if slightly dubious victory but it did the trick. The footage of Harry and Bolt racing each other at the track bearing the Jamaican legend's name was shown on news bulletins all over the world.

After just about everyone watching had stopped laughing at what they had just witnessed, Harry confessed that he had done it for a bet. When he told one of his close friends that he would be going head to head with the fastest man on earth, he had jokingly bet that he could win. What he hadn't told his friend was how he had secretly planned to do it, by making a false start that would go down in the history books.

'He's a cheat,' laughed Bolt when we spoke to him afterwards. 'If he wants a re-match when I come to London for the Olympics in the summer, I will be ready for him.'

While the unforgettable footage filled a double page in almost all of the British papers the following day, it said more about Harry than just his willingness to cheat. No other members of his family could have pulled off a stunt like that without looking cringingly awkward.

He was, after all, in Jamaica to represent his grandmother the Queen in her Diamond Jubilee year. The visit was a serious business for Harry, his first ever official solo overseas tour, and it was something he had to get right. Royals traditionally travel the world on behalf of the Queen and the British people. If they go well the rewards can be huge, boosting trade and scoring a goal for international diplomacy.

As ever, this tour had been carefully arranged by the palace and the British Foreign Office, and the itinerary had Harry visiting Belize and several Caribbean countries before jetting south to Brazil. Every conversation, handshake and official walkabout would be scrutinized to see if the so-called playboy prince would be able to pull off the serious business of representing his country.

Behind the scenes the men in grey suits at the palace were worried about whether Harry would be able to get through his first solo tour without controversy. The prince had of course, taken part in many set-piece visits and as a child had learned how to conduct himself in the limelight while joining his parents on all kinds of official engagements. And his track record was good. Harry has always been a major draw for coverage in the media.

Other members of his family could only dream of the level of interest shown when Harry took part in a public engagement.

Whether he was playing polo on Governors Island in New York, or meeting patients outside a hospital in Cardiff, his set-piece events were always well attended and gained wide coverage.

But a full-scale overseas Royal tour is very different from brief photocalls and mini visits abroad. There is so much that can go wrong and as a general rule, if things can go pear-shaped, they often do. Royal tours have a habit of going badly, with the odd off-the-cuff remark, or poorly thought through picture opportunity backfiring in spectacular fashion. The list of incidents that have caused Royal blushes or even more serious diplomatic incidents is almost endless.

Prince Philip's careless remarks have become the stuff of legend over the decades. The Queen's husband wears the crown when it comes to putting his foot in it during overseas tours. In 1965, on seeing an exhibition of 'primitive' Ethiopian art, he muttered: 'It looks like the kind of thing my daughter would bring back from her school art lessons.' In 1984, when accepting a figurine from a woman during a visit to Kenya, he asked: 'You are a woman, aren't you?' Two years later, while on an official visit to China, he told a group of British exchange students living in the city of Xian: 'If you stay here much longer you'll be slitty-eyed.' In 1994, he asked an islander in the Cayman Islands: 'Aren't most of you descended from pirates?' In 1998, he asked a British student who had been trekking in Papua New Guinea: 'You managed not to get eaten, then?' And at a reception during a tour of Nigeria, the Duke remarked to the country's then president, who had arrived in traditional dress: 'You look like you're ready for bed.'

Even Prince Charles has found himself in the centre of diplomatic storms from time to time, thanks to impromptu remarks made on official tours. In 2014, during a visit to Canada, Harry's father met with a group who had lost relatives during the Holocaust. He was heard to liken Russian president Vladimir Putin to Adolf Hitler – comments which caused a diplomatic crisis for the Foreign Office at a time when relations with Russia were already strained to say the least.

And during a visit to the United Arab Emirates in 2007, the Prince of Wales caused a backlash after seemingly suggesting the global fast food chain McDonald's should be banned. He was overheard talking to a nutritionist and asking her: 'Have you got anywhere with McDonald's, have you tried getting it banned? That's the key.'

So it was with understandable trepidation that in early 2012 the Royal advisers agreed to send Harry on a full-scale overseas tour, where he would inevitably be joined by a press pack hungry to jump on any possible gaffe or 'foot-in-mouth' moment.

If the pressure on Harry was building, then comments made by the Jamaican Prime Minister Portia Simpson Miller just weeks before the prince was due to arrive did little to allay palace fears. The politician had been quoted as saying in January that year that she intended to remove the Queen as head of state and turn the country into a republic. It was feared that Harry might be well out of his depth during what threatened to be a very difficult and politically loaded visit for even the most seasoned Royal.

Then there was the possible elephant trap waiting for the 27-year-old during the last leg of his tour. He was due to represent British trade on a visit to Brazil in what would mark the conclusion of his first solo tour. It was feared that tensions between the UK and Argentina over the Falkland Islands could lead to protests that would overshadow the visit.

Behind the scenes, palace and Foreign Office officials were getting increasingly anxious. One senior palace source said: 'The prince's first overseas solo tour would be a watershed moment in his life as a senior member of the Royal family. While we were confident that Harry's charm and natural ability in front of the camera would win over the crowds, there was a real concern about how he would cope with the more sensitive aspects of the tour. Playing the joker is one thing, but dragging the country into a political or diplomatic dispute because of an off-the-cuff remark or badly timed joke was a real worry.

'Before setting off, Harry was briefed at length by staff from the Foreign Office. He took these sessions very seriously and asked many questions about what possible pitfalls he needed to avoid. In many ways his inexperience was a help. He was clearly nervous about making any errors and wanted to know the ins and outs of every part of the visit. Perhaps in that way therefore he was even better prepared than other members of his family who have carried out dozens of official overseas tours over the years.

'It was admirable that Harry seemed determined to make the visit work. At the time he was still in the throes of training to become an Army helicopter pilot, and that had been his focus in the months leading up to the tour. But because 2012 was a jubilee year, the pressure on the Royal family to visit as many parts of the world as possible and represent Her Majesty was immense. Harry was keen not to over-prepare and risk coming across as anything other than himself. He naturally agreed not to enter into any discussions about politics and instead decided to focus on what he does best, charming the people he meets with his down-to-earth approach.'

Despite the queue of advisers waiting to brief Harry ahead of his visit, it was not to them that he turned for the key advice. The source went on to reveal that on at least three separate occasions as the set date approached, the prince went to meet his grand-mother for advice. The Queen, who after all came to the throne at a very young age, knew only too well how much pressure her grandson would be under. While the conversations between the monarch and Harry were private, there is little doubt that she would have told him to relax, to take the tour in his stride and to focus on being himself.

Perhaps it was with these words ringing in his ears that Harry decided to play the fool as he walked onto the Usain Bolt running track that morning in Jamaica. No one – least of all his advisers – was expecting him to provide what will surely go down as a vintage Harry moment. The 'race' against the world's fastest man was clearly Harry's idea and he instinctively knew he could pull it off.

Perhaps, if he had talked through the plan with his private secretary and team of press advisers beforehand, they would have been justified in trying to talk him out of it. The 'race' against Bolt was the first time for more than twenty-five years that any member of the Royal family had dared to play the fool in such spectacular fashion while the cameras were rolling.

The last time that happened has also gone down in Royal history but for very different reasons. In 1987 Harry's uncles Edward and Andrew had agreed, along with Princess Anne and Sarah Ferguson, to appear in a royal edition of the hit TV show *It's a Knockout*. In a bid to look trendy and down-to-earth, the then 'young' Royals had agreed to don Olde English fancy dress to cavort through a series of party games along with other celebs dressed as squires, damsels and minstrels.

The custard pie-style game show may have been one of the most popular programmes on television at the time, but its cringe-worthy outcome was the stuff of Royal nightmares. With 18 million people glued to their TV sets, the Royals opened themselves to ridicule. Their attempt to appear 'normal' backfired so spectacularly that the event was described as one of the most disastrous episodes in the history of the modern Royal family.

It was claimed that Prince Philip was furious at his son Edward's decision to take a leading role in the project, describing it as 'unwise and unwelcome'. In a candid exchange with a BBC executive, the Duke of Edinburgh apparently fumed that his son was 'making us look foolish'.

His assessment of the programme was shared by many Royal followers. Philip Ziegler, the distinguished royal biographer, said: 'It would surely have been possible for [the Queen] to take a stronger line over such an ill-judged enterprise as the *It's a Royal Knockout* on television? Perhaps the full horror of this extravaganza did not become apparent until it was too late; if so, the Queen was remarkably ill-informed. Someone should have warned her what was about to happen so that she could have taken steps to stop it, or at least moderate its excesses.'

And James Whitaker, the then royal correspondent of the *Daily Mirror*, went further, saying the show was a 'watershed' in the public's perception of the Royal Family. He said: 'If you really had to pin down where it all went wrong, I would always point to *It's a Royal Knockout*. That was the start of the high-profile thing that started everyone thinking, "Who are these appalling people?"'

By the time Harry pulled off his stunt in Jamaica he had already breezed through the first leg of his tour in Belize in Central America. There he had met the Prime Minister, watched a performance by schoolchildren and successfully completed his walkabout among what appeared to be an adoring crowd. The sight of children holding home-made banners saying 'We love you Harry' was greeted with a welcome sigh of relief by the palace advisers. Everyone seemed desperate to say hello, get a wave or better still a chat with the prince. His reception in Belize confirmed Harry as the Royal everyone wants to meet and was a testament to his global celebrity status. He was the Royal who got himself into scrapes, a party-loving prince with a glint in his eye, and the public adored him for that.

But mucking around on the track with someone so revered and loved by Jamaica as Usain Bolt could well have been a PR disaster. As Prince Edward and co. discovered to their cost, there is a fine line between trying to be funny and pulling it off. Miraculously for Harry, he nailed it. His 'race' was greeted with delight by the

Jamaican audience and the headlines around the world the following day were full of praise for the prince. Seeing this unfold must have left Prince Edward scratching his head. In an instant his nephew had achieved everything he himself had tried to achieve by agreeing to take part in a wacky TV show all those years ago. But where the failure of Edward's stunt still haunts him to this day, Harry's antics were greeted with nothing short of adoration.

It's a difficult skill to pin down, doing something outrageous in front of the cameras without the joke being on you. Politicians have long known of the pitfalls of trying to be funny. What may seem like a good idea at the time can make you look stupid and lay you open to ridicule.

But Harry is no politician. The Usain Bolt stunt demonstrates the scale of the gulf between today's generation of young Royals and those of the 1980s. People know Harry has his faults, and they love him for it. When he is in front of the cameras the viewers want him to succeed, not fail. People simply do not examine Harry through the same cynical glasses they wear to view other Royals, and his antics with Bolt during his first solo overseas tour prove this.

As we left the stadium on the media bus and headed to our next engagement, the Royal pack was still buzzing from what we had witnessed. One thing everyone was in total agreement about was the fact that Harry's stunt was both brave and hilarious. Brave because if it had gone wrong it could have been seen as another *It's a Royal Knockout* moment which would haunt him for years to come.

But hilarious because it worked. He had made what would have been a slightly dry, if newsworthy, photocall into something very special. The images of Harry darting down the track with Usain Bolt trying to catch up, and those of him pulling the famous lightning bolt pose, would mean nothing but good publicity for the young Royal. The pressure of representing his grandmother on such an important tour had not stopped Harry from being himself. High risk in PR terms, but then he rarely does anything by halves.

Without even seeming to try, Harry had nailed the photocall and there was no suggestion whatsoever that his antics would be seen by anyone in the same way as the infamous *It's a Knockout* debacle. Unlike his predecessors he simply managed to play the fool without looking foolish. People were laughing at him, but for different reasons than when viewers in 1987 had laughed at the young Royals. Where they had seemed awkward and almost as though they were trying too hard, Harry had simply been himself – the Royal with a gift for making people laugh.

But the tour was by no means over and the serious business of meeting the Prime Minister was a hurdle he still had to overcome. The high jinks with Usain Bolt were a long way from the pressure of meeting a politician who had only recently raised the thorny issue of turning Jamaica into a republic and breaking the historic ties with the British Royal family.

The following day, as we waited in the garden outside the official residence of the Governor-General of Jamaica in the capital Kingston, the team of dignitaries gathered on the steps looked nervous. This was to be perhaps the most politically sensitive engagement of the entire tour, and even the prince's media team couldn't hide their anxiety.

Harry was due to meet Prime Minister Portia Simpson Miller on the steps outside the immaculately manicured entrance to the white-washed colonial building. Everywhere you go in Jamaica the historic buildings serve as a constant reminder of the island's colonial past. It was in Jamaica where the British plantations made fortunes for their white owners. More than 200 years earlier the country was one of the main destinations for black slaves dragged out of Africa and forced to work in what were often terrible and cruel conditions. Feelings about those dark days of

Jamaican history are still raw when it comes to politics, and for many people the British Royal family are a symbol of the past.

As Harry's motorcade pulled up, the pack of waiting photographers readied themselves for what were surely going to be the most symbolic pictures of the tour. And as the dozens of television cameras started to roll, live footage was pumped around the world. No matter how much planning and nervous energy had been put into this moment, the pressure was now all on Harry. How would he react? His every move would be captured and a single awkward gesture analysed like never before.

As if the pressure of the occasion wasn't enough, a huge portrait of Her Majesty the Queen had been placed on an A-frame right next to where the prince would greet the Prime Minister as the photographers snapped away.

What happened next was to sum up the unique quality that Harry alone brings to his family. Instead of an awkward handshake, the young prince, who was wearing a smart linen suit for the occasion, smiled straight at Ms Simpson Miller as he approached. For her part, the Jamaican Prime Minister beamed back at Harry before throwing her arms around him and planting a kiss on his cheek. The greeting, which had been the subject of so much speculation, was as warm as it was natural. The obvious age gap between the two VIPs made it look more like a son coming home to see his mother than a politician greeting a foreign dignitary.

The Prime Minister seemed overwhelmed to be finally meeting the prince she doubtless would have read and heard so much about. After greeting him on the steps of the Governor-General's residence, she locked her left arm into Harry's and led him inside. The greeting was warm and without flaw. The Prime Minister seemed genuinely delighted to welcome Harry, and her feelings were shared by the officials looking on.

As Harry walked arm in arm with Ms Simpson Miller he sensed her warmth and without a second thought looked at the cameras and said: 'This is my date for the night.' As the people around laughed, the Prime Minister beamed with delight and showed no sign of being offended by Harry's flirtatious remark.

Standing next to me as we watched the events unfold that day was the seasoned Royal correspondent Phil Dampier. A veteran of many Royal tours, Dampier was well aware of the pressure Harry must have been under. He reckons the prince's natural charm is his biggest asset. 'He is brilliant at winning people over by just being himself. Rather like his mother, he has a natural way with people and doesn't talk down to them.'

Dampier, who has reported on the Royal family for thirty years and wrote *Prince Philip: Wise Words and Golden Gaffes*, added: 'The Queen and her senior courtiers were watching him very closely on his first trip to see how he did. After all, he was representing Her Majesty in countries where times are changing fast. In Jamaica he hugged Prime Minister Portia Simpson Miller, who had made comments about removing the Queen as head of state and the Commonwealth. The Queen is a pragmatist and knows that some countries will drop the British monarchy when she dies, but she very much wants the Commonwealth to hold together and for Prince Charles to become its head. So it's important for Harry and William and Kate to carry on her life's work and make friends.

'The Queen knows only too well how a gaffe can ruin a tour from her experiences with Prince Philip. She would never stop him being himself, but I have been on some tours where one of the Duke's comments has made headlines around the world for the wrong reasons. A notable example was on her Golden Jubilee tour of Australia in 2002 when he asked an aboriginal leader: "Do you still throw spears at each other?" The story made headlines globally and overshadowed the tour, much to the annoyance of some courtiers. Harry avoided any such comments and just spread goodwill everywhere, dancing with people, sampling local drinks, hugging politicians and visiting hospitals.

'I know that the Queen was delighted and sent him a note congratulating him and thanking him when he got back. He was absolutely chuffed with that. The last thing he or William would ever want to do would be to let their grandmother down, and so far on overseas trips they have passed with flying colours.'

Dampier's verdict on Harry's first overseas tour was shared by all of the Royal reporters who witnessed it at first hand. It was a flawless display of how to endear yourself to just about everyone you meet, from children to war veterans and politicians alike, and no one had anything but the highest praise for Harry throughout the solo tour. The only blip during the carefully orchestrated visit was not caused by any controversy that could have cast a shadow on events but simply by Harry's immense popularity.

On the final day of his visit to Jamaica Harry arrived in a coastal town near Montego Bay. There it had been planned for the prince to take part in what is referred to on Royal visits as a 'walkabout'. These less formal photo opportunities are when the Royal in question gets to press the flesh with ordinary members of the public. It was planned that Harry would walk through a market and meet shoppers and stall-holders along the route. What the organizers hadn't banked on was the fact that on the afternoon Harry was due to arrive, a vast cruise ship had docked in the bay. The town was heaving with tourists, including many Europeans and Americans, and word that the famous prince was in town had spread like wildfire.

By the time Harry stepped out of his motorcade as planned and began to make his way through the market, the place was swarming with thousands of people clutching cameras and pushing forward in a desperate bid to see the Royal visitor. What should have been a relatively low-key event had quickly grown into a full-scale scrum of people, and Harry's seasoned protection officers began to show signs of panic. Their usually calm and laid-back approach was visibly strained as the crowds surged forward and threatened to turn into a stampede. After just a few minutes they were forced to pull the plug on the walkabout. There were simply too many people being whipped up into an excited frenzy at the prospect of seeing the prince. Eventually they called in the vehicles through their radio earpieces and Harry was bundled into the back of the car.

The press may have underestimated Harry when he raced Usain Bolt, and the palace officials may have worried unnecessarily about how he would cope with the pressure of meeting the outspoken Jamaican Prime Minister. This time it was the protection officers who seemed to have been caught unawares.

Later that day one of them reflected on what had happened in Montego Bay and told me: 'Wow, that was quite something. We had not expected so many people to be there and some of them were getting almost hysterical as they pushed forward to see Harry. We had no choice but to abandon the walkabout for Harry's safety and the safety of the crowds. That is something you don't often see on a Royal tour, it was really rather overwhelming.'

The tour was a triumph. By the time Harry waved goodbye to the press pack after finishing the final leg in Brazil, he knew he had proved a hit, not least because of all the pages and pages of positive coverage which had documented each stage. For the men in grey suits it was time for a joint sigh of relief. Nothing had gone wrong and everyone was praising the prince's performance. But Harry's first major overseas tour was significant for another reason. His grandmother, who was by now approaching her ninetieth year, would inevitably have to scale back her duties, especially those involving long and gruelling foreign visits. The burden travelling thousands of miles to represent Britain needed to be shared among other senior Royals. And as Harry had proved, his popularity across the globe was matched by his natural ability to charm people everywhere he went.

Flying home from Brazil, Harry knew that his next few months would involve knuckling down as he prepared to return to Afghanistan as an Apache pilot. But while his military career was going from strength to strength, how much longer would he have before the demands on the family would mean him having to give it all up and embark on a life as a full-time working Royal? The problem for Harry in many ways was that he was in danger of becoming a victim of his own success. Yes, there was no doubt he was an accomplished pilot and an asset to the Army Air Corps, but in this role he could be replaced.

The truth was that by 2012, it was beginning to dawn on the Royals that Prince Harry had a magic touch, a spark that the House of Windsor desperately needed. Unlike other members of his family, Harry brought a unique take on what it means to be a Royal. In an earlier age it might have been concluded that the best way of 'dealing' with a wayward and controversial prince was to keep him out of the public eye. But Harry's fame was eclipsed only by his popularity with the public. No one cared about his mistakes, in fact these were precisely the reason why so many were captivated by Princess Diana's younger son.

In 2012 Prince William was already married but continued to insist he wanted to remain working as a search and rescue pilot. William's reluctance to commit to becoming a full-time working Royal meant the pressure on Harry was increasing. He was fast becoming the Royal family's star attraction, and an asset they wanted to utilize. But in his heart Harry wanted to see through the role that he had trained so hard for. He wanted to return to Afghanistan and, for the time being anyway, nothing was going to distract him from that mission.

CHAPTER 20

HARRY IN LAS VEGAS

'WHAT HAPPENS IN Vegas, stays in Vegas.' Well, that's what they claim.

The irony of this statement will not be lost on Prince Harry. Type his name into Google with the words 'Las Vegas' and the million-plus hits will lay bare what was one of the most high-profile episodes in the young prince's life – proof, if any were needed, that the famous advertising slogan dreamed up by Sin City's tourism department in 2003 should not be taken literally.

In reality the decision to join his pals on a lads' weekend in the gambling capital of the world in August 2012 will surely dog Harry for the rest of his life. In the newsrooms of Fleet Street there is a less well-known saying, used when the story seems too good to be true: 'You couldn't make it up.'

This was exactly how rumours of the party-loving prince's latest antics were greeted in London on the day the internet began to go into meltdown. As news and picture editors rubbed their eyes in disbelief, there was no denying that this time Harry really had landed himself in hot water. What was to unfold over the following few days would tell us more about the popular Royal than we had ever known before.

In the 2009 film *The Hangover*, three pals wake up in Las Vegas after a monumental night of partying. The problem is the groom, whose pending nuptials they were celebrating, has gone missing, and they have no memory of what happened the night before. Even when they discover a tiger in their hotel suite's bathroom, the frantic friends are at a loss to explain how the previous night's events had unfolded.

Doubtless when Harry woke the morning after the night before in his exclusive suite in the Encore hotel, his thoughts would have gone back to what was, until that point, one of his favourite films. While he may have been relieved there was no tiger in his bathroom, sadly for Harry he was not a character in the Hollywood comedy. This was real life, and as he contemplated the scale of his partying of the previous day his hangover was unlikely to be helped by what he could recall.

'Did I really take all my clothes off?' he must have thought. 'And who were those girls that came back to the room?' As memories of the night before began to come back to him, Harry's thumping head would have surely paled into insignificance as it began to dawn on him what had happened.

In order to understand what happened in Las Vegas, you have to go back to a night in the officers' mess at Middle Wallop, the home of the Army Air Corps. Harry and his chums were letting their hair down after a gruelling few days learning to fly. Everyone was in good spirits and it was the first evening for some time the trainees had been able to enjoy a drink. In the air corps, trainee pilots are banned from drinking for up to twenty-four hours before taking the controls. The so-called 'bottle to throttle' rule is rigorously obeyed and anyone caught drinking before a flight is immediately thrown off the course.

Despite his image, Harry isn't the biggest boozer. Sure, he likes a drink, but he is often more reserved than others, especially when he is surrounded by people he barely knows. Only when he is drinking with his closest and most trusted pals, many of whom he has known since childhood, does he risk letting down his guard.

'Naked bar!' went the cry, as the young pilots filled their glasses in the officers' mess. At that point one of Harry's comrades proceeded to strip down to his birthday suit, followed by a handful of others. After a few seconds several of the men were standing at the bar in the nude as they downed their drinks and laughed.

Sources refuse to say whether Harry actually took part in this ritual, but he was there and saw how the prank was greeted as a bit of light-hearted fun. There were no women present, and it was by no means the first time a military bar, safely tucked away inside a base, would have played host to a well-known Army tradition.

As one former member of the regiment put it: 'The mess at Middle Wallop is just like any other. When the guys are there without guests the drinking can get a bit comical. There was one time we played mess rugby after an evening drinking. We used a cabbage as the ball and the officers split into two teams. Whichever team managed to touch the wall with the cabbage won. On that occasion most of us stripped off our uniforms, mainly because we didn't want to get blood on them.

'The naked bar is not so much an Army tradition as something that happens from time to time. It is nothing more than high jinks but it only happens when the commanding officer is off the base. There are other stories about people having to streak round a base naked as a forfeit, but all these kinds of banter are just a way of people letting their hair down. If you have been training hard, and you are stuck on a base with just one bar to keep you enter-tained, it's not surprising that from time to time things can get a little lively.'

Even the Army Rumour Service, an on-line forum for troops, describes the 'naked bar' as 'a popular and enjoyable pastime in the officers' mess, particularly when female officers can be persuaded to take part'.

Since his first day at Sandhurst, being in the Army had undoubt-edly had a hugely positive influence on Prince Harry, turning him from a naive and slightly angry young man into a proud soldier who had served his country with distinction. But the day he checked into Room 2401 of the vast Encore Wynn Hotel in Las Vegas he was determined to let his hair down and enjoy a long weekend with three of his closest and most trusted pals. Little did he know that, a few hours later, one of the perhaps less positive influences the Army had exposed him to over the years would rear its head.

The trip promised to be the proverbial adventure of a lifetime. Harry, his old school chum Thomas 'Skippy' Inskip, rugby player Adam Bidwell, and boyhood friend Arthur Landon had agreed to visit Sin City to let their hair down.

It was the summer of 2012 and Harry was in need of a change of scene. From the start of that year he had been working flat out, mixing Royal duties with preparation for his second deployment to Afghanistan. In fact he was only weeks away from heading back to the war zone, where this time he would be at the controls of the fearsome Apache attack helicopter. For months he had worked hard, preparing for what would be a dangerous and very demanding stint back in the front line.

It was an important year for the Royal family because of the Queen's Diamond Jubilee. After making his successful first solo overseas tour in the spring, Harry – like all the Royals – had been busy marking Her Majesty's sixty years on the throne. In June he had taken part in the national jubilee celebrations, including the huge concert outside Buckingham Palace, having also played a central role in the build-up and hosting of the London Olympics earlier that month. In the first half of 2012 Harry's feet had barely touched the ground.

So it was hardly surprising that when his friends agreed they would join him on a holiday, Harry was filled with excitement. At last he would be able to relax and enjoy himself before facing the challenge of a second tour of duty.

The friends flew first to Necker Island, the opulent Caribbean island owned by British tycoon Richard Branson. There, they were able to relax, in the knowledge that when that part of the trip was over they were heading to a city famed throughout the world for its nightlife. What a contrast it must have been, flying from the beautiful and tranquil seclusion of the Caribbean island to the bright lights and bustle of Las Vegas.

It was Harry's idea to take his friends to Vegas. A year earlier the Royal had visited the city while undergoing advanced training at the Gila Bend air base in Imperial Valley, Arizona. At the end of his eight-week course, he had taken a break in the city and, after enjoying a day renting a Harley-Davidson motorbike, he sampled the Vegas nightlife. The presence of the third in line to the throne in a city famed for its partying had not gone unnoticed. When Harry visited the Tryst club in the Wynn casino he was spotted drinking Grey Goose vodka before hitting the dance floor with a mystery blonde.

One reveller who claimed to have been in the club that night told reporters: 'Harry looked very close to one girl who looked to be in her early twenties. He was dancing with her and they had their arms around each other. They were hugging and at one point he had his hands around her waist as they danced. They all left together at about 3 a.m., Harry still looking very close to the girl.'

Clearly the young prince had enjoyed his brief time in Vegas and flew home determined to persuade his friends to make a return visit as soon as possible. It was during that first visit that Harry had been introduced to Steve Wynn, the Encore hotel's millionaire owner, who was more than happy to issue the Royal with an open invitation, should he ever return to Vegas.

As invitations go, this was one Harry could hardly turn down. For a prince used to the dusty old corridors of ageing palaces and threadbare Royal apartments, the prospect of spending a couple of nights in the sumptuous surrounds of the best suite the Encore had to offer was simply too good to miss.

Room 2401 is not so much a hotel suite as a bachelor pad equipped with the kind of luxuries that were enough to make even a Royal guest's jaw hit the floor. Perched high above the bright lights of Vegas and looking down from the sixty-third floor onto the city's famous strip, the 5,829 square foot, two-storey suite is the biggest and most luxurious of the hotel's sixteen duplexes.

It boasts three master bedrooms, its own private lift, butler service, a room with a massage table, a gym – and, of course, a pool table. The ceilings are inlaid with mother-of-pearl, there are hand-blown glass chandeliers, and guests can enjoy jumping into their own whirlpool hot tub while they sit back and watch a vast 72-inch TV screen. And for guests willing to shell out the £5,300 a night, there is no need to worry about getting noise complaints – the walls are made of padded brown mohair, stuffed to absorb sound.

After checking in through a private lobby in the late afternoon, Harry and his friends went to the SW Steakhouse to line their stomachs ahead of what promised to be a long night of drinking. They then moved on to the brightly lit Parasol bar, less than twenty yards from the restaurant and adjacent to the casino. Sources say this was around 11.45 p.m. and Harry was already 'half wasted', leading to claims that he was targeted in a 'honey trap'.

Trainee dental hygienist Kim Garcia, twenty-two, from California, said: 'He made eye contact with a brunette in a group and immediately invited them all to join him and his buddies. We recognized him instantly, just like the other girls who were sitting a couple of tables away and getting noisier the more they drank.' Miss Garcia, who was with hair salon receptionist Gloria Bryant, twenty-four, also from California, added: 'Gloria and I clearly heard one of them say, "That's Prince Harry! Let's see if we can get him to take us upstairs with him."'

As the drinks flowed, Harry seemed increasingly less bothered about being recognized, which is more than a little out of character. When he has been known to party in London, the prince hates being spotted. In these celebrity-obsessed days, he can barely go anywhere without people staring, shouting his name and even coming over with offers of drinks.

Harry has grown well versed to this part of the baggage that comes with being such a high-profile member of his family. But he has little choice. The alternative is for him to stay indoors, to live a life cut off from the rest of reality. Anyone who has ever bumped into him on a night out will know the drill. His friends, aided if necessary by his protection officers, act as gatekeepers to stop strangers from getting too close. It is only on Harry's say-so that people are ever allowed to join him at the table.

It is something he has just had to learn to cope with, and even when someone has inadvertently outstayed their welcome, Harry's trusted protection officers are on hand to politely usher them away. If that fails, then the nuclear option is to discreetly ask the manager to have them removed from the premises. But things seemed to be different that night in Vegas.

According to the accounts of other revellers who spotted him in the club, Harry seemed to be far more accommodating than usual to the attention that engulfed him. Perhaps this was because he was thinking of his friends. He has often played 'wing man' to his chums, allowing girls to strike up conversations in the hope that his mates will have a good time.

But it is more likely that his seemingly carefree behaviour was rooted in a deeper desire to let his hair down. He was in Vegas to have a good time and that was that. A night when he could forget about being Royal, when he could simply enjoy drinking with his good friends and just let the evening go where it went.

This desire is understandable given that Harry was soon to return to Afghanistan. It is not uncommon for servicemen and women who know they will soon be out in a war zone to adopt a 'devil may care' attitude. Many soldiers talk about how an impending deployment makes them drink more, smoke more and party even harder. It's a natural side effect of coming to terms with the fact you will soon be in harm's way, unable to drink, focused on the job in hand.

By 4 a.m., when the group finally decided to return to their suite, there was a sense that the night was still young. The friends were in high spirits and determined to make the most of the incredible accommodation. Their number had now swollen to twenty-five, including fifteen attractive girls they had been drinking with earlier that night. No one will ever know what possessed Harry to let down his guard and take the extremely out-of-character decision to allow strangers back to his room, but it would have been his decision. In the wake of the stories about what happened that night, there was criticism of his protection officers for not stepping in and – if you like – trying to protect him from himself.

This is a common misunderstanding of the relationship Harry has with his protection detail. They are full-time police officers and part of Scotland Yard's elite SO14 diplomatic protection team. Their job description is simply to ensure the safety of their 'principal'. There is nothing in their remit that says they have the job of preventing people from taking pictures, or from speaking to their principal, and it is certainly not their job to act as though they are highly paid babysitters.

I have often seen Harry's protection officers looking frustrated at the way the young Royal is behaving. Frustrated because when he is under the influence of alcohol, surrounded by strangers, often in the early hours of the morning, their job becomes that bit harder. They have to be on high alert for anyone who may pose a physical threat to the prince. In many ways it is similar to the frustration felt when you are with a group but not drinking because you are going to be driving. While your friends drink more and more, you notice the volume going up, the disapproving stares of other people, and can't help but feel embarrassed as the behaviour deteriorates.

But a protection officer's role has one clear difference from that performed by a designated driver. They would rarely risk the wrath of the prince by challenging him about his behaviour. Some of Harry's protection officers have been with him since he was a child, and they do play a kind of mentoring, at times fatherly role. But there is a fine line between protecting the prince and being seen telling him what to do. Harry, and Harry alone, is accountable for his actions and his decisions. The protection officers are accountable only for his safety and security.

None of the group, least of all Harry, was in the mood to end the fun, and stepping into the lavish suite did little to dampen the spirits. 'Wow, this place is amazing,' whooped the girls, who must have been in a state of disbelief at being invited back. As if the lure of spending the evening with a real-life prince wasn't enough, these lucky few women were now catching a glimpse of how the other half lives.

The drinks started to flow as the girls admired the surroundings, going from room to room in amazement and peering down at the bright lights of the Vegas strip below. Eventually the group gathered around the pool table as they sipped their vodkas and puffed on cigarettes. The protection officers – contrary to popular belief – were not now in the room. With Harry safely inside the suite, they kept their distance and sat on a sofa well away from where the party was gaining momentum.

According to one account of what happened next, someone suggested: 'Let's spice up a game of pool' – a reference to the game of 'strip pool' where everyone takes it in turn to pot a ball.

Miss, and you have to remove an item of clothing. And Harry, far from offering a word of caution, was actually more than enthusiastic about joining in. He was said to have shouted 'Let's ＊＊＊＊＊＊＊ do it!

A source would later claim to the *Sun*: 'That was what jump-started the party.' Seconds later, Harry was really letting it all hang out. Harry pulled a petite blonde, who had been making eyes at him, up from her seat. He cued off, did not pot – and so, as he was only wearing swimming shorts, got naked straight away. The source added: 'Everybody was watching when he took his clothes off. It was exciting for the girls. He was in great shape.'

Despite some 'hands-on' instruction from Harry on how to hold the cue, the blonde then missed enough shots to lose her dress and underwear. 'She had her eyes on Harry so she was going to do anything,' the source claimed.

The pool game over, they put their clothes back on, he offered her a beer and they sat on a couch talking. Later, they both 'disappeared', the source said, when the wild party finally came to an end at 5.30 a.m., by which time most of the others had gone to bed. The source added: 'He was very into her. She was giddy to be in the company of the prince and he was flirting with her. I don't know where they went but they disappeared at the same time at the end of the night.'

That could have been that. A night of high jinks and a chance for the then 27-year-old to let his hair down. Clearly any fears the story could leak out were not at the forefront of Harry's mind for the rest of the weekend. The following day he was pictured surrounded by a gaggle of girls at the city's Encore Beach Club. They showed the prince without his top, splashing about in the pool without a care in the world.

Sadly for Harry, what must have felt like the mother of all weekends was about to morph into the mother of all headaches for his palace media advisers. With the prince safely back home, the now infamous pictures of the naked pool game, believed to have been taken on a mobile phone, were circulating. By the time they reached the desks of the US showbiz website *TMZ*, it was too late to stop the world from finding out what went on inside Room 2401 that night.

There was no denying what the grainy pictures showed. There was Harry, bare bottom to the fore, hunched over his pool opponent from behind and holding a pool cue. And another photo showed Army officer Harry, naked apart from a distinctive thong necklace and his Rolex watch, protecting his own modesty by cupping his hands over his privates while a naked girl – believed to be the same girl he played pool with – hides behind him.

The story was out, and the following day it filled the front pages of all the UK tabloids. At that stage the pictures were already circulating on the internet but so far the editors back in Britain were holding back. But what would be said if they agreed to a palace request not to publish photographs that were fast becoming the most talked about and searched on the internet?

It was a difficult dilemma. Readers of most of the British tabloids are predominantly pro-Royal and certainly pro-Harry. If they published the pictures there was a chance of a backlash, of readers siding with the prince and blaming the papers for hounding him. There was also the matter of where the snaps were taken. It was in a private suite in a hotel where, it would be said, Harry had a reasonable expectation of privacy. But how could the papers 'self-censor', make an editorial decision not to allow their readers to see pictures that were, after all, already splashed all over the internet?

These dilemmas are the moments when the editorial executives are supposed to earn their money. One way the *Sun* tried to draw the issue to the attention of its readers was to mock up one of the pictures on its front page, using the modelling services of a member of staff who had the misfortune of both sharing a name with and having a passing resemblance to the prince.

'These are the pictures the palace don't want you to see, but they have been mocked up by us to save Harry's blushes.' It was an opening shot from the country's biggest-selling newspaper and certainly did the trick of highlighting just how absurd it was for the palace to stop the media in the UK from publishing the pictures.

A day later, the *Sun* finally gave in to temptation and splashed the real pictures across its pages. While the palace, and Harry for that matter, were deeply disappointed by the decision, they refrained from issuing a formal complaint. In reality they judged that they couldn't be seen complaining about the public seeing pictures that were already freely available and clearly showed the prince in, shall we say, rather an 'un-Royal' series of poses.

The media team batted away all questions about Harry's behaviour with the simple 'no comment' response. But privately they defended the prince, stressing that he was entitled to let his hair down, not least because of his impending deployment to Afghanistan. And, in reality, this is how the vast majority of the British public felt.

'It's just Harry being Harry,' was the overriding reaction when people saw the pictures. Once again the popularity of the Teflon Royal, the prince who can do nothing wrong in so many people's eyes, won through. Even among Americans Harry's behaviour while visiting their country didn't seem to cause any offence. He was, after all, the prince famed for his love of partying and it wasn't as if any of the women who undoubtedly egged on their famous host that night were complaining.

Of all his high-profile misdemeanours, the naked pool pictures were perhaps the least controversial. His Nazi gaffe was a serious blunder for which he took the rap. The 'Paki' row led people to question his maturity, but because the story emerged a full three years after the comments were made, it never really caused any lasting damage. His night in Vegas at least proved there was one member of the Royal family who still liked to let his hair down in style.

At the time when Harry was once again on the front pages for all the wrong reasons, his brother and new bride Kate had faded into the background, seemingly focused on a life out of the spotlight. If it were not for the fact that Harry deflected attention away from his older brother, there is every chance William and Kate would have been put under pressure to face the public. After getting married in front of two billion TV viewers, they had settled back into a relatively peaceful existence, only undertaking a minimal number of official engagements. Behind closed doors, William's reluctance to give up his job as a helicopter pilot was prompting concerns about the workload being placed on the Queen and other senior Royals.

It was fitting that when Harry finally broke his silence about the Vegas trip, he chose to allude to the impact it might have had on the rest of his family. Speaking several months after the story, he said: 'At the end of the day I probably let myself down and members of my family down.' But he went on to reveal more about how he sees himself when he added: 'It was probably a classic example of me being too much Army, and not enough prince – it's as simple as that.'

This was one of the best examples of how Harry tries to compartmentalize his life, his way of dealing with being a Royal and a human being. In uniform, he was an officer, a soldier in charge of men and subordinate to his superiors. While surrounded by his fellow soldiers he was Captain Wales, one of the guys and a popular member of the team. When he is on Royal duties he is Prince Harry – grandson of the Queen and son of the heir to the throne. It is remarkable how he manages to pull this dual role off, but in reality it's something he has been doing all his life.

At Eton College he rarely acted like a prince. He played the fool most of the time and gravitated towards the less academic members of his class. When enjoying private time with his mother, he was simply Harry the son, enjoying jokes and fun time with the mother he adored. It was only when he stepped out with his parents on official engagements that the young Harry became a prince, the rest of the time he would try and be normal. This trait is shared to some extent by his brother William. When the pair of them are together, they are not Royals, they are buddies who have each other's back. Ever since William's marriage, the bond between the brothers has remained strong because they offer each other a release from the daily grind of being princes. But this desire to pigeon-hole different aspects of his life will always be a problem for Harry. When the drinks are flowing, when thoughts of his Royal status are washed away by the alcohol, there is always a risk he will get himself the wrong type of publicity.

Harry, like it or not, is a prince first and foremost. His role in the Army was second to that – even when the cries of 'naked bar' went up.

CHAPTER 21

THE WARRIOR PRINCE RETURNS

AS NIGHT FELL over the vast British and American military base deep in the Afghan desert, everything seemed as usual. The cloudless skies above Camp Bastion were lit by the brilliant stars as the thousands of servicemen and women readied themselves to bed down.

It was a Friday night, but life inside the dry base was a world away from the bustling high streets of the garrison towns back home. Outside the NAAFI in the British section of the camp, a handful of troops in their military fatigues tucked into piping hot pizzas and smoked cigarettes. Elsewhere the rows of tents and shelters that the soldiers called home were filled with the usual mix of Bastion's residents relaxing and killing time.

One of the camp's newest residents, Captain Wales, was already fast asleep in readiness for the following day's twelve-hour shift. He had only recently arrived in what was now a makeshift city, ready for twenty weeks as a gunner on an attack helicopter.

Everything seemed normal; it was just another night in the smooth-running hub deep in Afghanistan's Helmand Province. Suddenly and without warning the tranquillity was shattered by a huge explosion. As people rushed outside to see what was happening, the sky was bright orange as flames gushed towards the stars above. The eruption seemed to be coming from the

American side of Bastion, but it was immediately clear this was not normal.

In the confusion that followed, the air was filled with the telltale crack of small arms fire as it began to dawn on the troops the camp was under attack. Bastion's eight square miles are well protected. Its location far away from any other life meant any unexpected movement outside the wire was easy to spot. The fortified defences that scanned the entire perimeter were manned round the clock by British and American soldiers. And the perimeter of the base was constantly patrolled by heavily armed units, ensuring the safety of the 30,000-plus military personnel inside.

The attack was as audacious as it was carefully planned. In the weeks before, a group of insurgent fighters had posed as farmers tending a crop of poppies that flanked the northern end of Bastion. Their disguises had allowed them to pinpoint weaknesses in the camp's security, and when the moment was right, they donned stolen US uniforms and strolled inside the perimeter unchallenged.

The suicidal mission was one of the most serious breaches of security at Bastion since it had first sprung from the desert in 2006. By the time fourteen of the insurgents and been killed and the fifteenth captured, two US marines were dead and eight other soldiers injured. Catching their target off guard, the raiders had also fired rocket-propelled grenades at aircraft parked nearby, destroying no fewer than six $30 million Harrier jump jets before they were eventually shot dead.

Prince Harry, it was claimed, slept through the battle in his quarters more than a mile away on the other side of Bastion. But inevitably, when the news broke back home, questions were being asked as to whether this carefully coordinated attack had been sparked by the Royal's arrival back in Afghanistan.

Unlike his first deployment in 2007, Harry's return to the badlands had been well publicized in advance. Because he would this time serve as an Apache attack helicopter pilot, it was felt there was no need for the repeat of the media blackout that marked his first tour of duty. Even if the British press could have been persuaded to another blackout – which was ruled out as impossible – any increased threat to other troops was deemed far smaller than before. From the cockpit of his awesome £46 million 'flying tank', the Royal would be safely away from the insurgents he had faced while serving as a foot soldier the previous time. So it was with some angst that senior commanders deflected the 'Harry' line away from the September raid on Bastion.

Of course for their part the Taliban propagandists were keen to claim it was a targeted attack on the 'Infidel Prince'. Four days earlier a spokesman named Zabiullah Mujahid had indeed told the press: 'We have informed our commanders in Helmand to do whatever they can to eliminate him.'

But most military experts dismissed the claim as opportunism. The far more likely explanation for the events of that night lay in the insurgent reaction to a US video that had mocked the Islamic faith. Widespread anger at the film *Innocence of Muslims* had led to violent demonstrations outside Western embassies and attacks in Egypt that had claimed seven lives.

Even though common sense prevailed and very few people tried to link the attack to Harry's presence at Bastion, this was not the start to his second tour of duty that the military top brass had hoped for. Ever since his abrupt removal from the war zone in 2008, Harry had dreamed of making this return.

Not known for his academic skills, Harry had amazed everyone by making the grade as one of the Army's elite Apache pilots. He had trained for more than three years to earn the right to serve his country once more, and being back on duty in Afghanistan was the icing on the cake.

When Harry had first come up with the idea of switching regiments and training to be a pilot, he knew this was likely to be his only chance of returning to the action. But few people, least of all Harry, ever expected him to qualify to fly the Army Air Corps's awesome killing machines. The Apaches are equipped with Hellfire missiles as well as deadly cannons, and just the sound of their signature engines in the skies high above is enough to send insurgent fighters into hiding.

Harry would be based at Bastion for the duration of his deployment. From there he would carry out missions high above the dust-ridden planes of Helmand Province. Despite their awesome reputation as one of the most advanced pieces of military kit, the Apaches' primary role in Afghanistan was to save lives. They would be sent as air cover to provide ground troops with the vital support they needed in the event of them being engaged by the enemy. Nothing was more reassuring for troops on the ground than the sight of an Apache overhead. If they were being attacked, the Apache could easily pinpoint where the insurgents were firing from and wipe them out in seconds.

The other vital role the Apaches played was to escort other aircraft tasked with rescuing wounded troops on the ground. These so-called CASEVAC missions – short for casualty evacuation – undertaken by RAF Chinook teams made them a sitting target for rocket attacks. For his entire three-month stint, Harry would be ready to react at short notice to fly above the evacuation crews and ensure they were safe from enemy strikes.

Few of his fellow pilots had the same insight into what it was like for the troops on the ground in Afghanistan as Harry. His previous stint in the front line may have been brief, but it had given him a clear understanding of how important the air cover from the Apaches really was. Most of the other Army Air Corps pilots would have served with the regiment from the start and would probably never have been on the ground.

As he unpacked his kit and made himself at home in the relatively safer environment of Camp Bastion, Harry's thoughts went back to his previous deployment. For the next three months there would doubtless be occasions when the adrenalin would be flowing and the buzz of being back at war would return. But this mission would – he knew – be so very different to the last.

When not on sorties, Harry would be stuck at Bastion killing time and thinking of home. His new girlfriend Cressida Bonas would only be an e-mail away, but this would not be like before. The long hours sitting around Bastion would be very dull. It was in a war zone, but life on the camp was relatively tame. Every mealtime Harry would walk over to the mess hall, a series of large domed tents from where hot, comforting food would be served up like meals at a school canteen. If he fancied a change, the prince could visit the camp's own Pizza Hut branch or go and buy supplies from the well-stocked NAAFI.

This tame environment was a world away from what life was like outside the wire. In fact it would feel to someone with Harry's experience more like a three-month stay at a Butlins holiday camp than a tour of duty. The other downside for the Royal was the fact that here he would be denied much of the anonymity he had so enjoyed while serving on the front line.

Every time he went to get his hair cut, or to have a coffee in the café run by a Norwegian couple, he would be gawped at by the troops. They all knew Harry was among their number, and spotting the third in line to the throne wandering about became a new pastime for soldiers bored to tears with being confined to the camp.

If he needed some respite, he would look to the servicemen and women that formed part of his unit. For every Apache pilot there was a substantial ground crew of engineers, as well as support staff tasked with keeping the helicopters in the air. By the side of the runway where the Apaches were based, the Army Air Corps unit had its own area where the crew would kill time. Besides dusty sofas there were games consoles, TVs and even makeshift internet cafés where the troops could while away the hours.

This mundane routine would not come close to the excitement of being in the thick of the action like last time. Instead of feasting on food cooked by his Gurkha comrades as before, Harry would stroll over to the cookhouse and fill his plate with burgers, steaks and bacon rolls. Was this really what he had spent so long training for, he must have wondered after just days at his new base.

A source who got to know Harry during his second deployment shed light on his tour. 'Being based at Camp Bastion was by no means ideal for Prince Harry,' he said. 'In many ways it functions like a small town, there are always people coming and going. It is fair to say most people just got on with the fact he was there. But the novelty of having a Royal living among the troops was too much for some people to resist. On one occasion two girls from the RAF asked if they could have a picture with him but he refused. I think it actually made him quite angry, but he managed to be polite and walk away. It was a very different experience from his first deployment, when Harry really was out in the field, seen as just one of the guys. The people in his unit were briefed in advance not to treat him any differently and they respected that.

'He avoided going to Leatherneck [the section of Camp Bastion occupied by the US forces] because he feared that if he was recognized the American troops would be less reserved than the Brits, and the last thing he would have wanted would be to be seen as some kind of celebrity soldier. Most of the time he stayed with his men from 662 Squadron and only ventured around at meal times, which must have been quite boring after a while. It was fine when he was on duty because the time went quicker, but during downtime there really isn't that much to do in Bastion.

'A lot of guys spend time in the NAAFI, which is basically a pub without alcohol, but Harry rarely went near the place. I suspect that was because he didn't like being stared at or maybe he was worried soldiers might take his picture and try and sell it to the newspapers. Having spent so much time training to become a helicopter pilot, the tour must have seemed at times like a bit of a disappointment.'

The source's comments explain the reasons why, in an interview released at the end of his tour, Harry surprised many people by saying that he 'hated' being stuck in Bastion. 'My choice would have been back out on the ground with my regiment,' he said. 'That sounds quite spoilt when I'm standing in front of this thing – £45 million worth – but I think hopefully my friends and family back home know exactly what I'm talking about. It is a weird reality, being stuck in Bastion. For me, I hate it, being stuck here. I'd much rather be out with the lads in a PB [patrol base]. The last job was, for me personally, better. Obviously lots of guys like the luxury and comforts of Bastion, but what's weird, as I said, is we're stuck in Bastion and what's going on out there is completely separate.

'It is a pain in the arse being stuck in Bastion. Going into the cookhouse with hundreds of people – it's frustrating. I go into the cookhouse and everyone has a good old gawp, and that's one thing that I dislike about being here. Because there's plenty of guys in there that have never met me, therefore look at me as Prince Harry and not as Captain Wales, which is frustrating. Which is probably another reason why I'd love to be out in the PBs, away from it all.'

The comments were surprisingly unguarded from Harry as he reflected on his two tours, not least because the British taxpayer had invested more than £1 million in his helicopter training since his first stint in Afghanistan. But they show how deeply he felt about being stared at, singled out from the rest of his comrades. This frustration has always been a constant in Harry's life, and his love of the Army had initially been rooted in the fact that he could be anonymous.

Flying helicopters had been his way of getting back to the front line, but the stint in Bastion was nowhere near the kind of Army life he had craved. The truth was that in the busy surrounds of his base, he remained Prince Harry first, and Captain Wales second. Perhaps this is one of the underlying factors that contributed to his eventual decision to quit the career he had chosen. A reluctant facing of the facts – he would never again experience the buzz of being treated as a normal soldier.

Although Harry's second tour was not hidden from the public through a media blackout like before, there was still an agreement with the British media. They were asked to avoid offering a running commentary on his three-month deployment to allow him to just get on with the job. This was, in general, respected by the media, and in return Harry agreed to doing a series of set-piece interviews for TV and press reporters. These were to be kept under embargo until the Royal had finished his tour and returned to the UK.

True to his word, Harry agreed to talk in front of the cameras on three separate occasions during his deployment, with chosen crews being flown out by the RAF on the understanding they would have to share their material as and when the embargo was lifted. Once again this was not an ideal arrangement but it did seem to work. In fact, when the interviews were finally aired they amounted to some of the most revealing the prince had ever given. Perhaps it was the familiar surroundings that put Harry at ease, but his comments were full and frank and it seemed that for once nothing was 'off limits'.

When on duty Harry and his crew would be in a state called Very High Readiness (VHR), meaning that if a call came in they could be in the air within seven minutes. Confined to the unit, this meant Harry would have hours to kill, almost like a fireman waiting to be called on a 'shout'. To ease the boredom, he revealed a routine which would have tested the patience of any battle-ready soldier. 'Essentially we just sit inside the tent and play computer games, watch movies and play uckers [a board game] while we wait for the phone to go. I'm one of those people who, during my flying course especially, I was fine at flying. I should have probably done a lot more reading, and then every now and then a written test would come up and I'd be absolutely useless. I've been like that since stage one of my youth, exams were always a nightmare, but anything like kicking a ball around or playing a PlayStation, or flying, I just find it a little bit easier than walking sometimes.'

He explained what sort of missions he had flown when the phone calls came through and added: 'It could be anything from a CASEVAC through to troops in contact, or cover protection for troops on the ground that are vulnerable. Every time you run to the aircraft you get that adrenalin rush, and when you get to the aircraft you've got to try and slow yourself down because if the adrenalin is pumping too much and you rush, you're going to miss something. There's a lot of pressures obviously when we go and support the Americans or when there is a wounded soldier on the ground.

'It's better than being on the ground in a tank as far as I can tell, but when you fire you still get the cordite smell, which is bizarre. The whole floor vibrates and when you fire a missile the whole aircraft shudders.

'Obviously a lot of people would decide this aircraft is a strike platform, which it was in the beginning but now it has that capability but it's being used much more widely, mainly as a deterrent because the guys [insurgent fighters] recognize the sound and the shape of the aircraft – it's a case of "Right, they're above so we're not going to do anything".

'We're flying less, but when we're out there, once we're on the other side of the fence, essentially we are doing as much as we can to make sure that the guys on the ground aren't being shot at, and if they are being shot at we go to where they're being shot at and we do what we have to do.'

Sitting there in front of the cameras, Harry had alluded to something that would set him apart from generations of members of his family. Although the primary role of the Apache crew was to prevent insurgent attacks, it was a role that had also made him the first Royal to admit killing someone in a hundred years. That was the question every reporter who had made the journey to Camp Bastion wanted to ask. Had Harry killed enemy fighters from the air? His answer was matter-of-fact and extremely significant.

Asked if he had made a kill, he replied: 'Lots of people have. Take a life to save a live,' he shrugged. 'That's what we revolve around, I suppose. If there's people trying to do bad stuff to our guys, then we'll take them out of the game, I suppose. The squadron's been out here. Everyone's fired a certain amount.'

He also confirmed that he had come under fire, adding: 'Yes, you get shot at. But if the guys who are doing the same job as us are being shot at on the ground, I don't think there's anything wrong with us being shot at as well.'

Harry's comments about killing the Taliban were jumped on all over the world. In another interview recorded as he returned to the UK, he was again questioned about being the first Royal to have killed for many years. He said: 'It's not the reason I decided to do this job. The reason to do this job was to get back out here and carry on with a job.'

He explained how the roles of Apaches themselves and the CPGs inside the cockpit have developed since the aircraft were first introduced in Helmand. 'It used to be very much: front seat, you're firing the whole time. Now, yes, we fire when we have to – take a life to save a life – but essentially we're more of a deterrent than anything else. We're a hugely reliable asset and the main thing for us is the tricky escorts. If guys get injured, we come straight into the overhead, box off any possibility of an insurgent attack because they look at us and just go, "Right, that's an unfair fight, we're not going to go near them."

'But occasionally we get taken on, the guys get taken on, even when we're in the overhead. It's a pretty complex job for everybody involved. But it's not just about the shooting, it's about giving the effect to the [enemy] guys on the ground, and that's not always pulling the trigger.'

It was a soldier's logic and one that most members of the public would see as understandable and acceptable. You are sent to war to fight, and if the situation arises where you have to pull the trigger, then so be it. But it was a sensitive subject for someone as senior in his family as Harry to speak about openly. And it had the effect of making him an even greater target for terrorist attacks in the future. Since Harry returned from Afghanistan he has become one of the most heavily guarded Royals. In the warped logic of Islamic extremists, he would henceforth always be seen as a legitimate target because of his role as a soldier. Details of his security are a closely guarded secret for obvious reasons, but Harry's team of protection officers are heavily boosted by the security services whenever he appears in public.

The return home from Afghanistan was a time of mixed emotions for Harry. The anger and disappointment he had felt when his first tour of duty was cruelly cut short was now replaced with a sense of uncertainty about his future. Being back in the front line had not given him the same thrill he had felt when serving on the ground. Sure there had been some exciting moments flying high above the conflict zone and executing his role with distinction. But was it really what Harry wanted? His love for the Army was about the freedom it offered, being one of the guys, a normal officer doing the job he was paid to do.

But the role of an Apache co-pilot stationed at Bastion had fallen well short of this, and in his heart Harry knew he would never be able to return to the Household Cavalry and continue where he left off. The Afghan conflict was changing and the process of handing the fighting over to the country's national army was now at an advanced stage. Top brass were already planning how to remove British troops from the conflict zone as the political will to see the war out had faded away.

Without Afghanistan, what future would there be for an Apache pilot? The prospect of flying sorties over Salisbury Plain and spending month after month without an active role filled the prince with dread. But returning to the Blues and Royals would mean a lifetime of pen-pushing from behind a desk – something which Harry had openly ruled out from the start of his military career.

In an interview with ITN recorded as Harry arrived in Cyprus on his way home from his second tour, the Royal hinted at this uncertainty over his future. Asked how he felt about doing a 'normal' desk job, Harry was frank with his reply. 'I'd never want to be stuck behind a computer desk. Normal for me? I don't know what normal is any more, I never really have done. There are three parts of me, one obviously wearing the uniform, one being Prince Harry and the other one which is the private sort of me behind closed doors.'

Asked what lay ahead for his military career, Harry replied: 'I really don't know. The Army will have an idea, I presume. What it is, I will do. Given the opportunity, I'd like to take on some more Royal stuff, to the extent that my pre-deployment has been very busy, so hopefully there will be a few gaps that open up. As long as I stay current with my flying and can continue with the job, I can pay more attention to the charities and stuff like that.'

Although his words were somewhat lost in the sea of interviews he had given at the time, this was an admission from the prince that perhaps his focus on the Army was already beginning to flag. Ever since joining Sandhurst to train as an officer, Harry had thrown himself into military life. Since 2005 his feet had hardly touched the ground as he learned to be an officer and then prepared for war. After his switch to the Army Air Corps the intensity of his training increased as Harry focused on making the grade as a helicopter pilot. With his Army Air Corps 'wings' under his belt, it was then a full-on period preparing for the second deployment.

On the flight home from Cyprus, however, there was for perhaps the first time in seven years a huge question mark hanging over his head. As it turned out, this was to be the beginning of the end of Harry's military career.

CHAPTER 22

THE START OF THE REST OF HIS LIFE

THE UNMANNED DRONE took to the skies above the sun-scorched bushland as its latest mission to track down the enemy began. Crouched nearby, Prince Harry fixed his eyes on the small TV screen onto which the images were being streamed live. Beads of sweat were falling from his face; this was a nervous moment for everyone. Their armed adversaries had made their kill and were desperate to flee the area uncaptured. But if they managed to escape it would mark yet another defeat in the war Harry was now fighting.

As a soldier of ten years' experience and with two tours of Afghanistan under his belt, the 30-year-old Royal was amply qualified for this latest role. It was summer 2015, just a few weeks after he had officially quit the Army, bringing an end to his decade of service. But now he was engrossed in a new conflict and had a new enemy: the poachers who had illegally slaughtered endangered rhinos for their horns. And instead of the badlands of Helmand Province, Harry was fighting this war in South Africa's vast Kruger National Park.

The warrior prince was the newest recruit in the fight to save the beasts whose existence is threatened by the fact their horns are worth more than their weight in gold. Instead of his military regalia, Harry now donned the khaki slacks and green fleece of the Kruger rangers' unit.

Out there in the rugged bush of what is South Africa's biggest tourist attraction, the prince once again felt the reassuring feeling of freedom. He was there to do a job and to help protect one of the world's most endangered species. He was a ranger, not a prince; it was the kind of escape he had always been looking for. But was this three-month deployment to the African bush the answer for a Royal whose advisers had earlier that year confirmed he was looking for a new role?

We know that Harry had craved a life in the Army since he had been a little boy. And we know that what appealed to him was the relative 'normality' of a military career. It was because of this that many people on the outside were surprised to hear that at the relatively young age of thirty, the prince had decided to 'retire'. It has also been claimed that in making this decision he was defying the advice of his inner circle and, more importantly, his father, Prince Charles. The Army had given Harry a purpose and direction that seemed so crucial to the people around him. But returning from Afghanistan for the second time really had been a watershed for him.

The days when he could perform a useful role leading his men in the front line were numbered. In reality he would soon need to serve his commanders in a different way, leading men from behind a desk, managing, planning and passing on his skills to his juniors. Even promotion to major meant first going to Staff College.

This troubled Harry, the soldier's soldier who entered the job determined to be hands-on and out in the field. But any suggestions that he reached his decision quickly were wide of the mark. After returning from Afghanistan he had remained with the 662 Squadron 3 Regiment Army Air Corps and continued to live at the unit's base in Wittisham, Suffolk. But in the back of his mind the dilemma over his future began to dominate Harry's thoughts.

With this uncertainty in the background, in May 2013 Harry had made good on a promise he had made to some wounded American soldiers and agreed to fly to Colorado to support the Warrior Games. But even Harry might be forgiven for underestimating the profound effect this engagement would have in his life.

Run by the US Olympic Committee, the Warrior Games had been set up to allow wounded US servicemen and women to compete in an annual sporting competition. It was like a miniature Paralympics, designed to help them overcome their debilitating injuries. Harry was already well aware that in the United States, wounded troops were rightly regarded as national heroes. It was a legacy of the Vietnam War, when many former soldiers ended up on the streets, unable to overcome their physical and mental scars. In 2013 the Warrior Games were in their fifth year, and the attendance of someone with Harry's profile provided the event with a welcome boost.

As ever, Harry was happy to muck in, and he was pictured taking part in a game of seated volleyball with wounded servicemen and women. His involvement had the required effect of guaranteeing coverage in both the US and UK media, and it seemed to pass off like any of his set-piece Royal visits. But this one was different. While those who met Harry and enjoyed his support would doubtless have gone away feeling happy, it was actually the effect they had on him that would really have a lasting impact.

It was during that three-day visit that the penny dropped for Harry. It was a eureka moment for a soldier who was desperately searching for ways he could combine his Army role with that of a senior member of the Royal family. He thought: 'Why can't we have something like this in Britain?'

It was like his experience as a teenager, coming face-to-face with the plight of the forgotten children of Lesotho. During his gap year he had spent weeks working alongside volunteers in the tiny African kingdom where one of the world's highest HIV and

AIDS rates had decimated the population. The profound experience back then led to him founding Sentebale and throwing his weight behind the campaign to save lives. Returning home from Colorado, he was once again filled with the feeling that perhaps there was something he could do to get involved.

Harry is a surprisingly spontaneous person who will often act on instinct rather than carefully thought through plans. In some ways this has been a weakness, particularly when it has contributed to some of the less sensible decisions he has made. But when it comes to making something good happen, this spontaneity is a definite strength. Before his plane had even touched down in the UK, his head was awash with ideas. He began grilling his support team. 'What's to stop us bringing the Warrior Games to Britain?' he asked. 'What if we challenged the American troops and let our boys take them on – it could work,' he continued.

In fact the challenge had already been laid down. In a speech at the Warrior Games he had appeared wide-eyed as he told the competitors: 'I only hope in the future, the near future, we can bring the Warrior Games to Britain and continue to enlarge this fantastic cause. I don't see how it wouldn't be possible to fill a stadium with 80,000 people, not to watch Olympics, not to watch Paralympics, but to watch wounded servicemen fight it out amongst each other – not on a battlefield but in a stadium.' He then got a laugh from his American audience by saying: 'I hope this is something you will all take a huge interest in, as your nation will be coming probably second if not third to the UK team.'

Over the coming weeks the prince refused to let his idea drop. He gathered together his team at Kensington Palace and set about trying to persuade the Ministry of Defence to agree to the idea. At last the flatness he had felt since coming home from Afghanistan had been replaced with excitement about what was to come. It is testament to Harry's passion for an idea that in July the following year he was standing there at the opening ceremony of the inaugural Invictus Games in London's Olympic Park. Invictus – Latin for undefeated – summed up the spirit of the event for Harry as he stood beside Prime Minister David Cameron, his father Prince Charles, and William and Kate.

The games were also significant for another reason, however. As Harry immersed himself in the task of getting them up and running, it allowed him to finally draw a line under his role as an Apache pilot.

In January 2013, with preparations for the summer games in full flow, Harry's spokesman at Kensington Palace put an end to the speculation about his future with a statement confirming the prince would take up a staff officer role in HQ London District. According to the statement this would mean Captain Wales would focus his efforts in helping to coordinate 'significant projects and commemorative events' involving the Army. After Harry's three and a half years flying Apaches, his spokesman was conceding that a job behind a desk was in store for the prince, who had for so long resisted such a role.

The statement was a thinly veiled admission that Harry's military career was all but over. From now on, although employed by the Army, his focus would be firmly on his duties as a Royal soldier. Gone were the days when he would be yomping over Salisbury Plain, or soaring about the East Anglian coastline on training sorties in his Apache. It was of course a desk job, but it was a desk job that the prince would be able to control. The question now was how long would this continue before Harry decided he was ready to call time on his career?

And the answer came as soon as senior officers started to make noises about the next rung of the ladder Captain Wales was approaching. High-flying officers hoping to extend their Army careers beyond the rank of captain cannot be promoted to major until they have successfully got through Staff College. Unlike

Sandhurst, the focus of this course is almost entirely academic, with students sitting through lectures on politics, military strategy and history. There is very little time spent out in the field and even when the recruits do spend time away from the lecture theatres, their training is more about the strategic demands of commanding men than the hands-on skills of basic soldiering.

By his own admission, Harry was not academically minded, and the next step in his Army career would therefore present the toughest challenge to date. And even if he were able to prove himself wrong and get through the classroom-based Staff College course, it would still mark a turning point for the Royal. Once he achieved the rank of major, Harry would be expected to lead men from the background, proving the age-old saying that the higher your rank, the further you are from the front line.

Colonel Richard Kemp, a former commander of British forces in Afghanistan, explained that there was nothing unusual about Harry's dilemma about whether to leave or push on to Staff College. He said: 'All officers go through a process of making a decision whether to leave the Army or whether to continue trying to climb the ranks. By the time officers reach the landmark of nine to ten years in the Army they have a difficult decision to make. And once you have reached that level of seniority you know that from then on you will spend a lot more time behind a desk planning and preparing rather than doing the job Prince Harry entered the Army to do.

'It is not for everyone, and many officers decide that around the age of thirty is the right time for them to leave and pursue a new career. The question they inevitably have to ask themselves is "Do I really want to do this for the next three years or is it time for a new direction?" At Staff College there is some practical soldiering but most of the time is spent in the classroom studying conflicts and examining strategy and operations. It is a demanding and academic course that simply doesn't suit everyone.'

The people around Harry may have felt he was better off staying in the military than drawing a line under the experience. But in his heart Harry knew it was time for him to go. The role he had forged towards the end of his ten-year stint was increasingly seeing him focus on the ceremonial and Royal aspects of the job. As the deadline for a decision approached he began to wake up to the reality that his long-term goals would actually be better served away from the Army.

The first Invictus Games were an incredible success, not least because of the speed with which they had come into being. But in truth Harry knew that he was in an unusual position, where he could leave the Army but still commit his time to drawing attention to the issue of wounded heroes.

In reaching the decision, there is no doubt Harry reflected on the experiences he had had as a soldier. One of the most powerful of these had been his return from the first tour when he came face-to-face with the costs of the conflict. Royal Marine Ben McBean had been unconscious on the flight back to RAF Brize Norton in April 2008. His injuries were so serious that he had no idea at the time that he was joined on the flight back by the prince. But when Harry faced the media after his first deployment was cut short, he felt uncomfortable about being hailed a hero after sharing the flight that day with two seriously wounded men. He made a commitment to do everything he could to ensure the sacrifices of men like McBean would never be forgotten. And now, with the withdrawal of British forces from Afghanistan in full swing, he knew that he could do this best without being tied to a military career.

When the palace finally announced Harry's decision in March 2015, he released a statement in which he reflected on his time in the Army. 'After a decade of service, moving on from the Army has been a really tough decision. I consider myself incredibly lucky to have had the chance to do some very challenging jobs and have met many fantastic people in the process. From learning the hard way to stay onside with my Colour Sergeant at Sandhurst, to the incredible people I served with during two tours in Afghanistan – the experiences I have had over the last ten years will stay with me for the rest of my life. For that I will always be hugely grateful.

'Inevitably most good things come to an end and I am at a crossroads in my military career. Luckily for me, I will continue to wear the uniform and mix with fellow servicemen and women for the rest of my life.' He went on to say: 'I am considering the options for the future and I am really excited about the possibilities ... so while I am finishing one part of my life, I am getting straight into a new chapter. I am really looking forward to it.'

There are those who doubt the wisdom of Harry's decision to leave the Army, and think he may regret it, but this is to misunderstand his reasoning. By the time he approached his tenth year as a soldier he had achieved what he had always set out to do. He had proved himself as a respected and effective officer, leading men into battle and serving his country with distinction. The challenge of making the grade as an elite attack helicopter pilot was a huge bonus for a Royal who had always doubted his academic abilities. But he knew deep down that there was very little prospect of him returning to the front line. From the British point of view the Afghan War was over, and the prospect of spending the rest of his career behind a desk or training others never really appealed to the prince.

During the build-up to his second tour, Harry had spent at least four years working flat out, training to become an Apache pilot and preparing for a return to Afghanistan. This inevitably meant he could not commit as much time to his charities as he would have liked. By the time he returned from the war his determination to dedicate more time to his good causes was obvious.

Colonel Kemp, while accepting that Harry's decision was a loss to the Army, argues it was actually an inspired and unselfish move.

He told me: 'The contribution Harry has made to the military since leaving the Army is in fact far greater than if he had continued with his military career. Since he left Harry has raised the profile of wounded servicemen and women in a far wider way. The wars in Afghanistan and Iraq may now be over but for those who were injured in the conflict or for families who lost loved ones, the battle still goes on.

'By serving his country in Afghanistan, he is extremely widely admired within the Armed Forces. He is seen as a good and decent officer who went to war despite the fact his Royal status meant he could have easily ducked out of serving. Throughout his military career he fought a battle behind the scenes to get to fight for his country, and even those who may not be the biggest fans of the Royal family in the military admire him for that. It was a sensible decision leaving the Army when he did because he has become a far greater asset to the military than he could ever have been as a major doing a desk job.'

Colonel Kemp's assessment of Harry's decision to leave the Army sheds light on what the prince was feeling after returning from his second stint in the front line. Yes, he was a trained officer and Apache pilot, but ironically, leaving the Army when he did would allow him to convert his experience into positive results for the forces. He had, in effect, been there, got the T-shirt, and could now play a vital role in ensuring that the public's awareness and support for the military continued long after the troops returned from the conflict zone. Colonel Kemp was quite right in suggesting that quitting the Army would in fact free him up to promote his former employers and colleagues, and the Invictus Games legacy is just one example of that.

But of course the military is not the only worthy cause that he would now be able to help. His decision to pursue a more active life as a working Royal would see the other causes close to his heart receive a welcome boost. After his 'retirement' Harry's palace advisers released details of the causes he would now be focusing on, but they still insisted this did not mean he was embarking on life as a full-time working Royal.

Following his mother's legacy, Harry would continue to support his Sentebale charity as well as making a commitment to the Halo Trust – the landmine clearing charity that was famously backed by Princess Diana. And in the late summer of 2014, he would spend time in South Africa working alongside the rangers of the Kruger National Park in their battle against poachers. All these organizations were no doubt thrilled to be gaining the attention of Britain's most talked about Royal and thus the media spotlight.

But there were fears among the men in grey suits about how this change of direction would impact on the prince's image. Would the devil make work for his idle hands and lead to more of the kind of criticism he suffered before starting Sandhurst? But Harry was much older now and far more mature. Many of his closest friends – and ex girlfriends – were settling down to married life, lowering the likelihood the prince would resume his partying ways. At thirty-one, pictures of Harry leaving nightclubs in the small hours would inevitably lead to questions about what direction he was heading.

Any such fears have proved unfounded, and in the months and years that have followed his departure from a full-time job, Harry has kept his nose clean and avoided any high-profile slip-ups. But there was of course one nagging question that kept rearing its head whenever the prince faced the cameras for set-piece interviews. When would he settle down and find someone to share his life with?

The relationship with Cressy had fizzled out long before Harry's last day at work as a soldier. He was now both unemployed and unattached for the first time since he left school. In 2015 he was voted the world's most eligible bachelor in a poll about famous men yet to find love. It seemed ironic that someone with so many female admirers was finding it so difficult to find a match. This issue was famously raised by Harry in the course of an interview with Sky TV during a visit to New Zealand in May 2015.

Asked first how difficult a decision it was for him to leave the Army, he said: 'It is a crossroads. I'm in the same position now as most people in my year group or my rank would be in, and most of the guys I joined with have left for numerous reasons. It is the case that if we move on then more responsibilities come, and I suppose with wanting to take on slightly more of this [Royal] role I don't really feel as though I would be in the right position to take on the careers of more soldiers and to take on the responsibility of continuing to fly, for instance.

'So it is a balance, and I've been trying to get the balance right over the past six months to a year before I finished and it was getting hard. Inevitably what happens as you climb the ranks is that you will do more of a desk job. A lot of guys that get to my age leave, and that is partly because a lot of guys join for the outside, for the excitement of running around in the bush with the soldiers. And then there is a point where you have to take the next step and go to a desk and do Staff College and become a major and so on.

'With all that comes greater responsibilities and a lot of your time, which if I'm doing this [Royal duties] kind of stuff, doesn't work. It doesn't sit comfortably with me knowing that I'm off doing something while others are still at work looking after my soldiers. I don't want people to cover for me – that was never going to work.'

Harry's words confirmed the thought process behind his decision, but he remained coy when he was then asked how he planned to balance more Royal work with something new. 'There are a few things on the shortlist,' he said, 'but I don't want to speculate. But as long as people back home know they can trust me in making the right decision and whatever it is, hopefully it will be something that means I can still give something back, I suppose. This part of the job [Royal work] is fantastic but both William and I feel we need to have a wage, we need to work with normal people to keep ourselves sane and also to keep us ticking along.

'Surely in the future if we want to make a big contribution or a valid contribution and be taken seriously then we need to work alongside other people. But as I said, if people can genuinely trust that I'm going to make the right decision and that whatever it is hopefully I will make them proud, then so be it. I've got to a stage now in my life where I'm very happy. I've done ten years in the services, there is part of me of course that would love to carry on doing that, but there needs to come a decision about responsibilities in this role, therefore I need to find something that will have an even balance.'

In his interview Harry was setting down a marker to reassure senior members of his family that leaving the Army was the right decision. Both Prince Charles and the Queen had discussed the future with him, and sources revealed they were not entirely convinced he should leave.

One senior palace source said: 'At first the Prince of Wales in particular raised concerns about his youngest son leaving the career he loved and was so good at. It was his view that the Army gave Harry both a focus and a purpose. But in the end the senior Royals agreed that it was a decision only Harry could make. In his interview during the tour of New Zealand Harry was trying to reassure his father and grandmother that he would not let them down, that leaving the Army was for the best.'

The source said the concerns of senior Royals were most likely rooted in the experience of Prince Andrew, who had served with distinction as a helicopter pilot during the Falklands War. 'Prince Andrew was a very popular member of the "Firm", but when he left the Navy he struggled for many years to find a role that was suitable. He became a trade envoy, but that was the start of a string of controversies over the friends he made and his reputation with the public was damaged beyond repair.'

The interview coincided with the birth of Harry's niece, Princess Charlotte, and the questioning, perhaps inevitably, turned to when he might want to settle down and have children of his own.

Harry, looking a little awkward as he answered, said: 'There come times when you think now is the time to settle down, or now is not, whatever way it is, but I don't think you can force these things, it will happen when it's going to happen. Of course I would love to have kids right now, but there's a process that one has to go through and tours like this are great fun. Hopefully I'm doing all right by myself. It would be great to have someone else next to me to share the pressure, but you know, the time will come and whatever happens, happens.'

CHAPTER 23

MEGHAN

'WOMEN ARE LIKE teabags – they don't realize how strong they are until they're in hot water,' read the famous quote from former First Lady Eleanor Roosevelt. When these words were inked into that year's school book, no one at Immaculate Heart High could have ever foreseen their later significance. Above, on the same page, was glued the image of one of the more popular and outspoken students at the private Catholic school in central Los Angeles.

Twenty years after those eerily prophetic words appeared next to the photograph of the girl known to classmates as 'Sparkle', the front pages of newspapers all over the world would be carrying pictures of the same person. This time they would show the pretty brunette in a black lace bra, pinned against a filing cabinet and enjoying a passionate embrace with a male colleague. A gift from the tabloid gods that would instantly make her one of the most talked-about women on the planet. It was official, Prince Harry was indeed dating the stunning star of steamy American TV show *Suits*, and now the world was desperate to find out more. There was no getting away from it, actress and women's campaigner Meghan Markle was finally in hot water.

It is fair to say that the 35-year-old divorcee's arrival into the global limelight was more of an explosion than a gentle induction. Britain's *Sunday Express* newspaper carried the scoop after spotting that she and Harry were intriguingly wearing the same friendship bands. Their source had been tipped off about the relationship and this gave them the confidence to put two and two together and run the story.

As the palace stayed tight-lipped and refused to comment, the papers could not hide their excitement as they published grabs of Meghan's on-screen sex scenes with co-star Patrick J. Adams. The tsunami of information that followed was – even by Royal standards – unprecedented, which was hardly surprising in the circumstances.

Prince Harry had been single for nearly two years and as he focused on his Royal work in that time the issue of his eligible status was a constant theme in the media. 'When will Harry find love?', 'The lonely prince' and 'Harry's quest to find Princess Right' were just a few of the headlines from the glossy magazines whose readers were so obsessed by the popular Royal. Other comment pieces pointed to the fact that Harry's inner circle of school and childhood chums had one by one settled down and got married. Without his single pals to party with, surely – they insisted – it was time Harry followed suit. A year before Meghan burst onto the scene, there were front-page stories about a possible rekindling of the romance with Chelsy Davy, but this never materialized.

Another contributing factor was the marriage of William and Kate and the subsequent arrival of their two children, Prince George and Princess Charlotte. Their births had lowered Harry's status from third in line to the British throne to fourth and fifth respectively. No longer was he saddled with the tag of 'spare to the heir', a rather unkind title that Harry had always hated.

'You're an official gooseberry,' William said to his kid brother as the pair of them and Kate returned from an official engagement on the way back to Kensington Palace. It was a remark that would have made Harry very angry had it come from anyone else. But

William's words were meant in jest, and as the Royal protection officers drove them back home that night in the late spring of 2016 Harry was able to laugh them off in his usual way.

In reality, William was spot on. Time and time again, Harry would appear by his brother and sister-in-law's side as they attended events and posed for the cameras. The missing link in Harry's life was on display nearly every time he left his cottage in the grounds of Kensington Palace. With their young children needing space, William and Kate had moved to a much larger apartment at KP, leaving Harry to live the bachelor life alone. When the Range Rovers dropped the three of them back at the palace, Harry would return to an empty home. Even if he was buzzing from performing in front of the adoring crowds, this development in his personal circumstances simply underlined the void in his life.

Reflecting on this pre-Meghan period, a close friend of Harry told me: 'Although William would tease his brother for being single, and playing the role of gooseberry when he was at official engagements with Kate, it was increasingly difficult for Harry. He is very much a people person and hates spending time in his own company. But with the young prince and princess to look after, more and more of William and Kate's time was dominated by family life. There were times when Harry would have to spend hour after hour holed up in his cottage alone. It was not as though he could just pop out for a beer after work like a normal person. In many ways he was becoming a prisoner in his own home and would spend hours watching TV alone.'

With too much time on his hands, Harry would reflect on the failure of his relationship with Cressida Bonas, which he blamed almost exclusively on what he described as the 'baggage' that comes with dating a prince. Cressy was a free spirit, a pleasant and popular girl who would always cheer Harry up if he was feeling low. But she hated the attention of strangers as she walked down the street, and when they finally went their separate ways Harry was convinced it was the extent of the public interest in his girlfriend that caused their split. As we have seen, this was only one factor in the relationship's failure, but it was the only one he would accept. When on the odd occasion he showed frustration at the media intrusion into his love life, it simply fuelled the level of interest in when Harry would finally meet the right woman.

'WE'D LIKE YOU to meet a friend of ours, Harry,' insisted New York-based fashion designer Misha Nonoo, the wife of Harry's Old Etonian friend Alexander Gilkes. 'We think you'd like her, and she's coming to London in a couple of weeks.'

Whether a result of his frustration at his predicament or just a simple case of curiosity, to Harry's friends' astonishment the offer of going on a blind date was accepted. Alexander was a close friend of the Middleton family and had attended the wedding of William and Kate in 2011 with Misha, who knew Meghan well from the social circuit in New York. Although Harry and Alexander were not that close, Harry trusted his judgement and must have just thought to himself, 'What have I got to lose?'

As we have seen, making new friends when you are in Prince Harry's position is almost impossible. Either they are fame-hungry types looking to climb rungs on the social ladder, or they are people out to break into Harry's inner circle for more sinister motives. Every time Harry met someone new socially, he would ask himself whether this person could be trusted. What if they were just out to get close and then sell stories about the Royals and their closest friends?

This justified paranoia had accompanied Harry for most of his adult life and goes a long way to explaining why he kept such a small and tight-knit group of trusted friends. But the flip side meant he really hadn't met that many women – and when it came to turning on the charm if he spotted someone he liked, Harry's skills were surprisingly useless. He was awkward around women of his own age, almost blushingly avoiding conversations or cutting them short when someone began to break through.

So it was perhaps no small miracle that when Alexander and Misha suggested setting Harry up on a blind date, the shy prince agreed to meet Meghan when she visited London at the beginning of July 2016. The exact details of their encounter remain a closely guarded secret, but what we do know is that for both Harry and the beautiful American actress it was the closest thing to love at first sight.

Speaking on the day their engagement was announced in November 2017, Harry and Meghan reflected on that first encounter. In a now-famous interview with the BBC, Harry said: 'We were introduced by a mutual friend. And we met once, then twice; two dates back-to-back in London.' When Meghan was asked if she thought the friend that introduced them was trying to set her up, she replied: 'Yes, it was definitely a set-up – it was a blind date. And it's so interesting because we talk about it now, and even then, you know I, because I'm from the States, you don't grow up with the same kind of understanding of the Royal family. So while I now understand it really clearly and the global interest there, I didn't know much about him and so the only thing that I had asked her when she said do you want to go on a date was, 'Is he nice?' If he wasn't kind, then it just didn't seem like it would make sense. So we went and met and went out for a drink and then, I think very quickly into that we said, "We should meet again. What about tomorrow?"'

It has been claimed that Harry fell for Meghan after seeing the first series of *Suits*, then tracked her down and finally persuaded her to go on a date. Clearly, as is so often the case with Royal stories, this account of what happened is a long way wide of the mark. However, as soon as they went on that first blind date,

Harry was on a mission. Bowled over by the beautiful woman he had met back in early July, he was determined to learn as much as he could about Meghan. The source added: 'After meeting up with Meghan, Harry was like a schoolboy with a crush. Having spent so many weeks on his own, he now had a real focus. As her flight back to Toronto was leaving the tarmac at Heathrow Airport, Harry was back at his cottage busily watching back-to-back episodes of *Suits* on Netflix. He was up to Season 5 within a matter of days, having locked himself away and excitedly binged on episode after episode. He couldn't wait to see her again, but the problem was he was about to head off to Africa for a month to help with a conservation project in South Africa and visit his AIDS charity in Lesotho.'

To Harry's delight, Meghan agreed to fly from Canada to Botswana in August 2016 during a short break in her filming. For five wonderful nights the love-struck pair lay under the stars and spent time all alone in the Okavango wilderness. To some this may have seemed like an odd place for Harry to take his new girlfriend, given the fact that it was where he had spent so much time with his first serious love, Chelsy Davy. But as far as Harry was concerned, Botswana was the perfect location.

His first visit to the southern African country that shares a border with South Africa came just weeks after his mother's funeral. Harry's nanny had taken the 12-year-old prince there in a desperate bid to distract him from the terrible events back home, and the freedom he experienced was to have a profound effect on the young boy. Ever since then, Botswana has been Harry destination of choice whenever he has tried to escape the outside world. Their break may have been short, but by the time Harry and Meghan were on their way home from Botswana their relationship was in full flow. The blind date had blossomed and for the first time in years Harry started thinking that he might really have found 'the one'.

The importance of this first trip to Botswana cannot be overestimated, and the couple reflected on it as they faced the cameras to speak publicly for the first time on the day of their engagement. Harry said: 'I think it was about three, maybe four weeks later that I managed to persuade her to come and join me in Botswana, and we camped out with each other under the stars. She came and joined me for five days out there, which was absolutely fantastic. So then we were really by ourselves, which was crucial to make sure that we had a chance to get to know each other.'

Meghan – four years Harry's senior – was herself a free agent after her marriage to the film producer Trevor Engelson had run its course just two years earlier. The couple had enjoyed a magical start to married life, tying the knot as the sun set over one of the most beautiful beaches in Jamaica in 2011. Among the family and friends who waved sparklers and cheered as they celebrated the glitzy union, few would have predicted it was anything other than a lifelong commitment. They had been together since 2004 and had many things in common. Engelson had a promising career in the film industry ahead of him and Meghan was still overjoyed at landing her big break with the hit prime-time legal drama.

They were every bit the beautiful couple as they posed for photographs in front of the Caribbean that night. But it wasn't to be. The strain of two mushrooming careers meant their introduction to married life would be marked by long periods apart, as *Suits* was filmed on location in Toronto, while Engelson's budding career meant he was anchored to LA. In interviews at the time, Meghan insisted the couple would visit each other 'constantly', but she was often seen embracing the post-filming parties and drinking sessions that followed a long day on set. In one of her many posts on social media, Meghan revealed how she had stayed up playing board games with her co-stars and 'drinking Scotch into the wee hours of the night'.

The fledgling marriage was increasingly strained and even a romantic trip to the Far East failed to reignite the flame. There was clearly no argument over finances, a battleground that causes strain in so many relationships. When she filed for divorce, just eighteen months after their idyllic wedding, Meghan didn't ask for a penny from her wealthy ex.

With her split behind her Meghan could be forgiven for thinking that was the end of the matter – time to get on with her life, focus on her acting career and put the experience behind her. Little could she have expected the issue of her status as a divorcee to dominate discussions as news of her next relationship came out. When it comes to the Royal family, the issue of divorcees marrying into the 'Firm' has a long and controversial history. When King Edward VIII – Prince Harry's great-great-uncle – was revealed to have been dating twice-divorced American Wallis Simpson, the controversy that followed sparked a constitutional crisis in Britain.

The then Prime Minister Stanley Baldwin was forced to intervene when the King made his intentions of marrying Mrs Simpson clear. The issue was raised in Parliament and eventually led to the abdication crisis and Edward VIII giving up the throne. His brother Prince Albert – father of Queen Elizabeth II – then found himself unexpectedly being crowned king, as George VI.

Even though this sequence of events happened way back in 1936, when the Royal family's relationship with the public was a world away from today, it was inevitable that for someone as senior as Harry to be romantically linked to a divorcee, the old questions of suitability would rear its ugly head.

Meghan was born in LA in 1981, the only daughter of African American Doria and her white husband Thomas. Even at a young age it was clear that Meghan was preoccupied with her racial identity. In a number of interviews before news of her relationship with Harry broke, she recalled how one Christmas her lighting director father had bought her a 'white Ken doll for the dad and a black Barbie for the mum'. Her parents divorced when she was just six but she remained close to her father, often spending time behind the scenes as he worked on the popular sitcom *Married with Children*.

Even when she was as young as eleven she showed her ability to make a stand after taking exception to a TV commercial for a washing-up liquid that used the slogan 'Women all over America are fighting greasy pots and pans'. Irritated by the inherent sexism of the slogan, she wrote a letter to both the manufacturer and the then First Lady Hillary Clinton, in protest, and within a few months the word 'women' had been replaced by 'people'.

Meghan did well at school and earned a place at Northwestern University, Illinois, where she started taking theatre studies before deciding to add international relations to her workload. Her ambitious nature even saw her completing an internship at a US embassy and she ended up working in the Argentine capital Buenos Aires.

But it was not until a friend introduced her to an agent at a party that Meghan was persuaded to try her skills in front of the camera. In another interview, she was to reflect on the challenges she faced trying to make a break into the acting world. She said in a piece for *Elle* magazine: 'I wasn't black enough for the black roles and I wasn't white enough for the white roles, leaving me somewhere in the middle as the ethnic chameleon who couldn't book a job.'

Despite her difficulties, she won her first part in the daytime soap *General Hospital* and that was followed by roles in series such as *CSI: NY*, *90210* and sci-fi drama *Fringe*. Her presence on the small screen mixed with genuine acting ability finally led her to bag a big break when she auditioned for the part in *Suits*.

Being thrust into the limelight meant Meghan's divorce and subsequent fling with Canadian celebrity chef Cory Vitiello in 2014 were reported widely, while not attracting anything like the level of interest that was to come. This background shows Meghan is clearly an ambitious, likeable and driven woman, well used to being in the public eye and not averse to promoting herself.

The summer of 2016 was a whirlwind for Harry and Meghan. The more time they spent together, the more they realized that they were good for each other. Had it been any other normal couple, there's no doubt the pair of them would have stepped out together, boasting to friends, family and even strangers about the wonderful journey they were on.

But the priority for them both in that long, precious summer was to cram in as much time together before the rest of the world found out that they were an item. Privately, Harry was terrified that when the inevitable happened, the special bond he was making with this intelligent, affectionate and bubbly American would be compromised. His biggest fear was that the spotlight would scare Meghan off and destroy yet another fledgling relationship.

And less than four months after that first blind date, the inevitable happened – the secret was out. In October the call Harry had been dreading came in from his press secretary. The *Sunday Express* would be running a front page revealing to the world that Harry was dating Meghan. Sources have since told me that even though Harry knew the call would eventually come, he was furious and begged his taxpayer-funded media relations team to try to stall its publication. But in the end there was nothing they could do. There was no denying the story, and by trying to question its accuracy the team at Kensington Palace would risk being accused of trying to mislead the public. Just like the day the call came through about the Nazi outfit, there was little Harry could do but put on his tin hat and hope for the best.

He nervously called Meghan in advance to warn her that the story was coming out. They had been advised to avoid making any public reaction, a subtle way of warning Meghan not to put anything out to her one million followers on Instagram. They needed to sit tight and see what happened. Ironically, it was Meghan who calmed Harry down. She told him she was OK about it and reminded him they had already knew that this would be inevitable.

One source revealed: 'Meghan could tell Harry was very worried, not about himself, but about how she would react. Even though she was well used to dealing with attention from journalists and the public, Harry wasn't sure even she knew the scale of what was about to happen. Meghan insisted she was a "big girl" and that she was ready for news of their relationship to come out. She told Harry not to worry.'

The lack of a denial regarding that initial story prompted an avalanche of coverage, which even Harry couldn't have predicted. Within days of Harry and Meghan being romantically linked, papers and magazines on both sides of the Atlantic contained page after page of details about Meghan, her family, her divorce and her 'suitability' as a Royal girlfriend. Speaking less than a fortnight later, one respected Royal correspondent light-heartedly told me, 'We know more about Meghan after two weeks than we found out about Cressy in four years.'

And the reporter – whose words would no doubt have horrified Harry at the time – was right. Less than a month after that first story linking the pair was published, typing their names into Google would lead to more than six million 'hits'. In the UK, pictures of Meghan's on-screen antics were splashed all over the front pages, and on the inside pages commentators analysed the new relationship in minute detail. Some wrote articles with headlines such as 'You would have to be mad to marry a prince', while others questioned the motives of someone they saw as a publicity-hungry American divorcee.

On the other side of the Atlantic the interest in delving deeper into the life of Harry's new girlfriend reached fever pitch. Within days, Meghan's relatives, ex-boyfriends, neighbours, family friends and former classmates had been tracked down, some reportedly being offered money for dishing the dirt. There was something undignified about the fact that someone with Meghan's profile was seen as fair game, even though the media interest was understandable.

There is an old rule for Royals when it comes to their interaction with the media – 'never complain, never explain'. To be seen to break either of these unwritten rules is generally considered to be a no-no, risking being dragged into a wider row that could ultimately backfire. But when it comes to rules, Harry tends to tread his own path. His popularity is so great that he is one of the few members of his family who knows that if he goes on the attack against the media, the chances are the public will take his side. It is a risky tactic, but after riding the storm of stories that followed the revelation of his relationship with Meghan, Harry finally decided it was time to draw a line in the sand.

On the morning of 8 November 2016, Harry persuaded his advisors to issue a statement on his behalf, the likes of which we have never seen before. Not only did the statement openly go on the offensive against the press, complaining about the way his private life was being portrayed in the media, but it also took the unprecedented step of confirming his romance with Meghan.

At the time it was widely greeted as an error of judgement and a sign that Harry's tendency to wear his heart on his sleeve was once again going to backfire. But was it also proof that his advisors were unable to stand up to the prince? Exactly what lay behind this 279-word statement is now clear. Since their first date, Harry and Meghan's romance had seemed perfect, like the very thing he had been waiting for since adulthood. Harry knew that the only thing that could – in his eyes – cast the romance in jeopardy was Meghan deciding she simply couldn't cope with all the attention.

The *Daily Telegraph*'s respected chief reporter Gordon Rayner, himself a veteran of many Royal tours, wrote at the time: 'Never before has he [Harry] been so angry that he felt the need to go public with a statement confronting what has been written about a girlfriend by both mainstream media and by the public through the skewed prism of social media. The Prince is fully aware that in issuing such a public defence of his new girlfriend – and a plea to give her some space – "before any further damage is done" – he is confirming just how serious their relationship is.'

Rayner's analysis was spot on. Harry was in fact telling the world that in his view he was beginning to think he had finally met 'the one' – a fact that we now know for sure. Clearly, by November 2016 Harry was already feeling that Meghan was the person he had been searching for, the woman who could be the one thing that was missing in his life. Looking back at that statement, it was in fact the biggest clue to Harry's true feelings at the time and a sign that they were already deeply in love. But the problem still remained – from the outside it looked as though Meghan didn't tick a single box when it came to her suitability as a Royal bride. After all, on the surface there was no escaping the fact that Meghan was an American divorcee with more than a million followers on Instagram. Privately, many Royal watchers were deeply sceptical about this new romance and doubted whether Meghan's motives were based more on her ambitions for fame than her genuine attraction to the British prince. One veteran of the Royal pack even described it as a publicity stunt and feared Harry's heart was going to get broken once again.

These initial – and highly speculative – suspicions were understandable given that Meghan was such an avid user of social media to promote her profile. From the outside it looked as though she had hit the publicity jackpot, as her profile went into the stratosphere almost overnight. At the very least her 'fling' with Harry would boost her career in ways that were hard to imagine.

Unbeknown to Meghan, the moment her relationship went public was also the moment her every move started to be scrutinized. Every post she put on Instagram, every Tweet and every time she spoke in public would be examined in forensic detail as those desperate to judge her motives tried to find clues.

With the relationship out in the open, and with Harry's robust warning to the media for privacy in place, the couple entered a new phase. It is true to say that the six months that followed the statement would be make or break for the romance. Many expected it to buckle under the pressure of the media gaze – if there were cracks in the relationship, surely they would never survive months of scrutiny. They were, after all, in a long-distance relationship, which are notoriously hard to sustain even without the kind of stresses Harry and Meghan would be under.

But Harry was determined to make it work. And he was no stranger to trying to sustain a relationship from thousands of miles away. In his years with Chelsy Davy he had learned how distance can be disastrous for any relationship. But he had learned an important lesson from the days when his romance with his first love descended into a series of exotic holidays punctuated by long periods apart. Chelsy and Harry were never able to stay close enough to experience being normal, and the more Harry tried to impress his girlfriend with expensive trips and romantic getaways, the further they grew apart.

The secret to Harry and Meghan's success was the fact they both wanted the same thing – someone special with whom they could escape and feel normal. While filming in Toronto, Meghan's life was anything but normal, spending long days on set and long nights alone in her apartment. For Harry, his Royal duties were broken by time spent alone in the evenings at Kensington Palace pining for Meghan.

It is no surprise, therefore, that Harry and Meghan continued to be drawn together with the distance between them simply magnifying their affection for each other. They would spend hours on the phone, talking and making plans for when they could next be together. The impact this had on Harry was clear. He was in love with someone who just wanted to be with him for who he is. Meghan's old school friends have since described how affectionate she has always been. Damaged by the failure of her first marriage and forced to live under the spotlight because of her own career, the more Meghan got to know Harry, the more she found they had in common. And for the first time in his life, Harry didn't have to feel guilty for dragging his girlfriend into a media storm. She was famous in her own right and well used to life knowing there could be a photographer round every corner.

A source close to the prince insisted the impact of his romance with Meghan had a profound effect on Harry. For the first time in his life he had found someone who really wanted to listen to him talk about the past and who he was. The source even went as far as claiming that it was Meghan's friendship that finally allowed Harry to face up to the demons of his past.

The source said: 'Meeting Meghan and really getting to know her sparked a change in Harry. On the one hand he was like a school kid in love, but on a far deeper level his relationship with Meghan was helping him to address the things that had troubled him over the years. Anyone who knew Harry from his teenage years knew he could be angry, that he almost had a self-destruct button when he was in a bad place. This never seemed to damage his public image but it did mean there were times when Harry found it hard to cope with who he was. Finally he had in Meghan someone who understood him and who was willing to accept him warts and all. Surprisingly, on the inside Harry is quite shy and vulnerable, not quite the confident figure people always assumed he must be. Over the months talking with Meghan he gained in confidence and this was noticeable for all those around him.'

In April 2017 Harry stunned the world with an interview no one could have ever expected from a senior member of the Royal family. Harry, William and Kate were all committed to trying to do more to encourage people to speak up about their private struggles with mental health. In the build up to that year's London Marathon, the Royal trio wore blue headbands in support of their little-known charity Heads Together. A team of runners was taking part in the marathon to raise awareness of issues such as depression and grief that had had a devastating effect on each of their lives.

But Harry was to go one step further in his support – and in so doing propelled the issue of mental well-being to the top of the news agenda. Without warning, Harry agreed to take part in a podcast called 'Mad World' conducted by the *Daily Telegraph* journalist and mental health campaigner Bryony Gordon. The concept of the podcast was to get high-profile guests to speak candidly about this taboo subject and their own mental health experiences. When Harry accepted Bryony's request for him to be her first guest, there is no way anyone could have predicted just how far he would be prepared to go.

In an interview that made headlines across the world, Harry revealed that he had sought counselling after enduring two years of 'total chaos' while still struggling in his late twenties to come to terms with the death of his mother. He described how he 'shut down all his emotions' for almost two decades after losing her, despite his brother trying to persuade him to seek help. Harry went on to describe how he only began to address his grief when he was twenty-eight after feeling 'on the verge of punching someone' and facing anxiety during Royal engagements. Describing the 'quite serious effect' that losing his mother had on his personal and professional life, he told how living in the public eye left him feeling he could be 'very close to a complete breakdown on numerous occasions'.

The thirty-minute conversation was one of the most candid insights into Harry's battle to come to terms with his grief. He said that he spent his teenage years and twenties determined not to think about her. 'I can safely say that losing my mum at the age of twelve, and therefore shutting down all of my emotions for the last twenty years, has had a quite serious effect on not only my personal life but my work as well. I have probably been very close to a complete breakdown on numerous occasions when all sorts of grief and sort of lies and misconceptions and everything are coming to you from every angle.' Asked whether he had been to see a 'shrink' to offload his thoughts, he said: 'I've done that a couple of times – more than a couple of times – but it's great.'

The prince admitted that at times he had struggled with aggression and turned to boxing as an outlet for his frustration. 'During those years I took up boxing, because everyone was saying boxing is good for you and it's a really good way of letting out aggression. And that really saved me because I was on the verge of punching someone, so being able to punch someone who had pads was certainly easier.'

He eventually sought support with the encouragement of his brother and others close to him, who told him: 'Look, you really need to deal with this. It is not normal to think that nothing has affected you.' Since learning to talk honestly about his feelings, he said, he now felt able to put 'blood, sweat and tears' into making a difference for others. 'The experience I have had is that once you start talking about it, you realize that actually you're part of quite a big club.'

For such a senior Royal to talk openly about his innermost feelings was totally without precedent and went a long way towards explaining some of the occasions when Harry had found himself on the front pages for the wrong reasons. It explained, for example, why a young prince might have decided to throw caution to the wind and choose to wear a Nazi outfit to a fancy dress party. A rebellious act, deliberately trying to shock his fellow party-goers and raise a laugh. But also a naïve error that would provoke a reaction all over the world.

Lashing out at a photographer in the street was branded at the time by some as 'thuggish' behaviour, but could now be seen for what it really was. An understandable – if foolish – reaction from a young Royal who came face to face with the kind of photographers that in his mind were responsible for the death of his mother when he was just twelve years old.

And stripping off in a Las Vegas hotel suite in front of strangers could now be seen as the actions of a prince trying to escape from the demands of being in the public eye, with the exhausting pressure of constantly needing to behave in a certain way. Without the proper professional help that we now know Harry had sought, his were the actions of someone who had never actually come to terms with his grief and the pressure of what he always saw as his 'accident of birth'.

We may never know how great a role Meghan played in helping Harry make the unexpected decision to reveal his inner battles to the world at large. But it is far from a coincidence that his interview came in the weeks that would ultimately lead to Harry making the front pages for all the right reasons, sitting side by side with the woman he had chosen to marry.

CHAPTER 24

WINNER, WINNER, CHICKEN DINNER

STEPPING OFF THE tiny plane at Maun Airport, Harry must have been feeling a mix of nerves and excitement. It was a place he had visited many times before, but this visit, in August 2017, would change his life forever.

The official line is that Harry went down on one knee while he and Meghan cooked a roast chicken at his cottage in the grounds of Kensington Palace. While it is true that this was the moment in November 2017 when the pair could say they were officially engaged, in fact it was more than three months earlier during a romantic trip to Harry's 'second home' in Botswana that Meghan and he decided they would spend the rest of their lives together. In the African wilderness, miles from the outside world, Harry and Meghan agreed to take their relationship to the next level.

Sources have revealed that it was while the pair cuddled up in a camp on the edge of what is perhaps the world's most authentic safari experience that Meghan agreed to quit her job and move to London permanently. For most couples this might perhaps have been the moment they could announce to their friends and family that they were getting married. But as fifth in line to the British throne, things could never be that simple for Harry. Following the Royal Marriages Act of 1772 the monarch has the right to veto the marriage of a senior member of his or her family. Without the formal consent of the Queen, therefore, Harry would have to wait before being able to pop the question.

Despite this, by the time Meghan and Harry returned to Botswana – just over a year after they first met – the two lovers knew what the next step would involve. As an actress on a popular American TV show, Meghan would never be able to continue her career if she planned to settle down with her prince. Fortunately for Harry, Meghan had already decided that the seventh season she was already filming would be her last. Her role as the para-legal Rachel Zane would come to an end. What lay ahead for her was a decision about where to live once the final season was in the can. She could of course have returned to LA and continued with her acting career. But in the weeks and months since she had met Harry, she knew her life was heading in a radically different direction.

It was during this summer break in Botswana that the subject of their future came up. Harry knew there was a chance that Meghan might consider moving to London and giving the relationship a better chance of surviving. And it was on this trip that he was determined to discuss his feelings and the fact that he felt ready for them to move in together.

We will never know exactly what was said, as the remote camp where they stayed gave the happy couple complete privacy. However, what happened in the weeks after their return proved that they had already made a significant commitment to each other long before the 'chicken dinner' and the moment they agreed to make things official.

After returning from Botswana, Harry and Meghan embarked on a series of events that would pave the way for an announcement. The couple had agreed for Meghan to give an interview to *Vanity Fair*, the popular American society magazine. In the interview Meghan made her first public comment on her relationship with Harry and even went as far as to declare that she was head over heels in love.

This was significant because it cemented the fact that eleven months after the relationship went public, it was stronger than ever. Harry's fears that Meghan would struggle to cope with the pressure of dating a Royal had not been realized. In fact, Meghan's status as a celebrity and successful actress in her own right meant the traditional problems Harry had faced in his relationships were irrelevant. She was famous, he was famous and together they were more than able to cope with being in the spotlight. Months earlier Meghan had stopped posting on social media – a clear sign that her relationship was now more important to her than the need to maintain her public profile. By stopping her regular posts, Meghan could not be accused of trying to cash in on her elevated fame with Harry – something that instantly silenced even the most sceptical of Royal watchers.

By declaring her love for Harry in *Vanity Fair* Meghan was making a calculated step towards the doorstep of the Royal family. Their relationship was based on love – it was as simple as that.

The next significant step they agreed to take was to appear together in public as boyfriend and girlfriend. In September Harry took centre stage in Meghan's adopted home city of Toronto, where his Invictus Games for wounded servicemen and women gave the couple an ideal opportunity to send a signal to the world about how strong their relationship had become.

The rights and wrongs of making such a public statement were discussed with Harry's media advisors. If the Invictus Games took place in Toronto and Meghan stayed away it would send a negative signal. People would ask if their relationship was strained, or whether her absence was a sign that they were not so suited after all. Because nothing could have been further from the truth, Harry was determined that Meghan would be there – and he even decided to go one step further and invite his girlfriend to take part in an official engagement as part of the games.

Meghan and Harry stepped out together for the cameras, even holding hands and kissing as the photographers snapped away. It was a genius decision and one that had the precise impact that Harry had hoped for. By being pictured so publicly, Harry was flooding the market with the first really good-quality pictures of him and Meghan. This would, in effect, spike the guns of the bounty-hunting paparazzi photographers who would have made tens of thousands of pounds out of the first high-quality shot of the couple together. The last people Harry would have wanted to benefit from taking his picture were now coming to terms with the fact they would find it impossible to get better pictures than those seen all round the world in a controlled environment.

By the time Meghan and Harry appeared together at the closing ceremony of the Invictus Games the market was flooded with lovely pictures of the pair of them side by side. The combination of the *Vanity Fair* interview and their appearance together sent the media on both sides of the Atlantic into a frenzy of speculation about a possible engagement. As far as Harry was concerned, he didn't mind a jot. So what if people knew they were this close, that the relationship had spiralled into something very serious? By then Harry already knew that he and Meghan would be living together in London and he didn't really care who found out.

Often when media speculation about a birth a death or a marriage gets too far out of control, the palace quietly advises the media behind the scenes to back off. Officially they never comment on such private matters, but if speculation reaches fever pitch they have in the past tried to rein in the Royal pack. This was different. This time Harry and Meghan were on a deliberate and carefully planned course that would pave the way for her move to London and, ultimately, the official announcement of the engagement.

The fallout from the speculation about what was going on meant that, like all Royal reporters, my phone was in meltdown as journalists from all over the world wanted to know if the rumours were true. And with the palace remaining tight-lipped, it began to feel like a free-for-all. On 12 October I was asked to do an interview for Russian TV outside the gates of Kensington Palace. It was late afternoon and as the camera rolled I spotted the tell-tale signs of police outriders with their blue lights flashing heading towards us. The quick-thinking cameraman panned round in time to film a blacked-out people-carrier followed by two police protection vehicles as they sped past in the direction of the private entrance to the palace.

While it was obvious that either William or Harry must have been inside, I was struck by the fact that the police were escorting a vehicle with blacked-out windows. In almost all cases the Royals are driven in vehicles with normal glass, and you can often catch a glimpse of who is inside even at the speeds at which they are whisked about. But this time it seemed strange that whichever Royal it was had chosen to travel behind blacked-out windows.

I didn't have to wait too long before discovering what we had inadvertently caught on camera. Richard Kay, the *Daily Mail*'s legendary reporter who had spent so many years covering Princess Diana, was told by his sources exactly where Harry and Meghan had been that afternoon. The couple were on their way back from 'tea' with the Queen at Buckingham Palace, less than half a mile down the road. It was the first time Harry had introduced his grandmother to Meghan and by all accounts it had gone extremely well.

In their interview to mark the engagement Harry joked about how the Queen's beloved corgis had taken an instant like to Meghan, curling up on her feet as she sat with Her Majesty. Once again we will never know what was said that day, but it is quite clear that Harry would have told his grandmother of the couple's plans to live together.

People often ask Harry what his relationship is like with his grandmother. Although the formal structure of her as monarch is in place, Harry is actually very close to the Queen and their friendship is very informal. Technically speaking, this was the day on which the fifth in line to the throne was introducing his intended to the Queen. However, in reality it would have been a far less formal affair and a chance for Harry to show off his girlfriend like any grandson hoping for approval.

The meeting went well, and now Harry and Meghan's plans to move in together had been officially sealed. It was now surely just a matter of when, not if, the couple would announce their plans to marry. And the public didn't have to wait for much longer. Just after 9 a.m. on Monday 27 November 2017, a statement issued by the Prince of Wales confirmed what everyone had been thinking. Harry and Meghan would marry on 19 May 2018. Less than eighteen months after their first 'blind date', Harry's long wait for a bride was over.

By the time I made it to Kensington Palace that day for a round of interviews with foreign TV, the media circus was in full swing. Along the front drive next to the palace was a line of satellite trucks flanked by a wall of reporters holding microphones as they stood under lights telling the world of the breaking news. As is so often the case on these occasions, news teams from all over the planet were on hand to report back in their native language to viewers back home.

The news that an American was to marry into the British Royal family broke a few hours before those on the eastern seaboard of Meghan's home country were waking up. And the frenzy of excitement naturally seemed to be oozing from the news crews of the large American networks. There were teams from Japan, France, Germany, Australia, India – just about everywhere, it seemed.

Prince Harry remains such a popular and high-profile member of the British Royal family, and the fact he had finally found the person he wanted to spend the rest of his life with was a huge story. At 1 p.m. that day, Harry and Meghan emerged for the cameras in the Sunken Garden outside Kensington Palace and all eyes were on the bride-to-be's finger as the world caught its first glimpse of the engagement ring.

It later emerged that Harry had chosen the ring and used diamonds from his late mother's collection set around a large rock from, where else, but Botswana. As the army of commentators did their pieces to camera, one of the constant questions was whether Meghan could continue her job as an actress. In reality this is very unlikely, if not impossible. But to see her emerge, beaming with smiles and holding tight to Harry's hand to face the world's media, it was obvious this was in fact the start of a new acting career.

From that moment on, Meghan's every word, her body language, what she wore and how she conducted herself in public would be under the microscope. And unlike when she may have fluffed her lines while filming for *Suits*, from now on there would be no retakes. The first take would be the real deal.

The reality was there for all to see. The person who barely a year before didn't seem to tick a single box for a Royal girlfriend was now a confirmed princess-in-waiting. As an actress, Meghan may have seemed unsuitable. However, what better preparation for a life as a Royal wife? Clearly she is able to blend into this role with seemingly flawless appearances by Harry's side. When Diana Spencer first appeared in public following her engagement to Prince Charles, she looked shy and almost overwhelmed by the magnitude of the situation. Meghan, in contrast, nailed her first performance as a bride-to-be.

Three days later she and Harry took part in their first walkabout as a Royal couple on a visit to Nottingham to mark World

AIDS Day. Once again, Meghan's performance was incredible considering the pressure she must have been under. She and Harry were greeted by screaming crowds desperate to catch a glimpse of the woman who had made headlines all over the world. Meghan took to it like a duck to water, shaking hands, waving and exchanging small talk with the adoring public. Harry, meanwhile, looked more relaxed than ever and must have felt so pleased to have finally been able to make such an appearance with someone other than his brother and sister-in-law by his side. It was official – the Harry and Meghan show had started.

On the evening of the announcement, Harry followed William and Kate's example by giving a BBC television interview to be shared with the world. Sitting on a sofa inside his cottage at Kensington Palace and holding hands, the happy couple were able to reveal the moment when Harry finally popped the question. 'It happened a few weeks ago, here at our cottage,' said Harry. 'It was just a standard typical night for us.'

'Just a cosy night in,' Meghan added. 'What were we doing? We were roasting chicken, and it was just an amazing surprise. It was so sweet and nice, very romantic. He got on one knee. It was an instant "Yes". As a matter of fact I could barely let him finish. I said, "Can I say yes now?"'

'You didn't even let me finish,' Harry continued. 'You said, "Can I say yes now?" and then there were hugs and I had the ring in my hand, and I was like, "Can I give you the ring?" So it was a really nice moment. It was just the two of us, and I think I managed to catch her by surprise as well.'

Meghan went on: 'I don't think I would describe it as a whirlwind in terms of our relationship. Obviously there have been layers in terms of how public it has become, after we had a good five or six months of just privacy, which was amazing. I think we were able to really have so much time just to connect and we never went longer than two weeks without seeing each other, even though we were obviously doing a long-distance relationship. So we made it work.'

The couple looked so natural together, oozing that look of two people deeply in love and genuinely excited about their big day and future together. The overwhelming reaction from the public was one of happiness for them both. No one seemed to care about the fact she was a divorcee; the days when that might have been a barrier to a British Royal are confined to the past. The fact that Meghan was raised in a Catholic school could have been an issue under ancient British law. However, it was quickly nipped in the bud when the palace revealed that Meghan had agreed to be christened into the Protestant Church of England.

The last thing on anyone's mind that day were negative questions about whether the two were suitable. The reality is that Harry's place in the hearts of the British public is so strong that none of these stuffy old traditions were going to get in his way. At last it was clear that Harry had found the one thing that had been missing in his life since his teenage years. A person who loved him for who he was and someone he was going to marry for love.

It is perhaps this single fact alone that makes this relationship work. Being famous and successful in her own right meant Meghan was able to cope with the storm of publicity surrounding her relationship with Harry. Harry's clear infatuation with his 'blind date' grew into a deep love, and this enabled him to get to know someone without the pressure of constantly questioning whether he was doing the right thing.

Whether they admit it or not, it was a whirlwind in every sense of the word. But watching the two of them gleefully talk about how they had got to the point of engagement that day, most people were struck by the fact that this could actually work. Yes, they both have history, but neither of them seem to care, so what right does anyone else have to complain?

Meghan's confidence in public and her clear admiration for Harry make her a perfect match, and the fact that there is so much more to her than a perfect, upper-middle-class upbringing means she is far more likely to win the hearts of the public. No one can accuse her of being work-shy, as she has built a successful career in her own right. No one can say she is after Harry for the fame – she was famous already, and knew only too well the costs that come with being recognized everywhere you go.

Harry's journey has been a difficult one, but since his late twenties the hardest part for him has been trying to find the right person to settle down with. He never had the luxury of meeting someone in the same sort of relatively normal environment in which William met Kate. The relationships he has had were passionate and full-on, but ultimately never made it past the 'baggage' factor, as Harry puts it. Dating a Royal, let alone marrying one, means your life changes forever. The only way it can possibly work is if the relationship is based on mutual love and a willingness to commit to everything that comes with it.

The young prince who battled his way through much of his adult life has now emerged as the jewel in the crown of the modern Royal family. Harry, more than anyone, links the 'stiff upper lip' and traditions of the institution to a younger audience. He doesn't eclipse the Queen, or even his brother William. He complements them both, enabling them both to bask in the popularity of the 'Party Prince'. Those close to Harry say how desperate he is to have children, and it is likely the pitter-patter of tiny feet will follow in the not-too-distant future. With children in tow, the Harry and Meghan show is likely to become one of the strongest assets of the Royal family for years to come.

The only danger is that as the public go wild for their favourite couple, there could be an impact on William and Kate. Since their wedding in 2011, the Cambridges have steered a cautious path, fighting legal battles behind the scenes to protect the privacy of their children. At times it has seemed that William's desire to be regal, to live up to his role as heir to the throne, might have made him look a little aloof or detached from his future 'subjects'. Until now, Harry has been able to soften this side of his brother by appearing with them at as many official engagements as his diary would allow. But as husband and wife, Harry and Meghan are more likely to carve their own path of Royal duties and good causes to promote.

The challenge now facing the men in grey suits at Kensington Palace is how they can ensure that the Harry and Meghan show doesn't eclipse the more important need for William to grow into a suitable king in waiting. At the start of their married life, Harry and Meghan are likely to embark on engagements with William and Kate. It is likely they will also be encouraged to mix engagements in which Kate and Meghan appear together, while the brothers attend other events as a double act.

But as Harry reflects on his life to date, there must be worse things to worry about than being too popular. His battles as a young man, his service in the front line in Afghanistan and the success of his charity work have made him the popular figure he is today. It is hard, if not impossible, to imagine Harry's popularity dipping in the same way as it did for his uncle Prince Andrew. But that does not mean he can take his popularity for granted. Harry will need to continue his commitment to Royal work and at times he may find this frustrating.

It has been difficult for William to sustain a full work load at the same time as wanting to be there for his children. At times he has been criticized for not fulfilling enough engagements, an accusation that has yet to be levelled at Harry. In the first two years of their married life the public will be desperate to see Meghan and Harry. They will be asked to take part in overseas tours on behalf of the Queen, and it will be a constant battle for them to balance their own lives with those of full-time working Royals.

There is no doubt that there would have been times when Princess Diana may have looked down on her youngest son and been worried. There were periods – especially during his extended gap year – when the future didn't always look so bright for Harry. His understandable inability to come to terms with his mother's death made the early years of adult life tricky. But the Army did much to shape the young prince, giving him a focus and the discipline that comes with being a leader of men. Yes, there were still incidents that didn't cover Harry in glory. But these were few and far between, and they never dented his popularity with the public.

The path to finding a bride has perhaps been one of his hardest struggles, with long-term relationships fizzling out and shorter flings simply ending up as fodder for the press.

But in Meghan it looks as though Harry has come full circle. He is able to talk about the years when he let himself down, the public adore him and there is a genuine sense that with her by his side the best is yet to come.

ACKNOWLEDGEMENTS

I WOULD LIKE to thank the following people for their help with this book: Royal writer Phil Dampier; Royal reporters Emily Nash and Emily Andrews; former reporter for the *Sun*, Jamie Pyatt; Royal photographer for the *Sun*, Arthur Edwards; photographers for the *Sun*, Paul Edwards, Dan Charity and Scott Hornby; and thanks also to Chris Pharo for his support.

PICTURE CREDITS

Page 1, top: *Sun* / News Syndication

Page 1, bottom: Reuters / Kieran Doherty

Page 2, top left: UK Press via Getty Images

Page 2, top right: Reuters / Kieran Doherty

Page 2, bottom: *Sun* / News Syndication

Page 3, top: Reuters / Dylan Martinez

Page 3, bottom: Chris Ratcliffe / AFP / Getty Images

Page 4, top left: *Sun* / News Syndication

Page 4, top right: John Stillwell PA Archive / PA Images

Page 4, bottom: John Stillwell PA Archive / PA Images

Page 5, top left: *Sun* / News Syndication

Page 5, top right: Gareth Fuller PA Archive / PA Images

Page 5, bottom: Paul Ellis / AFP / Getty Images

Page 6, top: *Sun* / News Syndication

Page 6, bottom left: John Stillwell PA Archive / PA Images

Page 6, bottom right: Karwai Tang / WireImage

Page 7, top: Andrew Milligan / AFP / Getty Images

Page 7, bottom: Paul Cunningham / Corbis via Getty Images

Page 8, top: Chris Jackson / Getty Images for Invictus Games

Page 8, bottom left: Reuters / Phil Noble

Page 8, bottom right: Dave J Hogan / Getty Images